Opening The Secret Box

More than 100 archetypes to boost your energy, harmonize relationships, business marketing, money attraction, prosperity, and inner fulfillment.

Iolanda L. F. Silva

First published in 2022.

Opening The Secret Box
Illustrated by Kevin Sanders
Edited by Book Writing Experts

Paperback ISBN: 979-8-9874361-0-3

Hardcover ISBN: 979-8-9874361-2-7

eBook ISBN: 979-8-9874361-1-0

Published in the United States of America

Dedication

For every brother and sister from this
and the other side of life!

Acknowledgment

I thank and honor the great team who helped me transform my thoughts into words. This book is special to me, and I know it will help many souls who seek transformation. My agents, Selena, Amanda Kennedy, and Sam Jordan - thank you for your patience, kindness, and understanding as editors of this book. I'm grateful for the work of Kevin Sanders as editor and illustrator of this book; the inspiring, creative, and amazing illustrations representing each chapter of this book. It means a lot to me. I'm deeply grateful to the special person I ever met, Helio Couto, as my spiritual therapist, watershed, mentor, and professor who helped me become who I am today and everything I experienced, learned, and connected to archetypes and the Whole. I am also grateful to my family, who have always believed in me, sending blessings, love, and motivation to everything I do.

Contents

About the Author

Iolanda Lais Ferreira da Silva is a light worker, Reiki master, Tarot Reader, and Astrologer. A new conscience was developed due to her abrupt spiritual awakening through harmonious resonance therapy and exploration of the awareness of animals, plants, and symbols in herself.

She aims to transform sorrow into power, increase the perception of reality, unlock divine purpose, and elevate vibration and awareness through oneness with God after receiving the direct calling, love, and support from the universe linked to deeply interior transformation.

Preface

Life is vast. Whether you perceive it as Pandora's Box or a journey depends on your perception. Life is, however, more than an occurrence. Each day, every ounce of energy lived is a reaction of our actions against the catalyst we call events. These events further vary in nature. From getting up each morning to heading to our respective occupations, interactions, conduct, and speeches.

In short, life consists of experiences that have both positive and negative aspects of existence that are interconnected with each other to form what is called 'life 'itself; we call this 'soul, ' 'psyche,' 'heart,' 'mind, 'etc., depending on the culture, beliefs, and the philosophical perspective one takes when looking at things from their point-of-view and understanding of life as well as the universe.

Let's look at events based on the soul, psyche, heart, and mind. What are these things? These are matter that makes us. They are both physical and spiritual. We are a vessel of events – a box that holds more than memories and moments.

Every archetype, myth, symbol, fairytale, and metaphorical story is like a little box where there's the base of all civilizations of history. This little box might have wonderful things. For example, in our culture, we have all kinds of archetypes:

God – a father figure, Mother – a female figure, Brother/Sister, Chosen One, Hero – a brave and strong person who has achieved his destiny or become a god. Villain – someone who goes against this kind of good character (like in stories). Bully –

someone who tries to control others. Good guy vs. Bad guy – usually, the good guy will win because he has something more than the bad guy.

In our lives, we've all gone through circumstances that cross our paths, leaving behind a profound influence on its direction, but how? We are all so much more than the sum of our experiences, and it is the sum of our experiences that shapes us into the people we become; we're not born to be something other than what we are…but where do those influences come from?

For as long as humans have existed, the question has been asked: What was your mother like when you were born? Or your father, grandfather, etc.? How did they affect you? And now, with the Internet at hand in this modern age, the question can be posed in another way: "What do my online habits tell others about me?"

And though the questions may seem benign, the answers to them can be far more revealing than one might think. Let's look at some examples of these questions:

"There's a young girl called Hanna. She can't go home before stopping at some fast-food restaurant every day and feels guilty for being compulsive by gaining weight."

"There's a young boy called Peter. He catches everyone's attention wherever he goes. He shines bright and is attractive to everyone. His girlfriend is jealous, and sometimes they argue."

"There's a young boy called Patrick. He dreamt of becoming a musician. Now he's retired and sick after years of frustration as an engineer."

All 3 three examples are enough to shed light on the different archetypes each possesses, manipulated by something more that resides within them. Nevertheless, as different as these three are, they have a similarity. Can you identify what they have in common?

They're experiencing repetitive problems. They are going through the same events on a loop because of a certain barrier in their life that they either did not recognize or did not resolve. This is the key to understanding what's happening to you at any given time in your life right now:

You can't see your way out of it and therefore think it has no way out; That's the most important thing to remember when we come back to this theme again because if you've ever had one of those moments where you just felt like there was nothing else left for you to do but to sit down and accept it – if you have, then you know exactly what I mean.

Finding someone 100% balanced in all areas of their life is rare. The fact is that most of the repetitive problems one faces result from choices. I know that sounds obvious, but did you know that most of the choices we make are not ours? Science knows that 95% of our choices through unconscious motivation are influenced by content as subliminal messages, which are out of our control. The good news is that it is very easy to quickly change these subconscious beliefs with our conscious awareness. The changes will remain for an extended period since the neuroplasticity nature of the brain creates new neural pathways to reach any goal or achieve success in life if you believe in yourself and your abilities.

Ask yourself - How many times have you tried to set a goal and noticed the year is close to the end, only to find yourself saying, "I'll do this next year," "I'll start on Sunday," or "I'll do it later." These thoughts make you lose the meaning of life, resulting in the sentiments of being lost on the road because the car had broken down. But how many breakdowns does a driver have to face until they notice a factor preventing them from reaching their destination?

It is also important to learn how to control emotions. If not, you may be overwhelmed by negative thoughts that are out of your control and always influence your decisions and actions. In some cases, one's mind is so powerful and creative that it might cause unwanted effects on the body and mind when it is running wild, like anxiety attacks and depression. However, with an archetype, all of this can be altered.

This book aims to offer a piece of knowledge about how you can change your life and grow yourself by using an archetype as your helper. When I decided to write this book, I wished to help others by telling everything I learned about the archetypes, In addition, to sharing my own experiences with them. How can I convince anyone otherwise if not through my experiences? I believe in practicing what I preached, so I performed these archetypes on myself and monitored my progress and growth to know that archetypes can do wonders.

With my learning experience and success, I have decided to write this book to extend my learning. This book intends to present information in a simplified way for a better understanding, step-by-step to ensure there are no doubts or questions about how you can be the master of your mind, overcome repetitive problems, and succeed. Instead of being a byproduct of circumstances and external factors influencing your decision-making ability, I intend to unwind you from the aggravating cycle of mundane and setbacks to let you walk on a path where you embrace each challenge for its wisdom and rectify your future.

Sometimes we are in the circle of events that makes us think about how or why something happened, bad choices, actions, and attitudes that make us feel bad hours later. We experience different feelings when reading fiction books, metaphorical stories, parables, fairytales, etc. Our brains can take in many different experiences and make meaning of them, thus helping us understand our lives better and making us stronger and wiser in growing up and learning from life's lessons and difficulties.

The way we feel by receiving this information, science calls it neurotransmission - the chemical of persuasion, love, hard work, and stimulations that impulses us to behave right after reading, watching, or listening. But where is this information coming from? The archetype is the information our consciousness cannot notice; our unconsciousness can receive it. Have you ever thought about how many people succeed in their lives by thinking about how lucky they are? How they act, talk, write, perform, think, eat, dress, dance, walk, look, smile, react, sing, speak, drive, seat, move, swim, run, and even sleep is different from any other person. The truth is that some archetypes might influence them, and they don't even know about it.

What about the brain, now? Given it detects positivity subconsciously, does it mean emotions are processed in a specific area and not all over the brain? Or is there any correlation between the emotional states (anger, joy, fear...) and the particular part of the brain? And how much do they depend on each other, or are their interactions limited to certain stages of development? When you read these words, your heart starts beating faster; when I see you coming, my heart beats harder; when you touch me, my body reacts with adrenaline. Why is that? It's because of the chemical neurotransmissions produced in our brains.

Chemical Neurotransmission as Dopamine, Oxytocin, Serotonin, and Endorphin are the best ones we know and contribute to making us happy. You can develop them on your own through positive affirmations, physical exercises, actions, gifts, healthy meals, and so on. The answers will base on your feelings after practicing all these things. There are thousands of symbols and archetypes in the world, but in this book, I will show you the most common and influential symbols to help you in your daily life and how you can activate or deactivate it.

The archetype theory from the most famous psychiatrist Carl Gustav Jung shows us the main archetypes of personalities. Joseph Campbell inspired us by remembering the heroes of mythology and gods in cultures, who were the main foundation of all human physical and intellectual pursuits. Their influence on society and their deep connection to our unconscious mind play a role to date. However, what remains undistinguished is that we have the power to select what archetype to follow and what to let go of. Likewise, you can choose one or more symbols to see a natural flow taking place from inside to out of your life. Depending on your desired outcome, you can add or change these symbols.

The symbols and archetypes we will look at will tap into your consciousness with the information, wisdom, and knowledge you possess. Sounds like something you can search for on Google. If so, ask yourself if you can distinguish between information and conscience based on what you read online.

Information and conscience - what is the difference? If you think about the quote, "Everything in the Universe is information" and "We were all made from one consciousness," can you tell the difference? Sounds confusing, I know. This is the main challenge of this book: you must find the answer on your own. If everything starts to make sense by the end of this book, you've just started expanding your consciousness taking your first step, or maybe a higher jump.

I will show you how to identify the archetypes influencing your life, the light, and the shadow. How information affects your conscious ability to take charge of every event and situation, be it favorable or unfavorable. You can learn how to balance your life and set your goals every day, understanding why the shadow manifests and how you can turn it into the light.

I will ask a question that may seem strange at first because I have asked it before and gotten a response. Still, this time, I want you to think about it with greater depth than ever before, even if it means writing it down on paper or tapping out a response as I go along with my teaching process, then returning to it later for deeper consideration: What would happen if the darkness and mystery of God were suddenly removed from your experience? What might we lose?

When you read these words, you will see a different worldview. Why? Because you will take out an archetype, you may have adhered to as your groundwork, without which you will start to question everything else associated.

The most important thing you must remember is that the archetype is not something you "use." Of course, we can interact with it and extract its information and energy, but each archetype has its information and energy.

This book is to help you to think outside the box and see what you haven't perceived yet, showing you the exact meaning of each specific archetype as a symbol explained—the possibility to activate it in your life even if you are not influenced. After researching studies based on Carl Jung, Edmond Freud, Joseph Campbell, Marie D. Jones, Clarissa Pinkola Estes, Edward F. Edinger, Helio Couto, and Dr. Mabel Cristina Dias, I decided to unify those amazing works and develop all those in one.

The key is understanding its deep inner message and how to apply that knowledge in your life through visualization, imagination, meditation, and prayer to create changes in your consciousness. If you are ready to unlock the secret within you, let's turn it over and begin this book.

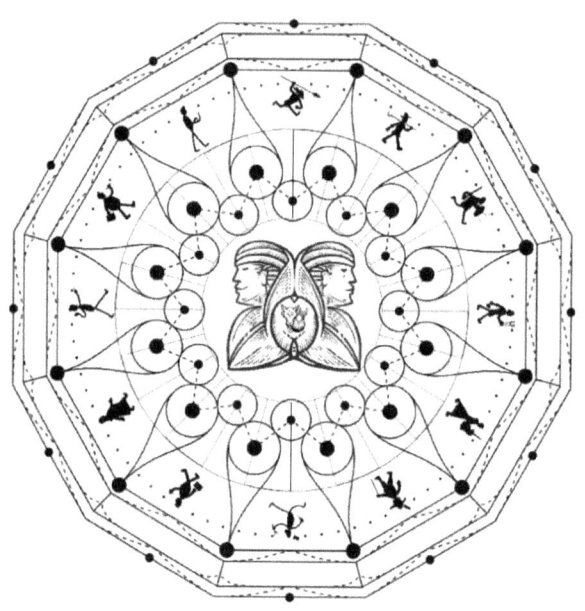

hunter	grower	warrior	craftsman	explorer	merchant	mechanizer	industrialist	oil driller	corporate executive	financier	startup founder
pre-history	10.000 B.C.	500 A.D.	1200. A.D.	1500 A.D.	1550	1800	1850	1901	1930	1960	2001

Chapter 1

Symbols, Archetypes, and Myths

Many people believe psychiatrist Carl Gustav Jung created the archetype, but that's not quite right. The first stories and ideas were found throughout the Plotinus scriptures, inspired by the philosopher Plato. Jung, who died in 1961, is credited with popularizing the idea of the archetypes, which he called "collective unconscious" or "archetypal patterns" (though these are more like universal principles). He was interested in the collective unconscious since his early days, and it was until 1928 that he began to write about them extensively in 'The Structure and Dynamics of the Psyche(1928-1934).

The archetype is an ideal, a concept, or a notion, which represents something fundamental to the human experience; it has deep psychic and emotional implications for humans and the collective psyche (also known as the unconscious). It can be an idealized image or pattern of a person, thing, or situation. In other words, archetypes are "a pre-conceived idea of what constitutes an archetype of a particular type." For example, Love, Justice, Motherhood, etc.

For many people, archetypes are the building blocks of personality and thus the basis for personality development in individuals and society, as well as the collective unconscious mind of humanity itself (also called the collective subconscious). Archetypes can be defined as images of the collective unconscious, and they may vary from culture to culture, as well as between individual cultures

Regardless, as per Plato, the idea was necessary for the existence of the physical world, the core idea, but what does that mean? The first energy or emanations before physical manifestations, the idea, the model, and the perfect being.

Plato's philosophy has two worlds: the idea and the manifest. For example, before an artist begins to paint, the image of the board already exists in his mind - the idea; he's merely a channel to manifest this concept into physical reality; there is always an archetype in the realm of ideas. There's a whole world beyond our awareness. The entire process is drawn from an archetypal idea that transcends time and space but is still anchored to a concrete place and time by its specific circumstances.

Archetype from Greek ἀρχή - arche: "pattern," and τύπος - type: "model," represents the principle behind something. Have you ever thought about why a woman doesn't need to study, pay for courses or look for someone to teach her to become a mother? The answer sounds obvious she is naturally born knowing how to do it independently; it's instinctive. However, archetypes have light and shadow.

If the woman wants to enjoy the light mother archetype, she will live unconditional love and happiness in maternity by feeding her children and caring for them. But if she lives in the shadow, the result will be abandonment and mistreatment. That is because she will ignore the archetype that exists to which her soul is somehow connected, but she has disconnected.

How many great leaders have we experienced in this world? The fact is behind their behavior pattern. There's an archetype backstage of reality. This archetype has the power to influence people's way of thinking, feeling, and behaving in ways that are beyond their conscious awareness, even though they may know all about them unconsciously!

An archetype represents a 'meaning 'or value system, which we absorb from our culture and pass on to future generations. An archetype can also be described as a type of 'energy, 'as it is not something physical but rather a dynamic, living force that influences human thought and emotion and creates 'patterns. '

Let's go back to a mother's example: a mother who is overly protective over her children will embody an archetypal image of a mother who takes care of others to give her children a safe environment. It is a principle passed down from one woman to another, though no proper training is ever acquired. How does this happen? It happens because of an archetype that is in existence. It is simply absorbed by the surroundings.

The archetypes have atomic foundations, just like everything else in the world. They are real, but they are in another dimension of reality. When we look at ourselves and others through the lenses of our archetypal patterns, we may see a reflection of the deeper order, or we may see a distorted reflection of it – just as when you investigate the depths of a pool and see a distorted image of what is underneath, reflected in the water surface above you. These archetypes exist in the collective unconscious of each person; collectively, we hold them as cultural myths that structure how we relate to one another and how we organize our society.

While there is a single truth, all truths come from the same source and are ultimately equal, so we can access the archetypes directly through our minds without being influenced by outside culture or society. It is one of the great secrets of the Universe that there is a special relationship between these archetypes and all the things that we call "natural" or "physical" – and between them and what we call the spiritual realm and the psychic world and the etheric world and the mental world and so on.

As soon as you start asking questions about the archetypes

and their nature, there is no way to explain them away or explain how they can be so powerful yet seem so ethereal simultaneously. So, we all must understand that archetypes aren't simply figments of our imagination; they're real!

The idea of an archetype is not a fantasy-type thing but a fact that every person on earth experiences and goes through life by following. This is an affirmation most people resist accepting. That's why the problems always grow. Because we live in denial about what we are going through and how it can benefit us to face our emotions instead of hiding from them when we do this, then they have more power over us than ever before because we are allowing them to control us or make us feel as if we did something wrong when really, it's nothing like that at all, it's just what every human being needs to go through to grow as a person and experience growth itself, it's part of life.

By being in denial, however, we empower problems. Because we don't want to hear about it, or get past it, or change our way of living and thinking about it, so it doesn't happen again in the future, and because we don't see any other way to deal with our problem but to find a "cure" or a solution to the problem or whatever it is we think is wrong with us or what others may say is wrong with us (the truth). In my opinion, we have all been touched by archetypes.

The truth is we all are aware of these archetypes around us, and we know that there is one principle to things, yet we desire to explore and overthink an archetype into its multiple existences. Regardless, an archetype doesn't need to be in many forms. Sometimes only one piece of information is enough to be recorded in your mind for years, maybe forever.

Science refers to it as a "mind program," since any information that cannot be deleted but must be reset, exactly like a computer, is referred to as reprogramming reprogram. It's not always a bad thing, though. For example, many of us have developed this "stuck" mindset during our lives (and even before) due to circumstances, such as:

- Inability to adapt to change because we've grown accustomed to an old way of doing things
- Being told how to behave and feel all our life by authority figures, which were probably insecure themselves
- Being born into a family with certain beliefs about how people should think and behave.

These mindsets can be very powerful and are used to keep you stuck.

Many people have been affected by traumatic events in their lives that have been ruined because of those memories. For example, after the death of a loved one or being raped, molested, abused, etc. They become so traumatized from the pain that it affects them in all aspects of their lives until the day they die, not even remembering how to do things anymore or even knowing what the word memory means. Such people may also have other problems, including depression, anxiety, panic attacks, chronic fatigue syndrome, chronic pain, fibromyalgia, insomnia, and more.

However, the more you use your brain for self-healing. The more you learn how to access and utilize the subconscious mind, the more you will be able to create the life of your dreams, rather than live out the same old, day in and day out, with little to no hope and an ever-growing sense of desperation and hopelessness as you attempt to make things work in your reality because you are stuck in what I call the mental prison of "the matrix."

This matrix is just as much of an archetype as is self-healing. The only reason you cannot navigate healing is that you trap yourself in the archetype of trauma. Nevertheless, you will manifest or understand the phenomenon when you understand that everything is atomic and how they act in all dimensions. The archetypes are energy, conscience, and symbols bringing feelings when we look at it, listen or perceive; it doesn't matter if it happens consciously or unconsciously. But what do we do with this information? How do we use it? We need to become conscious of our emotions to develop the ability to recognize them before they take shape into a belief system that is personality. Emotional maturity means accepting and releasing emotions to maintain your power and wisdom so that you may better utilize your energies for good.

The archetypal images that have been imprinted during our evolution (evolutionary memories) are activated when we live a certain kind of life (patterns). If you change your pattern, for example, if you change your inner image for a positive one, then you can change your emotions (feelings). You can change the behavior of others because the archetypes work on all levels of our being, from emotions to actions and behaviors, and even what we think and say, and this is possible only by creating new patterns of living.

Science has evidenced the manifestation of archetypes accessing the multiverses or the other side; modern technology built thousands of machines capable of accessing the other side. Otherwise, we would have no cell phones, Wi-Fi, TV, and all electronic toys. Nevertheless, in the next chapter, I'll show you the archetype through science and as a spiritual sign.

Archetypes have thousands of definitions: they can be sounds, symbols, attitudes, situations, behavior, touch, personalities, smells, and so on. One of the most common archetypal features is that humans experience emotions, whether pleasant or negative, strong or weak. Of course, positive results show up as self-growth, prosperity, happiness, love, health, etc. But the negative is depression, poverty, disease, addiction, separation, and so on.

When we feel a specific emotion, it affects our entire body. Our face shows it, our posture changes, and we react with energy in some way, either physical or mental, depending on how much we feel it in ourselves and how it impacts us on a physical level now (for example, by making us cry). If we know someone suffering from an illness, their faces will express the same symptoms that their bodies show, which means their emotions are very close to their body's emotions.

To understand archetypes generally, it is necessary to define what we mean by an archetype as a collective image of our mind and our emotional response when exposed to certain stimuli, like colors, smells, sounds, tastes, etc. Archetypes are universal patterns or principles that exist in all human beings, which can be triggered when we are emotionally aroused by something, such as the birth of a child, meeting your mother for the first time after many years.

This allows us to define more accurately the archetypes that exist in each individual's subconscious mind and help us to identify them if they have developed a strong influence on our identity and behavior patterns that we are not aware of or even willing to admit to ourselves, simply because we don't want to think about it and consider changing anything in our lives for fear of how this might affect our sense of security and happiness at the moment we start analyzing the problem further, which may be some time after all. When we do, it is too late.

Carl Gustav Jung, guided by Sigmund Freud, suggested that these archetypes were archaic forms of innate human knowledge passed down from our ancestors. The archetype proceeds from a platonic proposal into the world of ideas where there's primordial and terminal, where everything originates and returns to its source. It is a principle that applies as much to individual life as it does to the collective history of mankind itself, including in the most recent past. But archetypal experience is not something that man has built. It is an organic part of him, like the instincts (also a product of this universal creative activity). Thus, the mind becomes conscious of archetypes through images of things already formed. These images represent the original form of the thing and give us some knowledge about the inner being of things.

Jung used platonic thought to explain universal images

preexisting in the inner being since immemorial times. Jung described only twelve character archetypes residing within our collective unconscious as a primary type representing the range of basic human motivations. Four female and eight male archetypes can be described as the mother archetype, including all women. The father archetype includes all men. The lover archetype includes all humans. The shadow archetype includes all individuals who have suffered from abuse or abandonment and may include all humans.

Jung believed that the collective unconscious contained all of the knowledge and experiences humans share as a species. He also believed that the human psyche was composed of three components:

1. Ego
2. Personal unconscious
3. Collective unconscious.

All twelve are part of our collective unconscious and have some form of expression throughout history or across cultures, even though they may not be recognized consciously by individuals in any specific culture. The collective unconscious can also refer to Jung's concept of archetype inspired by Plato's philosophy, which held that there existed an original form into which all things were molded at creation and from which all later forms arose.

Jung's fantastic job helped millions of people to identify themselves the way they are, and I was one of them. The knowledge of archetypes can be constantly developed. It can also confuse different typologies; I decided to start with one typology in unified ways to describe the archetypes that humanity can live through their lives.

The first thing you need to understand is that human beings can have two main ways of living: The first way is called "ordinary," which means that we go through life like any other animal in nature; we work, eat, sleep, reproduce, etc. The second way is the spiritual or inner world of our mind based on a conceptual concept such as love, beauty, truth, power, wisdom, balance, harmony, etc....... This is what we call "spirituality."

Each archetype symbol has the meaning and power to manifest our life according to nature and potentiality. Still, we need to know what each archetype represents before proceeding further. The process of working with the archetypes can be a very powerful and profound tool in personal development if we are ready to use them wisely and have a deep understanding of them. This will help you overcome obstacles along your way to achieve success and happiness in life and increase your level of spiritual awareness in the process. By doing so, you can understand yourself better and get insights on how to live in harmony and balance within yourself, with others, and with the world around you to reach your goal in life.

To understand the meaning of each archetype, you must have an understanding of your personal history as well as a knowledge of what happened in your family's past, which will help you with this journey of self-discovery to find out what are the gifts that each archetype offers to you on your path towards a conscious awareness of who you truly are and how you can best express it in every aspect of your life: physical, emotional, mental, spiritual and material (financial). To do so, we need to connect the archetypes and our personal experiences so that the archetype itself becomes meaningful for us. So, if you are keen on discovering what archetypes direct your life, let's begin with our understanding of who we are and how we can unknot ourselves from a chain reaction of events and start anew.

Chapter 2

Archetype in the Science and Spirituality

"Archetypes provoke a response at the deepest level, unconscious, bringing up feelings, emotions, behaviors, primordial, filed deep in the human mind."

- Helio Couto

According to (Couto, 2015), "If you want to understand how archetype works through science, you may accept the atomic existence." You might assume that if there were no negative energy in the universe, all energy would be positive. Similarly, suppose you understand that electromagnet waves can work in all dimensional portals. In that case, you'll be able to perceive the manifestation of a phenomenon.

But how do you perceive these manifestations? How do you know their existence if it's only your perceptions that you have access to? That is the problem with how we view perception, and it's very similar to how we see life itself – everything depends on our perceptions! This is because what we perceive is directly influenced by the context we experience (mind). So, when we talk about "perceiving something," we usually mean observing or perceiving an object/phenomenon as existing outside of ourselves; this is not how reality works for most people.

Reality works and exists as an archetype model before anything else exists. Any symbol would show up as a true aspect in many forms. The only problem is the idea that you can be separate from your archetypal nature is just as false as any other belief system out there! So what happens when we get in touch with our archetypes? How does it change us? How do we relate to each other? We relate to each other through these archetypes surrounding us, comprising us, making us.

As mentioned before, these archetypes can be sound, touch, smell, personalities, etc. The easiest way to perceive it is by observing the results. Science can produce experiments, such as chemical tests, to see how the brain works after some archetypes stimulate someone. They can find these results through an electroencephalogram, tomography, MRI, and other laboratory exams.

Scientists can see the activation of other brain areas as neurotransmission - one of the main archetypes whose purpose is to send emotions into your mind using neurologist terms. Scientists can see the activation of other brain areas as neurotransmission - one of the main archetypes whose purpose is to send emotions into your mind using neurologist terms.

The best way to understand what I am talking about is through an analogy: Imagine you are on a train. At some point, you have a headache, and then you take two pills (aspirin or something else) to help you feel better in no time, and that's it! But imagine that you notice a change in your mood at some point, and you start smiling, laughing more, and finally feeling like a different person than you were before.

Well, this happens when we take our meds, but without any knowledge of the mechanism of action of those medicines, and only through intuition or feelings, which may not be always reliable.

When you see an archetype in the form of a product, your brain will associate emotions and feelings with the product. Science calls this neuro-association. This technique is made for product marketing. There are a thousand ways to create associations in some products. When the client wants to choose one product or another, the product that brings emotion will be chosen. When you buy any product, such as clothes or gadgets, you start thinking about how it feels to wear that item on your body, use a particular device at work, play games with a gadget, etc. A product can easily trigger neuro-association with similar characteristics to the previous one that has already been associated with those feelings.

The most important thing is to understand that you can benefit yourself with great potential. People must be aware of neuro-association, and the possibilities of feeling manipulation are huge.

It is very important to get a grip on this kind of knowledge because you will have much more control over the way you live and what happens in your daily life if you know how to influence people by means of archetypes or emotions as the main factors in their psyche (feelings). Archetypes are like a treasure box of different emotions, memories, attitudes, and behaviors that were used in the past to survive and thrive in some circumstances to be effective now as well as in future situations – they form the basis for our present actions, thoughts, feelings, behavior, beliefs, and decisions, as well as all of our relationships with others and ourselves.

Archetypal knowing is a practical tool to help you cope with the inner world of emotions and their outer manifestations in daily life. To help us begin this journey of understanding archetypes, we can utilize the archetypes to our benefit and have an increased understanding of ourselves and others, as well as learn how to manage and transform negative patterns of behavior and mental processes.

Neurotransmission

Neurotransmission is a chemical substance made through neurons to stimulate other nerve cells. Scientists believe that there are one hundred million neurons in the human body.

The brain and nervous system need to transmit information through neurotransmitters and hormones and electrical signals of action potentials (spikes) at synapses between nerve cells, which allows us to perceive our internal and external environment. The primary role of these chemicals is to transmit messages from one neuron to another neuron or cell and play an essential role in memory formation and learning.

Interestingly, we can also create emotions in ourselves and others by creating certain neurotransmission into a conversation. In fact, one of the best ways to increase your emotional intelligence is to pay attention to what you are saying and how you are saying it—or not! But I will tell you about relationships in the chapter 6; the possibilities are infinite when you know about chemical emotions.

The production of these neurotransmissions will depend on the archetype you are experiencing, but if you change your archetype, the neurotransmission can alter the type of conversation you are having. If you see the world as a series of dramas or if you see the world as an epic, it alters how you have conversations with people in your life and what sort of emotions you experience when you do so, which in turn affect your relationship to yourself, others and the world around you - which also has a significant impact on your physical health and wellbeing too!

Since the brain produces neurotransmission at high speed, stimulus time is important. Through an experiment, Dr. Eric J. Nestler proved that repetitive exposition provokes an alteration in the chemical brain. That explains why we must watch an announcement or commercial product several times to feel excited before buying it. When we understand human behavior, we can easily regulate it biochemically.

The brain functions are even more complex, but the information is enough in practice. There are a thousand ways to explain the archetypes, but people want to hear scientifically proven, which can be analyzed through neurotransmission. That's the reason why people sell, and you buy. Movies, series, and shows have audiences, and you watch them. A piece of music makes it to the top charts of the year, and you listen to it. The politicians are elected, and you vote. When I say you, I mean anyone in general, but the truth is that anyone can be controlled. There are a lot of neurotransmissions, but I'm going to show you the main of them.

Dopamine

Dopamine makes us feel happy, strong, confident, sexually empowered, ecstatic, powerful enough to overcome obstacles, and essential for well-being. Every time someone receives a positive stimulation, the brain creates dopamine that makes us feel happiness, living through the universe's vibration. A low level of dopamine leads to inferiority or insecurity.

Dopamine is extremely powerful neurotransmission, and it brings total control of a situation. Whatever the situation is, you can face any problem and challenges that life can show you through neurotransmission. When the neurotransmission of Alpha Male and Dominant Female occurs in your brain, your brain will start to produce serotonin, as well as release cortisol for stress relief and endorphins to create an overall sense of relaxation and happiness, which you can always feel and experience when the neurotransmission happens in your brain or your body!

Most of the greatest businessmen or executives need higher levels and continuous dopamine circles in their brains. They are not just on one level of being. They're at different levels throughout the day – like a rocket scientist is at different levels during an experiment, a doctor is at different levels as he performs surgery, and a painter is at different levels when creating a painting or when doing so in a state of flow – these are all different states that represent a level of consciousness in the brain, and this is why we have more than one part of the brain involved with consciousness.

Serotonin

Serotonin is a stimulation in the part of the brain and an inhibitor for others that relieves depression controls pain and humor, in addition to help you fall asleep. It is imperative to feel happiness. For example, a suicidal shows a lower serotonin level, which is requisite to regulate anxiety and change it into calm.

With serotonin, you are in peace with yourself and the world. This way, we can regulate the emotional state of any population by just changing certain archetype explosion. Serotonin is one of the most important neurotransmissions as its actions help cognition and behavioral aspects.

Endorphin

Endorphins are important for happiness, relaxation, ecstasy, and general wellbeing. Some medicine proprieties react as a relaxing pill as pain relief; it's connected to a certain level of dopamine in the organism. It generates a pleasant feeling, relieving depression; it controls an organism's response to stress regulation and liberates hormones of stress. Endorphins come from brain cells called neurons connected with pleasure centers of the body (brain).

Endorphin production is connected to good and positive things in life. If we receive a positive stimulus, we might produce endorphins. However, the opposite is true; if we experience negative events like pain, sadness, or loss, endorphin levels fall because of stress. Although endorphins are often thought to have a positive role in the body, they have several different functions depending on where they act.

Some endorphins relieve pain by reducing inflammation, whereas others block opioid receptors, preventing other chemicals from entering the brain cells that cause us to feel depressed, anxious, or tired. Endorphins also trigger the release of serotonin (a neurotransmitter) which helps us sleep better at night and makes us more likely to want to socialize.

Endorphins also promote comfort, a potential of the morphine encephalic, strengthen immunity, memory, patience, and humor, and decrease psychological stress, consequently delaying aging. That's the reason why depressive people easier get sick because their archetype does not stimulate endorphins.

Oxytocin

Oxytocin is most present during the breastfeeding period and childbirth. They can reach a long-term effect on men and women in many areas of their lives, especially when an emotion or a relationship is involved. Oxytocin is called hormone connection, responsible for mammal's survivor to be nourished by their mother right after birth.

At the beginning of studies, oxytocin was wrongly affirmed as a female hormone. It was discovered that it's present in men as well. Fathers have feelings, too, when they know their partner is expecting.

Fathers need to connect with their children, grandchildren, and descendants. The importance of oxytocin is present in our relationships with our friends, parents, relatives, and even with our pets. During a sexual relationship, both men and women release oxytocin, releasing Ambiental and cervical stimuli. Oxytocin slight desire to be kissed and cuddled by their lover.

Oxytocin is the only hormone in the human body that is released during sex with someone you love, and it's also what makes people fall in love in the first place; however, oxytocin alone does not cause a person to become a romantic or a loving partner, as we know from personal experience and research about oxytocin and other hormones like dopamine and serotonin, which are responsible for creating a feeling of love within a person. So, they need a partner with similar traits to trigger those feelings.

For men and women, there are different chemical levels in the brain. The level of a man's chemistry is higher than girls. A woman needs more oxytocin if she wants to feel orgasm, eventually, multiple orgasm if her brain is full of oxytocin.

We use term oxytocin as 'love drug' for its ability to form strong emotional relationships and boost emotions. Oxytocin helps individuals recover quicker from sickness; married people have the advantage of living longer and contributing to groups that care for cancer patients; therefore, there are so many lovely people in hospitals attempting to make children and people of all ages happy while fighting against cancer.

There are a lot of diseases caused by stress; studies believe oxytocin is a chemical key to calm, stress relief, and consequently healing diseases.

Oxytocin, or "The Love Hormone," –is one of the best natural health remedies for treating anxiety disorders and various types of depression; research has been going on for decades now and continues even today to find out more about this incredible hormone; we're talking here about the chemical responsible for labor contractions during childbirth, milk letdown, and parturition, as well as the chemical responsible for social bonding and attachment among individuals and within families, which makes us feel safe, loved and cared for.

Acetylcholine

Acetylcholine is a stimulus that controls movements, memory, focus, emotions, sexual activity, and other organs. It also controls pituitary gland liberation during the learning involved.

Acetylcholine is a stimulus that controls movements, memory, focus, emotions, sexual activity, and other organs. It also controls pituitary gland liberation during the learning involved.

The chemical acetylcholine is used in our body to control the heartbeat rate and breathing function of our lungs as well as the muscles of our limbs, tongue, and vocal cords that make sounds such as words and phrases are controlled by nerve cells in the brain's motor cortex, which receives signals from sensory neurons in the skin and inner ears that inform us about what we feel and hear and from nerves in other parts of the body that inform us about where we touch and move.

Acetylcholine is important to our ability to remember positive notions. Acetylcholine is released in the hippocampus when we hear new information or learn new things about something, or in the brain's olfactory bulb when we smell pleasant odors like food, flowers, perfume, etc.

Acetylcholine also regulates the release of dopamine (a chemical associated with motivation), oxytocin (a chemical linked with love, care, affection, trust), serotonin (psychosis, depression, anxiety, mood), endorphins (pain relief), cortisol (stress) and prolactin (motherhood). Acetylcholine can be produced from choline in the body or dietary supplements.

Archetype as a Spiritual View

The tarot card is one of the most common tools to explain archetypes as a spiritual guide. There is all archetypical architecture in the spiritual world. Some readers use it for a riddle and other purposes, but my focus here is on the symbols that need to be interpreted, which we will see in the next chapter.

Since the Judaic period, symbols have been present until today; religions have used symbols as their representative since their foundation. They are essential to them. In some cases, they represent a single idea, while others represent the entire religion or a particular belief. They play a role in defining and creating a religious culture and community and transmitting traditions, beliefs, and rituals from one generation to another.

Once archetypes are preexistence, everything you see, like temples, candles, images, and statues, has a significant meaning well designed before being created. The symbolism behind the construction of the pyramids is still an enigma to us today. Still, we can use our imagination to guess at what it was about them that drove people to build them in the first place—and why they were built by so many different cultures in Egypt, Greece, Mexico, India, Central America, Asia, etc., for tens of thousands of years and across two continents (North and South).

Archetypes are not just about the past; they also exist in the present and future. All creators feel inspired before starting their works, but where is this inspiration coming from? Do they have the same consciousness as you and me? Can we access the same spiritual plan as they do? Can we think like them?

Archetypes represent some universal idea that we all must deal with, a theme so common in our lives, or a feeling which has been passed down through generations for a long time that we sometimes don't realize how much it exists in us and around us (think about the old saying 'it's in the blood.')

For spiritual believers, independent of their religion, we all have a divine within us. That explains why there are so many religions. Since the beginning of this world, human beings have deeply needed to connect to a divine spark. There are many reasons why some people let go of religion to find God independently. Others let go of everything, including their faith, maybe because they never gave themselves completely into the spiritual path because of paradigm, family teaching, culture, etc. Whatever your situation may be, we can all benefit from connecting to our inner source, tapping into divine energies for guidance in life, and healing ourselves spiritually, emotionally, mentally, physically, and energetically.

Anyone can find the truth within themselves, whatever they are, even in the most horrible places. There are thousand books talking about the enlightenment in social media, but a few amounts of people interested in listening, why? Because of the paradigm. We must break free from this prison that society has built around us, a prison of beliefs, attitudes, opinions, judgments about others 'guilt, self-hatred, fear, envy, aggression, violence, hate, selfishness, lust, greed, anger, jealousy, insecurity, lies, dishonesty, dishonor, shame, condemnation, blame, competition, possessiveness, greed, envy, hatred, resentment, etc.

The first scientist's studies information was never shared before developing their experiment creations, medicine, chemical weapons, etc. Why? Because research about occultism, black magic, Bible, miracles, and Egyptian stories to accomplish a goal may result in a new perception that any material being were linked to the other side of reality. We need to see how we can use our free will and take charge of this life instead of being a slave to all these things around us that we don't even know are enslaving us! The more you learn, the more you realize that there is much more in life than just money, power, and status!

"Witches and sorcerers are scientists who didn't attend college". This proverb reminds us that a witch has no idea how to solve a chemical equation or calculus, still, they know how to make a perfect circle to manifest results in somebody else's life.

It also means that witches don't need money because their power comes from a higher source, and they have plenty of it on hand anyway! You might think you're working for magic, but, you're being used by the higher powers to create what you desire.

Through spiritual eyes, archetypes are all inside us; everything is unified. So, to get your desired result, you need to open up and access the archetype that corresponds with it – whether it be a dragon or angel archetype, there's one that relates to that particular goal/desire - this will help you move toward it much faster.

When we align with our true nature, we will feel like one with the universe and be in love with ourselves, others, and life itself; we can experience a sense of oneness with the world around us — even if we don't believe it yet!

Archetypes aren't just the inner qualities that help people get through their daily lives – they are also the very fabric of existence itself, the nature of matter, and energy itself.

The archetypes we will discuss are not meant to be used as a guide for how you should live your life but rather as an understanding of what exists inside each of us and how it can influence our behavior in certain situations or relationships. If we know this information about ourselves, we will be able to recognize the archetypes in others and understand why they act and react as they do (and not always the way we think they would).

To make these connections, we need first to recognize them.

Chapter 3

22 Main Archetypes

Now I will show every detail of each archetype's characteristic influence. We can start with the leading 22 archetypes. They are:

1. The Artist
2. The Luminous
3. The Magician
4. The Detachment
5. The Priestess
6. The Hedonist
7. The Mediator
8. The Revolutionary
9. The Hero
10. The Mother
11. The Sage
12. The Master
13. The Leader
14. The Lover
15. The Resurrection
16. The Integrated
17. The Rebel
18. The Curator
19. The Lucky
20. The Courage
21. The Fairness
22. The Pure

1. The Artist

Creativity, beauty, expression, inspiration, feeling.

The artist needs to express their feelings through paint boards, lyrics, craft, and so on. For an artist, everything that can be imagined can be created. The artists can also be recognized as the innovator, the creator, the inventor, the musician, and the dreamer. It is a person who sees the beauty in his world and expresses it through his paintings, drawings, sculptures, films, or music so that people around him can experience what he has seen and felt by listening to the voice of the soul of the artist hidden inside himself and came out on canvas with the use of colors and brushes.

An artist's primary goal is to create something lasting, create a culture and express their worldview. The artist wants to reflect the human essence through aesthetic beauty and harmony, representing a receptivity symbology and new ideas.

Artists are creators of culture: they make artworks that have a deep connection with our humanity, and that can be a symbol of universal values, for a better understanding between people, for peace, love, and mutual respect. In other words, an idea that is more than just a product or material thing but a way of thinking and feeling becomes a living part of us. It connects us to the universe in general and ourselves and each other. This is why art can be a powerful expression for spiritual awakening and transformation.

The artist invites us to see the hidden perfection from imperfection. The artist shows us that we all have some shadow within, turning it into light as a transformation. The artwork allows the viewer to experience a deeper connection with the human condition and life.

The first level is to be creative or innovative, imitating others. The second level is shaping their vision, and the third level is creating structures that influence the culture and society.

Examples of myths: Greek Goddess Hecate and Yoruba Goddess Yemoja.

Examples of personalities: Mozart, the Polymath Leonardo Da Vince, Salvador Dali, Frida Kahlo, and Oscar Wild.

Examples of cultural creators: Sesame Street, Madmen, Frida, Shakespeare in Love, Amadeus, and Cinderella.

Examples of myths: Hecate (Greek), and Iemanja (Yoruba).

Examples of personalities: Oscar Wilde, Carl Gustav Jung, and Pablo Picasso

Examples of brand creators: Lego, Post-it, S singer, and Bombay Sapphire.

Some products encourage self-expression, offering consumers choices when they don't know what they want. It helps to promote innovations. What these brands do is that they make the consumer believe they have the creating power by supplying their idea, like an artist. The brands share their concept, expressed through a product that can further create the consumer's desired product.

The main goal is to find perfection where is imperfection.

Some products belong to a creative camp, like marketing, public relations, art, and technology innovation such as software development. Other items like the Lego shop encourage consumers to let their imaginations run wild. As S singing company, the product encourages consumers to make their own decisions and save money.

Light: if you choose to live this archetype fully, you'll develop behaviors like:

- ✓ Creativity
- ✓ Loves something new, open to new possibilities
- ✓ Feel a deep need to express themselves
- ✓ Personal charm
- ✓ Take the responsibilities from their attitudes
- ✓ Likes to bring impact into other lives through entertainment and seduction
- ✓ Imaginative

- ✓ Sensitive, they make choices through emotion instead of reason
- ✓ Never mind living in a disorganized environment
- ✓ Doesn't accept rules and boundaries easily

Shadow: if you resist living this archetype fully, you'll develop behaviors like:

- ✓ Psychological stress
- ✓ Difficulty meeting schedules
- ✓ Anxiety
- ✓ Anguish
- ✓ Sadness
- ✓ Addiction
- ✓ Narcissism
- ✓ Wanting to escape reality
- ✓ Clinging to the past
- ✓ Hypochondria
- ✓ Financial difficulties
- ✓ Jealously
- ✓ Emotional instability

If this archetype influences you, you can have a successful vocational profession in areas such as:

- Architecture
- Art Design
- Theater
- Music
- Dance
- Photography
- Esoterism
- Psychoanalyze
- Craft
- Design
- Literature

- Cinema
- Performing Arts
- Psychology
- Philosophy
- Writer

Powerful symbols of the artist are:

- Musical Instruments
- Fish
- Crab
- Paint Palette
- Moon
- Paintbrush

The tarot arcane is: The card XVIII La Lvne – The Moon

2. The Luminous

*The luminous archetypes seek self-acknowledgment
and expand awareness.*

The luminous understands that we were all made from one consciousness - the universe- and understands that anything can be transformed by expanding awareness and broadening the perception of reality. The luminous understands that there is a great source of light in every person; that we are all part of this same consciousness which is the Light of all Life; and that everyone is here to help bring on the New Age by sharing their knowledge, wisdom, and talents with others so they may help in creating an enlightened society that will be for the betterment of all beings everywhere.

Dr. Mabel Cristina describes "The luminous notices that there's no more ego but the self-awakening or divine spark that is wise, pacified and eternal on the inner being. The luminous now comprehend why they think and behave, consequently, they notice that whatever they are emanating is returning to them." (Dias, n.d.)

If the mind sees its thoughts as though from the outside, it will be free of these thoughts and no longer need to control them. If it does not see itself as it is, the mind will always be controlled by emotions, which are just thoughts in another form that arises from the body. Suppose it observes itself without judging or evaluating. In that case, it will become conscious of its true nature and then work on freeing itself from this consciousness and returning to a state where there is only pure awareness.

We can feel true happiness we did not live before; we survived. We become light to be a light for everyone around us. We can feel true happiness we did not live before; we survived. We become light to be a light for everyone around us.

I want you to imagine the most powerful being in this world is standing next to you, and that person says, "I have come here to give you power over everything you are experiencing." And if you say yes, what will happen?

Now imagine a second person who comes from the same place, and she says, "I've come to help you with all your problems." What would you choose? Which one do you think will make you happy? The first one? That's because it gives you more power than the other. So, when you ask yourself which one you want, it's like asking, which one of these two people will make me happy? You'll choose the second person, even though she will take away some of your power.

Expanding awareness, we can see everything clearly and notice that:

- We are all multidimensional being
- We are all connected to the same electromagnet camp
- We can create our reality; we are not victims
- God's will be the only thing that matters
- We are free willed to make choices

- What we are receiving from the universe are the same things from our thoughts and feelings

The luminous invites us to connect to the cosmic energy that organizes the world. It offers energy to conquer our deepest wishes and desires, especially our most significant purpose. This is a potent invitation! Our lives are organized by desire; this is how we express our creative impulses, unique gifts, and the possibilities of what we want for ourselves in life and relationships with others in the community and at work.

The same energy extends at home in our family, neighborhood, and town or city, state, province, country, and on a global level where all people and living things interact together as one planet and all resources are shared by all species as we make decisions about how we will live sustainably and responsibly in our own personal and cultural context.

Examples of Myths: Egyptian Aten, Greek God Apollo, Greek God Ra, Yoruba God Logun Ede.

Examples of personalities: Dalai Lama, Deepak Chopra, Eckhart Tolle, and Buddha.

Examples of Culture: Here Comes the Sun by Beatles, Little man Tate, Good Will Hunting, Finding Dory, and Jimmy Neutron.

Light: if you choose to live this archetype fully, you'll develop behaviors like:

- ✓ Never try to change people's perceptions of their prospective gifts, skills, and abilities and use it as a source of positive reinforcement.
- ✓ Accept that everyone has their evolution path. That's why they don't judge
- ✓ Understand that your reality will change if you change first
- ✓ Success in ventures, happy with all your goals being successful

✓ Recognize your shadow and look forward to healing it
✓ Admitting mistakes and not being afraid of asking for forgiveness
✓ Careful with the action that can impact the world as you understand that every action brings a reaction
✓ Love to learn something new
✓ A fully happy and wellbeing feeling brings happiness to everyone
✓ Never searching for guilt as they take responsibility for everything that happens in their life, whether bad or good.
✓ Understand that health is part of spiritual evolution. They love to exercise, consume healthy food, and feel elevating self-esteem

Shadow: If you resist living archetype entirely, you'll develop behavior like:

✓ Proudness
✓ Egocentrism
✓ Manipulation
✓ Disorganization
✓ Exaggerated ambition
✓ Pessimism
✓ Narcissism
✓ Excessive self-importance
✓ Arrogance

If the luminous archetype influences you, you might have a successful vocational profession in areas such as:

• Entrepreneur
• Landscape
• General Therapy
• Physical Education
• Esoterism

- Spiritual Coaches
- Music Therapy
- Plastic Art Design
- Performing Arts
- Marketing,
- Business Administration
- Sports
- Publicity
- Music
- Cinema
- Dance
- Yoga instructor

Powerful symbols are the sun, the sunflower, the light lamp, and the eye.

The tarot arcane is: The XIX Le Soleil – the Sun

3. The Wizard

Experiencing the Wizard archetype provides you a life with good Communication, Initiative, Intelligence, and skills for transformation and personal power.

You can be The Visionary, Catalyst, Innovator, Charismatic Leader, Mediator, Shaman, and Healer.

You are a wizard of your world who will help others to grow their powers as well as to make them feel secure in life and in their relationship with the universe or religion they believe in serve or worship, especially if you choose to do so on your terms without feeling obligated to do something that you cannot be proud of doing or is unethical or immoral in some way (such as killing innocent animals or harming yourself). Your main concern is to become a better person by helping those around you to do the same.

The wizard can manifest their ideas into reality through

these gifts and abilities. Thus, it becomes a change agent in society, becoming influential in politics or business to make positive changes happen in the world around them or simply make themselves happy, confident, and secure within their skin, all the while making a difference in others 'lives as well. They are successful in whatever they do, which ultimately benefits them and those around them.

- Basic desire is knowing the main law of the universe.
- The goal is to turn dreams into reality.
- The strategy is to develop a vision and experience it.
- The gift is finding a winner's results.

Myths: Hermes (Greek), Mercury (Roman), Thoth (Egyptian), Mage Merlin (Welsh), Eshu (Yoruba), and Moses (Judaic).

Some examples of the wizard archetype personalities are Paulo Coelho (writer), Deepak Chopra (writer), Jackie Onassis (ex-first lady), Osho (guru), and Aleister Crowley (mage).

The motivation is a premonition, extra-sensorial experience, or synchronistic.

Level 1: Magic moments and transformation experiences.

Level 2: The flux experience

Level 3: Miracles, the passage from vision to manifestation

Some examples of wizard influence on the culture are Merlin, Gandalf, Yoda, Don Juan, Harry Potter, and Maleficent.

Examples of brand wizard archetypes are RedBull, Absolut Country of Sweden Vodka, Sony, MasterCard, and Disney. The product or service is part of the transformation.

It promises to transform the consumer. The product shows a new age or creative culture to the consumer. It introduces a friendly technology to the user, a spiritual or psychological component, and a new and contemporary product, from medium to high price. Wizard people make the consumer believe that everything is possible and makes dreams come true in 1 million possibilities.

The wizard is an object with a power that can be obtained

through magical rituals and a person who can help us under-stand our reality and change it into something better if we fol-low his advice and accept his recommendations for our life improvement process. This person is like a shaman who guides us through an initiation process of a product we do not need.

The wizard is the main archetype we are influenced by, es-pecially during our youth—the need to experience new things and thoughts of the infinite possibilities offered.

The wizard has strong communication power with others, with natural elements, especially different communication with different layers of the mind.

Our mind has integrated divisions such as:

The conscience: is responsible for logical reasoning, focus, and discipline. The conscience is a small part of our psyche uni-verse as individuals. The voice inside us speaks to us about what is right and wrong, good or bad, and who we are concerning God and other people in society, etc.

The personal unconscious: is a big part of our mind that has no logical reasoning capacity. Its function is to save most of the information from the conscience, such as thoughts, feelings, impulses, and contents we don't want to experience.

Collective unconscious: is the life experiences of the hu-mans and archetypes around us. It comprises collective experi-ences, reasoning, thoughts, and feelings experienced as a unified community.

Superconscious: is the mind of the Universe and knows everything, and it's the consciousness that connects people to universal wisdom.

The wizard has a great skill in bringing information from the unconscious to the conscious mind, taking hidden ideas, and bringing them to the physical world to execute, just like an artist who creates the paint board in his mind and then produces the same drawing that was thought.

In this process of bringing those hidden ideas into our body, we can feel good or bad emotions like fear, happiness, sadness, etc., which we can identify as an emotional experience. Still, if you look at it more objectively, you will realize that these are just feelings in your brain and nothing else. Therefore, they cannot be real experiences unless you believe them as such. Consequently, they become real experiences for you. In other words, a wizard archetype takes these experiences and focuses only on the good ones to create something positive and meaningful out of them.

It's an archetype that expresses the solitude deeply - alone we came into this world, alone we will leave. The wizard believes everything is connected, and the sacred is something above or distant from us and a powerful force within us. Everything is possible. The wizard is constantly connected with the universe's law and in harmony.

"As above, so below, as within, so without, as the universe, so the soul...."

- Hermes Trismegistus

The wizard can manipulate all four materials elements: Earth (material), Water (emotions), Fire (intuition, sexuality), and Air (mental), and transform them into sacred. That way, the wizard can use all four conscience functions: Sensation (sand), feelings (water), thought (air), and intuition (fire). The wizard can use those for something greater, and that allows them to become a curator of bodies and souls.

It is not about having more power but using your existing ability with a purpose beyond the physical realm to create something profound.

When everything seems connected, events, people, conscience and unconscious, dreams and reality, it is called synchronicity that comes from wizards because it can transit to the interior and exterior world from different dimensions of reality.

It is the time when we are here on Earth. However, we are still connected with our higher self and other beings who live on another dimension or parallel universes. It brings us together through synchronicities which means that we all understand each other's situations and experiences. For example, a dream that may come true later becomes a real experience and vice versa.

> *"But I say to you that when you work you fulfill a part of earth's furthest dream, assigned to you when the dream was born, and in keeping yourself with labor you are in truth loving life and to love life through labor is to be intimate with life's inmost secret."*

> **- Khalil Gibran**

Through their work, the wizard makes all possibilities become probabilities; it is the archetype that "makes it happen." and promotes self-transformation in the world.

The most beautiful creations come about through this method of creativity: art, music, literature, dance, science, philosophy, and even love – all are forms of expression that manifest out of one source and then, in different ways, express the human being's inner nature.

The wizard helps people influence their transformation.

Light: If you choose to live this archetype fully, you'll develop behaviors like:

- ✓ A person who understands their mind creates their reality and uses this power
- ✓ Self-confidence. Understands that they can take any situation and transform it for the better
- ✓ Believes they have everything on their hand for success
- ✓ Great personal power
- ✓ Power to heal
- ✓ Great ability to work
- ✓ Open-minded about the new
- ✓ Excellent entrepreneur
- ✓ Great communicators

✓ Persuasive
✓ Strong connection with nature and see it as an ally
✓ Wish to innovate and create a new project
✓ Able to make a material thing into spiritual and sacralize what is profane

Shadow: If you resist living this archetype, you'll develop behaviors like:

✓ Have many ideas that they cannot put into practice
✓ Might feel depressive by not getting into action
✓ Might become selfish when they lose life's sacred connection
✓ Laziness; staying in the comfort zone
✓ Betray people around them and their ideals
✓ Because of great persuasion power, they might become manipulative
✓ Impulsivity, making an early decision that might cost them peace and money
✓ They don't continue the work they started like courses, projects, and relationships, making them stuck in life
✓ Procrastination, making them leave everything for later

If the wizard archetype influences you, you might have a successful vocational profession in areas such as:

- Journalism
- Publicity
- Marketing
- General Therapy
- Chemistry
- Art
- Medicine
- Sales
- Entrepreneur
- Architecture

- Translation and Interpretation
- Public Relations
- Real Estate Brokerage
- Spiritual Coach
- Writer
- Any other jobs involving communication, personal power, or intelligence.

Powerful symbols are the sword, Magic wand, Cup, Hat, and Pentagram

Tarot arcane is Card I, Le Bateleur - The Mage

4. Detachment

Fluidity and life trust.

The detachment archetype is a symbol that influences the attitude of letting it go.

This archetype is associated with all types of things, including animals and people and your environment and circumstances in life like family, friends and work colleagues or even government policies and laws and so on... What are you attached to? What do you think about it? Why do you hold onto things? Are you attached to something in your life because of what it means for you? What if this attachment hinders your ability to become freer from its influence? Are you attached to anything that makes you feel safe, comfortable, or confident?

Letting go can be difficult, and we may not always know what we are letting go of or what we want to detach ourselves from.

Examples of Myths are the Tower of Babel, The labyrinth of Minos (Greek), Prometheus (Greek), and Obatala (Yoruba).

The cultural influence examples are Yes Man (movie), Chaos theory (movie), Good Morning Vietnam (movie), Shallow Hal (movie), Up (movie), and Believe (music) by Cher.

Let it go means set it free, something you are clinging to. It could be because of fear, anxiety, or things that do not allow us to be our true selves. When we want something and request the universe, it won't work if we don't let it go. We must let go of things that no longer serve us to move forward with our life goals and dreams.

For example, when you go to the restaurant and request some food from the menu, do you need to get anxious or call the waiter every time to ask if your food is coming? Of course not, because you are sure that your food is coming. You ask and let it go. You have no idea what the cooks are doing in the kitchen, and you know there's no reason to worry about it - you trust the staff at the restaurant. So why is that so hard to feel this trusting when we ask for anything from the universe?

The simple question is the ego within us. The ego doesn't want to lose control; hence it clings to things we should let go of. Let things go; set yourself free. You don't have to worry or lose your peace anymore. The attachment delays our requests from the universe or even nullifies it.

Letting go is the most powerful attitude we commit. When we let go and allow things to happen naturally, everything we ask naturally becomes a material reality. To become an effective practitioner of the law of attraction, one must first understand that it works best when we are free from our own limiting beliefs about what will or will not manifest in our lives, what we can or cannot have, how much money we can make, etc. This means letting go of whatever you believe you already know because if your belief system doesn't align with your new understanding of how the Universe works, then your desire won't be able to take root and develop fully.

You must let go. You must learn to get up and not stay in bed all day or do nothing. We must do our part as universal lovers. Remember that God does things that we cannot do on our own. Letting go means not feeling anxious or pressured about what you want. If you ask something from the universe with a deadline and involve another, the universe will give you everything you need.

You are an infinite being! You have no limits! You are pure energy, with no restrictions or limitations of any kind! In our everyday life, we tend to think that we can't be without anything because it's impossible, but there is nothing that we can't get because we have limitless resources inside us! When we let go, we open the gate to unlimited possibilities! When we stop searching for something, then it appears! We live in this world full of illusions.

We can wish for something and work for it, but we cannot depend our happiness on the results. True happiness doesn't depend on external results; it stems from the inner self you can develop. It is known as life's satisfaction.

In relationships, letting go doesn't mean you stop loving someone or stop helping others. Letting go means you do not trap someone. Love is a feeling of freedom, just like the universe sets us. If we are always holding on to something or someone, then that can only mean one thing: We have more fear than love in our life! We need to let go of everything that holds us back and gives us no freedom or happiness; we need to give up all kinds of attachments and start giving ourselves fully to our own lives and what truly matters most – as this will bring us inner peace and the ability to love unconditionally and freely!

Sometimes we believe that life owes us something, but we wish life must be the way we want it to be. It doesn't work like this; our lives are shaped by our decisions and things around us, sometimes without our knowledge or control, and that's how life works for us all!

Have you experienced the moment of receiving something you were fighting so hard to get, but you only received it when you stopped fighting? This is a metaphor for how we receive many things in our lives that we believe are gifts from God, but we don't realize them until we stop trying to have them and live in faith with Him (I am not talking about faith-based actions). That's because you freed yourself from the attachment of wanting something.

The Detachment archetype teaches us that when we lose

fear, we experience freedom.

Light: If you choose to live this archetype fully, you'll develop behaviors like:

- ✓ Flexible, easy-going
- ✓ Integrity
- ✓ Disciplined and patient
- ✓ Humility
- ✓ Feel the pain without suffering
- ✓ Make plans and work hard, but detached from results
- ✓ Honesty
- ✓ Believes in the wisdom that transcends understanding and in the flow of life
- ✓ It's persistent but never creates exaggerated expectations
- ✓ Do not put pressure on situations or people
- ✓ Non-action
- ✓ Loyal to principles and values
- ✓ Great personality and attracts a high presence of attention

Shadow: If you resist fully living this archetype, you'll develop behaviors like:

- ✓ Attachment, possession
- ✓ Pessimism
- ✓ Anxiety
- ✓ Anger
- ✓ Self-victimization
- ✓ Self-destruction
- ✓ Fatalism
- ✓ Depression
- ✓ Conformism
- ✓ Self-charge
- ✓ Loneliness

If the Detachment archetype influences you, you might have

a successful vocational profession in areas such as:

- Physics
- Inventions
- Science
- Tourism
- Engineering
- Social Assistance
- Esotericism
- Priesthood

The most Powerful Symbols are lightning, Tower, Chaos Star, and Maze

Tarot Arcane is the Card XVI La Maison Diev – The tower

5. Priestess

Intuition and connection with the female sacred.

The priestess is a great depth and beauty archetype, the sacred female within us.

In her, we are healed of our wounds and made whole in ourselves and the world. We are set free to be precisely who we were intended to be: whole, complete, radiant beings in this universe and our own unique personal power, light, joy, creativity, and healing for all! She comes with the promise of learning from her errors and mending them along the road by recognizing the value of love in the healing process and utilizing that love to heal ourselves and others.

Myths examples are Persephone (Greek), Eros and Psyche (Greek), Isis (Egyptian), Virgin Mary (Christian), Sophia (Gnosticism), Ishtar/Inanna (Mesopotamian), Nana (Yoruba), Astarte/Ashtoreth (Hebrew).

Some personality examples are Clarissa Pinkola Estes (writer), Robert A. Johnson (writer), Lorraine Warren (medium), and Maria Orsic (medium).

Examples of cultural influence are the book of secrets (music) by Loreena Mckennitt, Ancient Mother (music) by Robert Gass, Moana, The Little Mermaid, The Red Tent, and Melisandre from Game of Thrones.

(Dias, n.d.) writes: The Priestess symbolizes the connection to your inner being, the unconscious, something hidden behind the veil. The unconscious is a deep world full of riches, with the potential to develop, such as our primary personality.

That part that is our ego, our sense of self which we all have in some way, and there's something else deeper down that can be explored, which is the archetypal part of ourselves, the collective unconscious – it's full of these deep truths and insights and wisdom and beauty that we are not necessarily aware of, but that connects us to everything, to the source, to nature itself, to the divine, to all things on this planet and beyond in an enormous network of connections.

According to Chinese philosophy, there's Yin and Yang in this duality plan. They are opposite but complementary, holding a seed with each other. They are part of everything that can be manifested in the universe. That's why we can find it within us; whatever gender or sexual orientation, anyone can live. This archetype feels a deep connection with your female aspect, the Yin.

The female is the one who is united and integrated. She doesn't oppose anything but includes and welcomes. The female awakes the love capacity.

She doesn't create a problem out of any negative experience or feeling. She welcomes it and the person and the whole process of existence itself! She has an open mind; she does not cling to her ideas or those of others; she is free from fear and anxiety; she is at ease with herself and others; she is compassionate towards all beings; she is generous, selfless, and loving and she knows how to use these virtues in every situation of life! She is the mother of the spiritual evolution of humanity.

The Priestess is a female sacred archetype that regains inner wisdom, self-acknowledgment, intuition, femininity, and sacred sexuality. It's the Goddess. The priestess has a gift of waiting because she knows that the universe and human timings are different. She waits until it's ready to unfold, like an orchid blooming after many months of hibernation inside its chrysalis!

The priestess is one of the most potent archetypes to embody in modern times because it represents the feminine expression of the divine feminine.

The Wizard represents the primary Yang, the male creation and active aspect. The priestess represents the primary Yin, the receptive creation. Once they are united, everything is created.

The priestess represents the untouchable part of us, a deep, pure, and confident side like a forest that has never been explored. That is where our potential lies. It's an archetype that can bring a wish to learn and study, affectivity, inspiration, and patience.

It wants us to grow, mature, and become more in tune with who we are and what we want out of life, but it also tells us to stay within ourselves so that we do not become lost or confused; to stay grounded even in a world full of change and constant flux; to listen to our intuition to understand what makes us unique, special, and valuable; to see beyond the surface, to find the deeper meaning; to know who we truly are and what we truly stand for.

The great virtues that the priestess can bring is a deep connection to our unconsciousness, dreams, feeling, and intuition. The Priestess guides us to discover our deepest desires to fulfill them through dreams, meditation, and rituals with symbols. She brings to our mind the power of femininity and its role as a healer, guide, and nurturer, which has been forgotten.

Light: If you choose to live this archetype fully, you'll develop behaviors like:

✓ Great intuition and the ability to listen to your inner voice

✓ Pure and Ethereal
✓ Compassionate
✓ Mystical, feeling attraction to any mysterious things
✓ Very receptive to everything that comes from the spiritual world
✓ Discreet, known to keep secrets
✓ Knows the right moment to tell things
✓ Mediumship, able to canalize information and go into a mystic trance
✓ Harmonious to the feminine side
✓ Serendipity, once you follow the eternity time
✓ Sensibility and perception of what happens to people and places
✓ Introspective means vital inner force

Shadow: If you choose to resist this archetype, you'll develop behaviors like:

✓ Life will feel 'stuck'
✓ Cold-hearted and distant
✓ Attachment to the spiritual world, at the point you feel useless to live around people and lose material pleasures and nature connection
✓ Denied your sexuality, at the point, you'll try to find excuses based on moral and religious teachings and develop your taboos and prejudices
✓ Close-minded and closed off to the new
✓ Waste time analyzing people and situations
✓ Difficulty in demonstrating feelings
✓ Develop spiritual vanity, believes that anything bad will happen to you because you are spiritualized

If the priestess archetype influences you, you might have a successful vocational profession in areas such as:

• Occultism
• Literature

- Philosophy
- Numerology
- Symbology
- Esotericism
- Music
- Nursing
- Psychiatric
- Acupuncture
- Social Service
- Pedagogy
- Homeopathy
- Alternative Medicine
- Transpersonal Psychology
- Obstetrics
- Writer
- Chef
- Food Engineering
- Tarology
- Mysticism
- Astrology
- Any profession that involves feelings and intuitions

Powerful symbols are the triple moon, Solomon's columns, God Mother, Vase, Water, and Cat.

Tarot Arcane is the Card II La. Papesse – The priestess

6. Hedonistic

The main virtues are pleasure, realization, and sensuality.

This archetype represents the search for pleasure in all areas of life. Some people who take up this archetype look more sexually liberated, while others might just want to try new things they wouldn't otherwise do without being "forced" into it by a partner or a situation. This archetype is all about exploring and trying new things.

Examples of myth influences are Seth (Egyptian), Bacchus (Greek), Dionysus (Greek), Pan (Greek), and Iyami (Yoruba).

Some personality influencers are Madonna, Michael Flocker, Oscar Wilde, and Robert Greene.

Some cultural influences are Killer Queen (Music) from Queen, Sympathy for the devil (Music) from the Rolling Stones, South Park (Anime), Constantine, The Wolf of Wall Street, The Great Gatsby, Lucifer, and The Devil Wears Prada.

Sigmund Freud called the pleasure principle the instinctive search for pleasure, avoiding pain and suffering, and satisfying biological and psychological needs. For him, pleasure is mortifying, guiding the personality and the stronger impulse in everyone's life.

The hedonistic has a great libido (vital force) that develops potential creativity when canalized. It is this creativity that takes anyone to personal success. A person may not be able to use the potential of their creativity in their job or business, but they could at least use it to create an environment where other people can take advantage of it and enjoy life more!

The worldly life is not a problem for the hedonistic because it has great intimacy. The archetype represents great seduction power and uses it to get what was wished.

It represents intelligence, refinement, sensuality, and charm. Looking for the beauty and everything that can stimulate your sensations.

It's an excellent strategy. Use does whatever it takes to live a great passion or get what it wants, which could be someone's love, work, or material things.

This archetype reminds us of those who give into beauty, pleasure, and daily life's joy, feel happier every day, and have fewer chances to get into depression when things get tough.

Stimulates the human being to make peace with the material world and never give up looking for happiness, peace, and pure pleasure.

Light: If you choose to live this archetype fully, you'll develop behavior like:

- ✓ Creativity
- ✓ Passion
- ✓ Force
- ✓ Desire
- ✓ Ambition
- ✓ Strategy
- ✓ Intense sexuality
- ✓ Sensuality
- ✓ Power
- ✓ Personal Magnetism
- ✓ Charismatic
- ✓ Domination over material
- ✓ Insight

Shadow: If you resist living this archetype, you'll develop behavior like:

- ✓ Abusive
- ✓ Excessive Materialism
- ✓ Possessiveness
- ✓ Uncontrolled Sexuality
- ✓ Narcissism
- ✓ Arrogance
- ✓ Lust
- ✓ Violence
- ✓ Addictiveness

If the Hedonistic archetype influences you, you might have a successful vocational profession in areas such as:

- Culinary
- Jewelry
- Fashion

- Hospitality
- Architecture
- Designer
- Oenology
- Business Administration
- Real Estate Brokerage
- Investor

Powerful symbols are the Snake, Trident, Wine, and Antler
Tarot Arcane is the Card XV Le Diable – The devil

7. Mediator

The main virtues are balance, temperance, and harmony.

The myth influence examples are Iris (Greek), David (Hebrew), and Osain (Yoruba).

The personality influences are Robert Cialdini (Writer), Deepak Malhotra (writer), and Terry Taylor (Writer).

The cultural influences are Gandhi (movie), Avatar (movie), Hitch (movie), Up (movie), Imagine (music) from John Lennon, Patience (music) by Guns N 'Roses, and Heal the World (music) by Michael Jackson.

The mediator archetype represents balance and temperance.

Temperance is a virtue of acting sparingly with prudence without exaggeration. Temperance is to control the passions in your attitudes and decisions, to avoid the excess of your appetizers, wishes, and desires.

 It is good to be moderate in your desires and ambitions because they can lead to an imbalance or excess in one's life that is harmful to one's health. It leads to self-destruction when indulged in continuously or excessively for long periods. The temperate person acts in moderation according to his knowledge, judgment, and experience, and with the greatest discretion to not harm himself, his family, and others around him through selfishness or greed and live a happy and peaceful life free from worry and anxiety.

It represents harmony, the right measure of things, and benevolence. It is an archetype that improves self-communication (transpersonal) and invites the harmonization of thoughts, emotions, and attitudes.

The meditator represents the intellect and imagination in their purest state, the ability to understand cause and effect and create something out of nothing – literally! The meditator can be very creative. As such, they have access to all the hidden resources of the subconscious mind, including powers to influence other people's behavior or destiny, for good or bad.

The mediator has a gift of active listening, showing genuine interest in what the other says, making it easier to create bonds. The active listener is the ally to the word gift, allows help to people, and conciliates their problems. Active Listening is not just hearing, but taking time to hear; not just listening for words, but listening for feelings, which allow you to empathize with the other person's needs, wishes, fears, etc., and then using your wisdom to respond appropriately and constructively.

The mediator represents life's flexibility, the capacity for adaptation to any circumstances, and balance in any situation. This archetype has patience and understanding and has no rush for things to happen, which gives the great capacity to make decisions.

The mediator is often misunderstood because it can be a passive person or a procrastinator. Still, suppose you know how to harness its powers. In that case, this archetype will guide you through every step of your spiritual journey with clarity and wisdom, always helping you see the bigger picture of the universe unfolding as it should be and making sure that you are not getting stuck anywhere along the way by taking time out to look at everything from different perspectives and angles until you come up with the answer you need.

Light: if you choose to live this archetype fully, you'll develop behavior like:

- ✓ Discipline
- ✓ Peace
- ✓ Union of Opposite
- ✓ Harmony
- ✓ Patience
- ✓ Diplomacy
- ✓ Consciousness
- ✓ Charity
- ✓ Confidence
- ✓ Mercy
- ✓ Serendipity
- ✓ Cooperation
- ✓ Sociability
- ✓ Moderation
- ✓ Justice
- ✓ Complacency
- ✓ Wisdom
- ✓ Reason and emotion to interact harmoniously
- ✓ Self-awareness
- ✓ Capacity to make things right at the right time

Shadow: if you resist living this archetype, you'll develop behavior like:

- ✓ Arrogance
- ✓ Indiscretion
- ✓ Indifference
- ✓ Selfishness to legislate
- ✓ Superiority feeling
- ✓ Intolerance
- ✓ Miss personality
- ✓ Negligence
- ✓ Mental disorder

✓ Dissatisfaction
✓ Irritability
✓ Discord

If the Mediator archetype influences you, you might have a successful vocational profession in areas such as:

- Chemistry
- Law
- Holistic Therapy
- Homeopathy
- Esoterism
- Biology
- Genetic
- Biochemistry
- Human Resources Activist
- Naturopathy
- Pharmacy
- Telecommunication
- Meteorology
- Esoterism
- Ecology
- Engineering
- Social Assistant
- Community Leadership
- Philanthropy

Powerful symbols are Glass Cup, Angel, Jug, and Wings. Tarot Arcane is the Card XIV – The temperance

8. Revolutionary

The Revolutionary virtues are transformation, metamorphosis, and evolution.

Myths influences are the Shiva (Hindi), Kali (Hindi), Hades (Greek), and Iku (Yoruba).

Some personality influences are George Orwell (writer) and Richard Simonetti (writer).

Some cultural influences are Scooby-Doo (anime), Casper (movie), Hannibal (movie), The Man in the Castle (series), Ghost (movie), Across the Universe (movie), V for Vendetta (movie), Blackstar (music) from David Bowie, Eyes Without a Face (music) from Billy Idol.

The death of the old is required for the change to occur for a new rise to replace it. It means that it's important to break things that no longer serve. Let go of the beliefs, models, behaviors, and lifestyles that made you obsolete.

A person who has been given their freedom can only be taken away by someone else – because when we allow our ideas of what we should think or do to constrain us, we lose our ability to act in any way but as they dictate; we become slaves to ourselves and our fears, not realizing that this self-imposed servitude will ultimately result in our demise – as there is nothing that is more self-destructive than believing that one's existence is contingent on how others perceive them.

Just like a caterpillar that must die to become a beautiful butterfly, we must get into metamorphosing phase to become meta-human.

Meta-human is the human who finds themselves in a higher conscious state beyond normal. Use your capacities and potentialities without limiting yourself. It's a higher jump through species evolution, enjoying new worlds and new experiences that bring knowledge to you where nobody has been before.

The power of Meta-Human is their ability to make conscious decisions regarding how we want to live our life based on what we desire to create in this world, not on what we think others will judge us for or what we fear may happen to us if we don't do what others say we should be doing, but rather on what we truly want to experience in our lives and what we would like to contribute to the greater good in this world, so when it's time to die we can look back at all the things we have created with our heart and soul instead of regretting something we didn't accomplish during our lifetime.

The revolutionary eliminates superficial, limited, and transitory (ego) and preserves profound and eternal (essence). That's why it is an important evolution to be an agent.

This archetype represents the revolution in a way that is a radical and quick change that so many times show itself necessary to win from life stagnation.

Light: if you choose to live this archetype fully, you'll develop behavior like:

- ✓ Transformation
- ✓ Planner
- ✓ Profundity
- ✓ Freedom
- ✓ Detachment
- ✓ Metaphysical thought
- ✓ Constantly renovation
- ✓ Transmutation
- ✓ Not scared of left behind the past
- ✓ Logic
- ✓ Honesty
- ✓ Intelligence
- ✓ If you fall, you know how to rebuild your life

Shadow: if you resist living this archetype, you'll develop behavior like:

- ✓ Stagnation
- ✓ Fear of death
- ✓ Exaggerate attachment
- ✓ Self-destructive (addiction)
- ✓ Depression

✓ Pessimist
✓ Frustration
✓ Suffering
✓ Unforgiven
✓ Fear and resistance to changes

If the Revolutionary archetype influences you, you might have a successful vocational profession in the areas such as:

- Philosophy
- Art
- Politics
- Activism
- Landscape
- Science
- Activism
- Medicine
- Gravedigger
- Any funeral-related job

Powerful symbols are the Wheat, Open Gates, Fenix, and Butterfly.
Tarot Arcane is the Card XIII – The death

9. Resurrection

The virtues of this archetype are authenticity, renovation, and rebirth.

Examples of Myth influences are Hermes (Greek), the Psychopomps (Greek), Final Judge (Hebrew), Christian eastern (Hebrew), and Ifa (Yoruba).
Influential personalities are Allan Kardec (educator and spiritual leader), Ken Wilber (writer), Mike Robbins (writer), and Carl Gustav Jung (psychiatrist).
Cultural influences are Starman (music) from David Bowie,

Coco (movie), Wall – E (movie), I am Legend (movie), 2012 (movie), The Book of Eli (movie), and War of the worlds (movie).

The Resurrection archetype represents the need for continuous personal renovation. We can evolve in consciousness. If we do, we change how we see ourselves and our world, which changes everything around us, including the nature of our relationships with others (especially with ourselves). This archetype says, "I don't want to be trapped anymore; I want to break free!"

To become a fully awakened individual, you must understand how much you still need to learn about yourself and your world—and about others too—to live in true harmony with them and the environment in which you find yourself (both physically and mentally/spiritually). You must accept yourself as a constantly growing, evolving being who is always changing.

Sometimes it's important to do an honest self-analysis to identify how we walk through the light path over the conscious lightness or when the resistance stills have its domination, and we are lost through the darkness. When the analysis is made, it's enough to correct the route.

The most challenging thing for many of us is to realize that we don't always make the best decisions in the process of evolution of ourselves. Sometimes, in the end, there is no way back from where we are going because we can only go forward as our inner experience guides us on the light path of consciousness and reality at any given time in our life on Earth.

This archetype shows that we can renew ourselves daily to who we are. We become authentic; every human being is part of the whole. We can be good or bad; we can choose love over hate, compassion over judgment, forgiveness over revenge, joy over suffering, and so on and so forth.

Most people resist living according to the essence of self because of fear of not being accepted by society or changing the patterns taught their whole lives. The only way they can find life is to do everything everyone is doing.

It's easy to fall into this trap when you have been indoctrinated from childhood that there is no right and wrong, no good and evil, just a variety of behaviors that are acceptable in certain circumstances – or even necessary for survival – and that everyone else does it too so it must be okay for you to do it as well! As long as you go along with what everyone else is doing, your ego gets its own little 'fix 'and is satisfied.

What steps to take for transformation?

- Know yourself – look within, put yourself in front of the mirror and find the answers to who you are.
- Know your fears – open yourself, feel it, write on paper what you are afraid of, find the answers of why; free yourself from it.
- Be honest – Tell the truth, and face the consequences of this attitude.
- Celebrate who you are – The most difficult challenge in life is loving ourselves as though we were children, which is called acceptance. Commit to your light side, just as you would to your darkness, and choose to enjoy the only person you are.

The resurrection is the archetype that revel's vocational of the human being to realize something bigger than himself, letting a legacy in the world. It can happen only through freedom. Let go of the past and go straight to the rebirth of eternal consciousness.

It is achieving freedom from the illusions of life and death, from the material realm of time and space, and from the prison of the ego that has been shackling one's true self for eons on end! The resurrection is a metaphor for how we re-create ourselves, transforming into a higher form of existence where there are no more separations, attachments, limitations, or fears.

You might constantly feel a calling in you, for the new, for rebirth. Sometimes you like to review your goal and general attitudes; from these things comes the transformation. If we are to change our personality, or even if it is only our body, we must first change ourselves mentally and spiritually, and that means we have to transform ourselves into what we desire to be rather than think about being someone else physically, who we don't know yet, but imagine in some abstract way as if they existed already.

You look for innovation but for the power of now believer, look for breaking the old beliefs and open yourself for the new. If you allow this archetype to influence you, you might become someone spiritualized, ready for the realization life is offering. I firmly believe in your ability to achieve anything you set out to do, and with hard work and dedication, it can be done! I also believe that we all have our destiny, and if we want it badly enough, we will get there no matter what obstacles or challenges come along the way!

Strong mediumship and musician, see the music as a profound life transformation, guiding your feelings and emotions in the depths of light.

Light: if you choose to live this archetype fully, you'll develop behavior like:

- ✓ Fast thinker
- ✓ Honor
- ✓ Success into difficulties
- ✓ Protection
- ✓ Creativity
- ✓ Observation capacity
- ✓ Talent
- ✓ Self-consciousness
- ✓ Innovation
- ✓ Idealism
- ✓ Reviewing values every time
- ✓ Dedication

Shadow: if you resist living this archetype, you'll develop behavior like:

- ✓ Fear of the new
- ✓ Possessively
- ✓ Prejudice
- ✓ Illusion

- ✓ Skepticism
- ✓ Stagnation
- ✓ Pride
- ✓ Rigidity
- ✓ Anxiety
- ✓ Excessive judgment
- ✓ Spiritual responsibility

If the Resurrection archetype influences you, you might have a successful vocational profession in the areas such as:

- Acupuncture
- Medicine
- Sexology
- Holistic Therapy
- Engineering
- Esotericism
- Spiritual Healer
- Law
- Biology
- Psychology
- Psychiatric
- Architecture
- Priesthood

Powerful symbols are Trumpet, Egg, Fenix, Angel, and Organ (instrument).

Tarot arcane is the Card XX Le. Iugement – The Judgment

10. Integrated

The integrated archetype represents the duality transcendence being.

Someone who unifies both polarities, male and female, material and spiritual, Yin and Yang. It's the Whole archetype, the totality, the united.

The archetype of the united is the feminine principle, as it represents the balance between opposite principles, an understanding of the masculine and feminine sides of oneself and their interconnection, rather than anyone side dominating or taking precedence over the other(s), which would be unbalanced in the first place – such as when only one polarity is being represented instead of both, or when one side is being presented as 'better 'than the other.

Myths influences are Hermaphroditus (Greek), Shiva (Hindi), and Alafia (Yoruba).

Some influential personalities are Osho (spiritual leader), J.C. Coopie (writer), and Wilhelm Reich (medicine doctor).

Cultural influences are Adventure Time (anime), 2001: a space odyssey (movie), Interstellar (movie), XXY (movie), and The Danish Girl (movie).

The integrated reminds us that when there's a unit, there's no poverty and wealth, male and female, ugly and beauty, material and spiritual, intellectual and emotions. Everything is part of the totality, and everything is incorporated because the Whole is everything that exists above any duality.

People that embody this archetype walk in the middle, without polarities; they don't require others to feel fulfilled; they are fulfilled themselves.

When they get into a relationship, one overflows the cup full of love for another.

It's the archetype of body movement, anything related to dance or music, where the body and soul work together. They are strong development from integrated.

How many people are so full of life's problems? Diseases, mental disorders, etc. People who stopped life's dancing in the material world later became frozen at heart, rude, in hard aspect. Because they don't feel any more energy flowing through the blood, muscles, nerves, brain, and skin, only their "inner be-ing" can be heard, but not see it!

But when you allow yourself to dance with life, move your body, move the skeleton, naturally, the muscular armor is dis-solved, setting the body free from the mind, problems, and society.

For that reason, the integrated archetype is deeply con-nected to dance and body conscience. The more you dance, the more you allow your soul to be free. The Integrated in your abundance doesn't have armor.

The integrated has no boundaries, so when a situation arises that causes them pain, they will let go of it and come back into their true self – the infinite creator who always gives birth to its own life and reality. We are all "infinite creators," but some-times we forget our true selves and become attached to what we think is normal for us and what everyone else does (in other words, what society says).

For example, we feel unhappy because something happens to us. Regardless, if we look at our inner being, we see that this situation brings happiness and freedom to us because we can do anything now, at any time, without limits.

When you allow this archetype to express itself, you become comprehended, sensual, self-love, and complete.

Light: if you choose to live this archetype fully, you'll de-velop behavior like:

- ✓ Good sense and wisdom
- ✓ Confident and free
- ✓ Life's enthusiasm
- ✓ Great realizations
- ✓ Love traveling and expanding horizon
- ✓ Feelings of balance and completeness
- ✓ Overcoming capacity
- ✓ Life flows, dance, and music existing
- ✓ Compassion, love the others, and self-love

Shadow: if you choose to resist this archetype, you'll develop behavior like:

- ✓ Depression of not reaching goals
- ✓ Lower self-esteem
- ✓ Arrogance
- ✓ Isolation
- ✓ Consider only your perceptions to be the truth
- ✓ Deny your weakness
- ✓ Self-devaluation
- ✓ Restlessness
- ✓ Anxiety
- ✓ Contempt for poverty
- ✓ Inconsistency

If you are influenced by the Integrated archetype, you might
have a successful vocational profession in the areas such as:

- Dance
- Tourism
- Life Coach
- Spiritual Coach
- Art
- Sexology
- Psychology
- Tantric Therapy

Powerful symbols are Tai Chi, Yoni Lingam, and Androgyny.
Tarot Arcane is the Card XXI El Mundo – The world.

11. Rebel

Peaceful rebels, no-action, and renounce.

The "no-action" is the main thing, though a renouncement is
also needed. For that, you have to be a pacifist - not just for one

day or even several days or weeks...but forever!

Myths influences are Prometheus (Greek), Osiris (Egyptian), and Oba (Yoruba).

Influential personalities are Gandhi (lawyer), Jesus (leader), Paul of Tarsus (missionary), Mother Tereza of Calcutta (missionary), James Dean (actor), and Robin Hood (character).

Cultural influences are Woody Woodpecker (animated cartoon), Rebel Without a Cause (movie), Breaking Bad (movie), Invictus (movie), Rock (musical genre), Hip Hop (musical genre), and Funk (musical genre).

Influential brands are Rolling Stone, Jack Daniel's (whiskey), Apple (tech), Harley-Davidson (motor company), and Converse All-Stars (shoes).

The Rebel archetype shows a new worldview, changes paradigms, and improves the perception of reality. It's absolutely against the status quo and all dominant belief systems. A rebel is not a passive agitator but an active agent of change who acts as a catalyst for transformation in the minds and hearts of others through their own lives and actions.

The rebel is anti-authority, anti-system, anti-institution, and anti-established norms or traditions of any kind; the rebel seeks to change things to better our lives so that they can live more freely and happily. Rebel has no loyalty to anything or anyone other than what works best for them and their inner self-growth, which does not conform to society's rules.

Rebels are not a revolution as many think; revolution means violent action against the opposite beliefs using force. The rebel's archetype means non-obedience through pacific resistance. To be a true rebel, we must question authority and make sure we do what is right instead of what society wants us to believe is right because it makes them feel good about themselves or their beliefs.

The strongest rebel action is the non-action or Wu Wei (Taoism). The principal says the best way to face a problem is not forcing anything, no precision, but letting it flow naturally.

The rebel is moved through ideas. Jesus was a great Rebel

example, coming into this world to teach a new life's perspective and set everyone free from hatefulness and violence by teaching love. Jesus was the greatest rebel ever to exist, a rebel for love meditation, and was loyal until the end of his life just to see everyone free.

The rebel proposes making a personal sacrifice for the sake of the greater good. That is why the rebel foregoes its interests in exchange for the sacrifice. It's an inner mentality to volunteer for a cause for the greater good, even if it means paying the price.

To be a rebel, you have to sacrifice yourself and your interests to the greater good of society as a whole, or at least a particular group that shares similar goals with you, who are not necessarily part of the government either... A rebel isn't just someone who has a different opinion on how something should be done, but one willing to make sacrifices (or "sacrifices") for that goal regardless of the cost to oneself or their peers, if necessary.

Light: if you choose to live this archetype fully, you'll develop behaviors like:

- ✓ Wisdom
- ✓ Meditation
- ✓ Self-love
- ✓ Allowing yourself to see the world from a new perspective
- ✓ Knowing when to wait
- ✓ Resist what you do not agree with
- ✓ Non-violence
- ✓ Respect
- ✓ Calm
- ✓ Self-domination
- ✓ A critic of social conventions
- ✓ See the facts in different situations; do not agree with everything that is an impost
- ✓ Able to sacrifice for the cause or ideal

Shadow: if you choose to resist living this archetype, you'll develop behaviors like:

✓ Grudge
✓ Incapable to act
✓ Aggressive rebel
✓ Ideal impositions
✓ Hatefulness
✓ Sorrows
✓ Suffering
✓ Feeling mot world belonging
✓ Self-punishment
✓ Hurt
✓ Difficulties
✓ Liar

If the archetype of the rebel influences you, you might have a successful vocational profession in the areas such as:

- Art
- Music
- Medicine
- Sociology
- Social Assistance
- Nursing
- Fire worker
- Philosophy
- Pedagogy
- Psychology
- Community Leaders

Power symbols are Sneakers, Tattoo, Tongue, Skate, Cross, and Motorcycle.

Tarot Arcane is the Card XII Le. Pendu – The Hanged Man

12. Curator

*The main virtues are healing, charity,
hope, and benevolence.*

The influential myths are Asclepius (Greek), Meditrina (Roman Myths), Pandora (Greek), Oshun (Yoruba), and Ariadne (Greek).

Personality's influences are Joel Goldsmith (spiritual healer), Carl G. Jung (psychiatric), Deepak Chopra (M.D), and Louise Hay (motivational author).

Cultural influences are Toy Story (movie), Wall-E (movie), Awakenings (movie), The Physician (movie), 50 First Dates, I feel good (song) from James Brown, and Eye of the Tiger (Song) from Survivor.

The Curator archetype represents the capacity for healing. Everyone is capable of healing anything themselves, others, animals, and the earth. The Curator works with the emotions and instincts to create a balance between the two to learn how to protect oneself and care for others while learning from one's experiences and knowledge of things that happen around them in life (such as the environment).

This archetype is associated with the moon since it is about the natural process of growth and change and is also seen as the feminine side of the moon because of its association with nurturing and protection. Healing is the process of restoring equilibrium to sick organs to regenerate and heal themselves, and the truth is that anybody can heal somebody.

Physical and mental disease happens when the organs lose their essence of self, love, happiness, light, and consciousness. When this reconnection happens, the energy camps mental and spiritual reorganizing to send energy and information to the body cells. When the body receives the wisdom of transformation, the regeneration starts afterward.

The curator turns everything easier; it happens when it emanates love, peace, happiness, and harmony wherever it goes. The curator awakens hope where there is sadness. They open doors to understanding where there is incomprehension; make clear the way where there is obscurity or darkness; show the path to the lost ones, and lead them home where they can find themselves again.

The curator can easily heal others because they have healed many lives before. The curators have a great capacity to help people transform pain into a healing process. They understand how to channel energy for emotional, physical, mental, and spiritual development.

The curators are aware that when a person experiences emotional trauma, they need to develop certain abilities to release the emotional pain and get rid of it from their life through different channels like meditation and other forms of exercise so that they may move on with their lives in a more positive way. They are available as a catalyst of change when needed, whether it is someone who needs to heal themselves or one who needs to be healed.

This archetype reminds us that all answers are within us, just like healing. Every time we ask questions and listen to the solutions that life brings to us through intuition, everything flows better; that moment is when the miracle happens.

The curator represents life's confidence, a better world. For that reason, it invites us to live in harmony, take care of nature, and help others give ourselves. It's not about getting your best done; it's about getting your maximum done. Don't do 99%, do 100% of yourself. If you want a miracle, your faith must reach 100%.

That means you mustn't just believe that you can be healed; it means you are sure that you are healed already. And there's no limit to how much you can do if you just keep trying harder than you ever thought possible – by curating yourself, you'll be doing more than you ever imagined! It's about getting things done for yourself and others and finding inspiration in unexpected places and people around you!

If you want a miracle, be a miracle.

Light: if you choose to live this archetype fully, you'll develop behavior like:

- ✓ Lovely
- ✓ Sensible
- ✓ Confidence
- ✓ Power to heal the world and be healed by them
- ✓ Ecologist
- ✓ Charity
- ✓ Donation
- ✓ Faith
- ✓ Peaceful
- ✓ Find your place in the world
- ✓ Hopefulness
- ✓ Harmony
- ✓ Creativity
- ✓ Inspiration
- ✓ Altruism

Shadow: if you resist living this archetype, you'll develop behavior like:

- ✓ Utopia
- ✓ Lust
- ✓ Abusive
- ✓ Distraction
- ✓ Anxious
- ✓ Quackery
- ✓ Opportunism
- ✓ Indifference
- ✓ Ironic
- ✓ Insensibility

If the Curator archetype influences you, you might have a successful vocational profession in areas such as:

- Medicine

- General Therapy
- Tourism
- Ecology
- Coaches
- Meteorology
- Oceanography
- Esoterism
- Agricultural
- Landscape
- Zoology
- Agronomy
- Vet
- Geography
- Nursing
- Health Sector

Powerful symbols are the Ocean, River, Hummingbird, and Star.

Tarot Arcane is the Card XVII L'Estoille – The Star

13. Lucky

The main virtues are change, movement, and co-creation.

Influential myths are Moira (Greek), Parcae (Roman), Norn (Norse), and Oshunmare (Yoruba).

Influential personalities are Rhonda Byrne (writer), Napoleon Hill (writer), Robert Kiyosaki (entrepreneur), Bob Proctor (Lecturer), and Esther Hicks (writer).

Cultural influences are Jimmy Neutron (anime), Rick and Morty (anime), Adventure Time (anime), Vanilla Sky (movie), Russian Doll (series), The Butterfly effect (movie), American Gods (series), Inception, and Samsara (documentary).

The Lucky archetype represents blessing and luck. Things

don't come to us as coincidences but through our thoughts, feelings, and behaviors. This is why it is often said that "luck happens when preparation meets opportunity" - preparation can be a conscious effort or an unconscious one. In contrast, opportunity can be the right timing for change, the right environment, or the right person at the right time for you to manifest what you want in your life and on your journey of becoming the best version of yourself!

The archetype teaches us the co-creation of our realities and that we're not blessed through expectations. We create what we receive by our choices about how we respond to what is presented to us. So it's always up to us whether we accept or reject the gift of a reality given to us. We are responsible for creating the world in which we live, with all its good and bad elements and manifestations, as well as the opportunities it provides for us to grow, learn and change for the better or not.

If anyone wants to reach success, circumstances may happen in your favor, just like a butterfly effect movie. Even if the event changes or one different detail happens for some reason, everything else changes, just like the theory of chaos.

In fact, life is exactly like that, unpredictable. However, we decide to determine our luck or bad luck. If we decide to live by the law of attraction, then bad things will happen because we have decided for them to occur in our lives...and this is not the way to create a better life for ourselves and others! When you are having doubts about your ability to manifest what you want, ask yourself, "What am I afraid of? What do I need to feel safe with? What makes me happy?" Get clear on what these answers are to begin to think and act from a place of abundance instead of scarcity.

The lucky archetype represents destiny, which determines through nature laws and reminds us to let life flow and not resist natural changes. At the end of circumstance, everything comes for good. The lucky know that everything passes and that life is constantly changing without attachment.

This doesn't mean that we don't get angry, but it means that we accept things as they are, with humility and gratitude, without trying to change them in our will or even blaming them on other people or circumstances. We accept what has been given to us and let go of the next turn of events, without attachment and fear, as if there is no tomorrow (as a gift). Actions, choices, and decisions are very important when you wish to make yourself luckier.

The Lucky don't miss any opportunity. It is always ready to change. It knows that change is needed to reach its goals. It makes its luck and knows that the unpredictable might happen. Understand that today we might be on top; tomorrow, we might be on the vale. No matter what happens, the lucky always have a solution for everything!

If you want to be on top again, you must be prepared for the chaos. Chaos is not a disorder. It is just circumstances that happen only to impulse us to move and change.

This is where your will and belief system come in handy because what we think about we get more of, and what we focus our attention on, creates reality, which is why we need to develop a stronger belief system when dealing with such issues as anxiety, stress, lack of energy, illness, addictions, and depression (or all of them). Beliefs are also powerful when we are dealing with ourselves. They create inner worlds that help us understand and learn about ourselves better than external opinions or situations could ever do.

The best way to deal with chaos is to keep your center of focus and purpose in life, so when things get chaotic or confusing, they won't take over all aspects of your life to derail you from what you are working towards! That's what happens when you get disheartened and feel like giving up when those feelings of frustration, failure, and despair come into play because if you don't keep your center of focus, you will lose control, and your goals will slip away! When you stay centered, your energy remains focused on your goals.

Light: if you choose to live this archetype fully, you'll develop behavior like:

- ✓ Good luck
- ✓ Fluidity
- ✓ Create reality without efforts
- ✓ Dynamic
- ✓ Long term vision
- ✓ Prosperity
- ✓ Happiness
- ✓ Balance
- ✓ Anticipation ability
- ✓ Progress
- ✓ Renovation capacity
- ✓ Aware of impermanent
- ✓ Sagacity

Shadow: if you resist living this archetype, you'll develop behavior like:

- ✓ Attachment
- ✓ Selfishness
- ✓ Comfort Zone
- ✓ Doesn't accept changes
- ✓ Instability
- ✓ Unnecessary risk
- ✓ Exaggerate greed
- ✓ Inertia
- ✓ Dissatisfaction

If the lucky archetype influences you, you might have a successful vocational profession in areas such as:

- Hospitality
- Internet
- Marketing

- Economy
- Entrepreneur
- General Freelance
- Tourism
- Manager
- Businessperson
- Commercial
- Seller
- Banker
- Casino
- Aviation
- Automobiles

Powerful symbols are Lucky Clover, Orchid flower, Diamond, Gold, Cards deck, Chest, and Pyramid.

Tarot Arcane is the Card X L'a Roue De Fortune – The wheel of Fortune

14. The Courage

The main virtues are self-mastery, willpower,
and emotional intelligence.

Influential myths are Artemis (Greek), Samson and the Lion (Hebrew), Ewa (Yoruba), Leda and the Swan (Greek), and Hercules (Greek).

Personality's influences are Martin Luther King Jr. (Baptist minister).

Billy Graham (evangelist), Nelson Mandela (political leader), Sir Edmund Hillary (mountaineer), Rosa Parks (activist), Harriet Tubman (activist), and Tiradentes (military personnel).

Cultural influences are The Lion King (movie), Hercules (movie), Zootopia (movie), Million Dollar Baby (movie), Chasing Mavericks (movie), The Pursuit of Happiness (movie), and The Blind Side (movie).

The courage archetype represents the deep desire over instincts and emotions. The courage faces itself and its fears. A person with this archetype lives in a constant state of readiness to face challenges and adversity, as well as new opportunities and rewards that may arise through taking risks or by overcoming obstacles in his life. The Courage is the first character you encounter on your journey to find true purpose in life, what we call the purpose quest!

Self-control is the ability to keep our desires from manifesting, make everything good, and avoid confrontation with others. However, it is based on the repression of instincts, not on emotional intelligence. Emotional intelligence is the ability to be aware of your emotions, understand them and use them constructively to get what you want without losing yourself or harming others along the way. It is the ability to regulate your own emotions, not necessarily those of other people.

Repress generates inner conflict and psychological disorders. Later it comes out like an explosion as if a balloon popped before being pressed by the air. A lot of people are in pain because their repressed thoughts have not been released from the body and mind but have been kept inside for many years, even decades, and finally come out in the form of anger, anxiety, depression, or other mental disorders that cause them to suffer physically and mentally and become depressed or get sick more frequently than usual (they can also be referred to as repressed emotions).

People who are aware that they are suffering from repressed thoughts will want to get rid of them, so they go through self-analysis or self-mastery.

Self-mastery is the capacity to observe our thoughts, emotions, beliefs, and instincts instead of opposing them. When it's understood those feelings are brain responses conditioned throughout our defense system unconsciously, and our limited belief system was programmed during childhood life, they are naturally dissipated.

We become free from fear, anger, pain, and suffering when we learn to be conscious of these emotional responses in their true light and not feed them with attention. We become free from anger and aggression when we realize that these thoughts are nothing more than a projection of our consciousness of reality – as if we were an outside observer looking at a movie.

Self-mastery is emotional intelligence. This is beneficial not just for our social lives but also for our mental health. Once we no longer need to control and repress these contents in our unconscious mind, we create fewer shadows and inner conflict. That way, we become someone balanced. The personality grows more harmonious when the shadow content is out of us.

When you are stuck or feel overwhelmed with something, stop for a moment and ask yourself, what is it? Is there an aspect of yourself that you don't like about this situation? If so, who are you being right now? Do you identify with the shadow that has surfaced at this time? The more you can acknowledge and understand your shadow nature, the easier it will be for you to change your behavior in future situations where you want to avoid repeating old behavior patterns or deal with new ones.

There's no greater power than self-mastery, and this virtue creates and manifests magnetism and personal power. The Courage Archetype represents the sexuality dominium, allowing libido canalization (vital force) to creativity.

One of the strong chemical stimuli any person receives from the courage archetype is dopamine; sleeping late and waking up early are basic habits.

Light: if you choose to live this archetype fully, you'll develop behaviors like:

- ✓ Faith
- ✓ Discipline
- ✓ Self-mastery
- ✓ Emotional intelligence
- ✓ Courage
- ✓ Intuition
- ✓ Determination

- ✓ Trustful
- ✓ Personal magnetism
- ✓ Objectivity
- ✓ Sensibility
- ✓ Charism
- ✓ Sexuality dominium
- ✓ Caution
- ✓ Frankness
- ✓ Honesty
- ✓ Strong and balanced sexuality
- ✓ Physical disposition

Shadow: if you resist living this archetype, you'll develop behaviors like:

- ✓ Perversion
- ✓ Manipulation
- ✓ Lust
- ✓ Brutality
- ✓ Perfectionism
- ✓ Unhealthy sexuality
- ✓ Explosive temperament
- ✓ Revenge
- ✓ Self-charge
- ✓ Dogmatism
- ✓ Anxiety
- ✓ Act through an emotional moment
- ✓ Use force to impose its wishes
- ✓ Greed
- ✓ Stubbornness

If the courage archetype influences you, you might have successful vocational profession areas such as:

- • Esthetical
- • Psychoanalyze
- • Sexology

- Physical Education
- Body Therapy
- Firefighters
- Psychology
- Zoology
- Vet
- Medicine
- Biology

Powerful symbols are Lion, Tiger, Lemniscate (infinity), and Trident.

15. The Fairness

The main virtues are justice, balance, and ethic.

The influential myths are Athena (Greek), Maat (Egyptian), Themis (Greek), St. Michael Archangel (Christian), Asteria (Greek), and Shango (Yoruba).

Personalities influences are Allan Kardec (educator and author), Jesus of Nazareth (religious leader), George Orwell (novelist and journalist), Joan Ruth Bader Ginsburg (lawyer), Thurgood Marshall (lawyer), Sandra Day O'Connor (lawyer), John Grisham (novelist and lawyer), and Thomas Jefferson (statesman).

Cultural influences are The Shawshank Redemption (movie), Monitory Report (movie), 12 Angry Men (movie), Conviction (movie), and Justice League (comic book and film).

The Fairness archetype represents the discernment of what is right and wrong. It's not human morals and justice alone because sometimes it fails, but ethical and divine justice. The Fairness archetype can have an inner voice that can guide you in your decisions, as well as guide others through you when you need help with a moral dilemma or issue related to life circumstances where you must decide how to handle the situation without being dishonest to yourself or someone else about your intentions or motives; you will be seen as fair to them and honest to yourself.

The moral changes according to a cultural context, but ethics represents immovable and eternal universal values. It's that thing we do when nobody is watching. The same thing happens when human laws change according to the time and cultural context of different civilizations. But morality doesn't change because it's a timeless value that exists in every culture worldwide.

The divine justice or cosmic is based on laws that rule the universe's workings, grounded in the intelligence and the universe's love, that it is pure conscience.

Fairness expresses the universal law that says, "For every action, there is an equal and opposite reaction," from Isaac Newton.

This law is not for punishment; it is pure and simple oriented to human evolution. Forgiveness is always received for failures, but it is needed to repair damages equal to proportion. It doesn't matter how long it takes; the debt must be paid off.

This law is not a law of retribution or revenge. Rather, it is about restoring balance in the universe and the person themselves so that they can evolve more easily in the future by following their natural path in life and not being influenced by past experiences (good or bad), which would lead to failure.

The fairness archetype is full of intelligence, balance, impartiality, great assessment capacity, analysis, and decision power. It has a very good understanding of life and work, the ability to solve problems creatively, think out of the box, and have a strong sense of responsibility and duty for others; it can achieve results without relying on others 'help, but it needs people's trust and support to complete its work smoothly and effectively, and it does not like to be forced to do something, especially by authority or bossiness from others; it is an independent person who likes to think things through first before making decisions or actions.

For the fairness archetype, everyone is equal; as a principle, every consciousness originated from the same conscience. The challenge allows everyone to conquer these practical conditions.

Light: if you choose to live this archetype fully, you'll develop behavior like:

✓ Obeying the law and the order
✓ Wish for your rights to be recognized
✓ Search for the truth in any situation
✓ Everybody sees you as fairness and righteous person
✓ Listen to both parts and look for work impartiality
✓ Enjoy correcting an unfair situation
✓ Don't care about your act's consequences
✓ Search for life balance in every situation
✓ Honest
✓ Objective and keeps their word
✓ Logical and strategist

Shadow: if you resist living this archetype, you'll develop behaviors like:

✓ Authoritarianism
✓ Destructive criticism
✓ Prejudice
✓ Unfair
✓ Intolerable
✓ Tendentious
✓ False moralism
✓ Exaggerated proudness
✓ Impatient

If the Fairness archetype influences you, you might have a successful vocational profession in areas such as:

- Lawyer
- Chemist
- Judge
- Diplomat

- Arbitrator
- Politician
- Journalist
- Accountant
- Anthropologist
- Physicist
- Business Administrator
- Sociologist
- Auditor
- Sociologist

Powerful symbols are Beam balance, Eye cover, Sword, Hammer

Tarot Arcane is the Card VIII La Justice – The Justice.

16. The Pure

Main virtues are purity, optimize, and faith.

Influential myths are Dionysus (Greek), Hercules youth (Greek), and Ibeji (Yoruba).

Personality's influences are Sandy (singer), Tom Hanks (actor), Doris Day (actress), Henry D. Thoreau (writer), and Meg Ryan (actress).

Cultural influences are Caillou (anime), Finding Dory (movie), Winnie the Pooh (movie), Lord of the rings (series), The Green Mile (movie), Forrest Gump (movie), Imagine (song) from John Lennon, Ronald McDonald (character), and Pollyanna (character).

The pure feels a depth desire for purity, goodness, and simplicity. The archetype is the opposite of the persona, which is all about covering up weakness or vulnerability to hide from the world and maintain control over others through manipulation and intimidation (the opposite of vulnerability).

Pure archetypes feel that they are the purest version of themselves and, therefore, will not tolerate any compromise in their identity, beliefs, or actions. Still, at the same time, because the pure archetype has nothing to prove, they can remain calm and unruffled under pressure—they can be still while the rest of us are running around like chickens with our heads cut off! Archetypes have firm boundaries—their ideals of what's right and wrong for them and how they behave towards other people and things in life.

Level 1: Simplicity, naive, dependent, obedient, confident, idyllic.

Level 2: Renovation, positivity, reinvent, restructure, purify, back on the Promised Land.

Level 3: A mystic sense of unity. Innocence comes from values and integrity. There's no external experience; it is "being" and not "doing it."

The pure archetype represents innocence as a quality with no ill feelings in the heart. It represents youth mentality, full of curiosities, hope, desiring for life's experiences, and exploring.

This archetype is associated with the element of air and is linked to the color green in Feng Shui. The pure archetype also represents the true nature of all things, an undivided state where nothing is left to be discovered or known about anything in life. Everything is revealed and understood without any hindrance or obstacles to prevent it from reaching its fullest potential to achieve the enlightenment of one's true self-nature (to reach "true self-realization.")

The pure represents the beginning journey or restarts through a lifetime. What does that mean? Life is made by cycles. We start at the initial point, walk throughout the world, and finish simultaneously. But at the upper level, we experience wisdom, knowledge, and information during our journey. We are not the same anymore because our awareness has been expanded. The body is changing, so the mind, heart, emotions, and senses are also changing to a new level of beingness, a new dimension of selfhood, and a new state of consciousness and energy flow.

The pure is the main archetype we experienced when we

were children, especially in the first year. We are allowed to live this archetype for the rest of our lives, which changes our worldview, thoughts, feelings, and behaviors.

The world is not as simple as it seems; we can only experience it through our perception filters or paradigms, our consciousness that is formed by our life experiences and beliefs throughout time—that are inherited from our parents, culture, society, education, family, etc., that make us who we are today, and that may cause us to repeat some aspects of ourselves again and again in different contexts, and hence, become habits... or patterns... or addictions.

The pure represents the freedom to run, experience, and look at things for what they are—the dreamer - able to create a perfect world.

Trusting in life's benevolence, the focus is always to be positive in people and situations. It carries conscience optimization, always willing to give a chance to opportunities that life is offering. In this way, it makes an effort to live harmoniously with others, giving preference to good over evil, truth over falsehood, health over illness, well-being over adversity, prosperity over poverty, and love over hate; on the other hand, looking for the best interest of everyone else; so, it tries to make a difference in this world, not only through its actions but also by supporting those who are working in favor of social justice and peace, while trying to promote respect among nations and peoples, respecting their differences.

The pure feels vital impulse, good mood, and energy to search, walk, and experience. The pure represents chaos, not in a disordered way but the infinity potential of the universe, able to create order when organized through intention. It is an energy that flows freely, with no obstacles, like water from a faucet or steam from a kettle.

In essence, the Pure is characterized by living happily. Happiness doesn't come from the external world or material things but from depth connection with the infinite possibilities that life offers and letting it go throughout existence flux.

Light: if you choose to live this archetype fully, you'll develop behavior like:

- ✓ Optimistic, trust that everything will be ok, even during difficult situations
- ✓ Someone who is always happy and believes not everything must be taken seriously
- ✓ Believes that you will be treated well in life and by others since you are kind and exceptional.
- ✓ Charismatic in virtue.
- ✓ The optimistic perspective of life and purity in beliefs
- ✓ Dreamer
- ✓ Spontaneous and honest
- ✓ Enthusiastic for projects
- ✓ Sociable
- ✓ Honest, honorable, and polite
- ✓ Easy-going and simple
- ✓ Believes in happiness above everything and in fairness where everyone can be whoever they want
- ✓ Loyalty when promises are made
- ✓ Believe that people are good and can learn from mistakes. That's why it is good at forgiveness
- ✓ Curious and explorer; loves to discover new things and new people
- ✓ Don't see bad things in the world; chooses not to focus on evil when facing it.
- ✓ Because of trust, it can open itself to knowledge and seek realizations
- ✓ Innocent - believes what people say
- ✓ Self-trust, trust in people, and confidence in life's perfection
- ✓ Believe that your need will be fulfilled one way or another. Tend not to worry
- ✓ Faith in life that can make the world a better place
- ✓ People must be trusted, as a principle

✓ It feels like an impulse to go into the unknown and seek intuition; trusting in life's flux

✓ Feels that the world is a safe place to live

Shadow: if you resist living this archetype, you'll develop behavior like:

✓ Suffer from depression because of nostalgia and homesickness

✓ Might refuse self-growth. Developing Peter Pan syndrome - forever childlike and become dependent on others

✓ Might become a perfectionist because they believe in an ideal world - psych utopia

✓ Vulnerable and dependent, manipulator like a child when cranky

✓ Everything is a joke in a serious moment

✓ Accts like a child; waiting for others to take care of them

✓ Due to a lack of trust, you might take unnecessary risks

✓ Fear of being surrounded by manipulative people because of your worldview. This fear might attract people with bad thoughts

✓ Comfort zone - believe that a savior will come and solve all problems

✓ Limit beliefs - because of its trusting ability, it believes in everything people in authoritative position says without questioning it

✓ Deny reality as it shows bad things from others' mistakes. For this reason, you might not recognize when you have been hurt by someone else and when you need help

✓ Repression

If the Pure archetype influences you, you might have successful vocational professions in areas such as:

• Commercial Exterior

• Search

- Tourism
- Music
- Comedian
- Theatre
- Inventions
- Entrepreneur
- Geology
- Flight Attendant
- Mountaineering
- Archeology
- Anthropology
- Explorer
- Business Owner or Freelancer
- Exploration/Travel/Arts

Powerful symbols are Children, Daisy flower, Lotus Flower, White Lilly, and Dolphin.

Tarot Arcana is the Card 0 Le.Mat – The fool

17. The Hero

Main virtues are courage, strength, and direction.
"A hero is someone who has given his or her life to something bigger than oneself."

- Joseph Campbell

A hero archetype is called a warrior, super-hero, soldier, winning athlete, dragon killer, competitor, team player, and liberator. In some cases, the hero has no name or no history at all. However, this does not change his nature of being a champion who fights for what he believes in and always strives to be a hero for others around him and helps them become heroes!

All heroes have a reason for doing what they do. Many often misunderstand them, who see them only on their terms, or do not understand that they are helping people out of the darkness and into the light of hope, freedom, and happiness.

Level 1: Overcome challenges, develop competence and mastery, expressed through realization and motivations tested in competitions.

Level 2: Like a soldier fulfilling duties for the country, organization, community, or family.

Level 3: Use force, competence, and courage in something that makes a difference for itself and the world.

Influential myths are Ulysses (Roman), Theseus (Greek), Achilles (Greek), Hercules (Greek), Arjuna (Indian), Ares (Greek), Ogun (Yoruba), Lancelot (Round Table), and Saint George (Catholic).

Personality's influences are John Wayne (actor), John F. Kennedy (ex-president), Martin Luther King Jr. (Activist), Nelson Mandela (ex-president), and Dom Pedro I.

Cultural influences are Classic Heroes (characters), Super-Heroes like Batman, Spider-man, Wonder Woman, Black Widow, Superman, Captain America, etc. (characters), Star Wars (movie), James Bond (character), Mission Impossible (film/series), Troy (movie), Constantine (movie), Revengers (movie), Gladiator (movie), Matrix (trilogy movie), Incredibles (cartoon movie), X-men (cartoon movie), The Powerpuff Girls (Cartoon series), Heroes (song) from David Bowie, Iron Man (song) from Black Sabbath, and Hero (song) from Mariah Carey.

Influential Brands are BMW (automobile), Star Wars, Nike "Just Do It" (sports outfit), Adidas (sports outfit), FedEx (transportation and e-commerce), and Olympics Games (world sports competition)

A hero archetype helps people improve their performance at the highest level. The force of the services or product is to make good things efficiently a difficult work.

The hero archetype represents the people who perceive world problems and feels an inner call to solve the problem. They are the master that teaches powerful tools and shows the way. A hero wants to get out of his/her comfort zone and overcome his/her fears, walking ahead into the unknown. They fight battles and win external challenges and themselves. Returns victorious, bringing knowledge to share with your people.

The Hero influences us to take control of our lives and work hard in the world, and look for an ideal. It faces a battle for its ideals.

The hero is an archetype moved by the desire for victory, realization, and success. It feels the courage and force necessary to face life's situations, let go of fears, and do whatever it takes to fulfill what must be done, paying the price if needed for its mission.

The hero has a clear set of values and morals and will always try to remain true to them even in the most difficult times; they will not bend nor break their principles and will never compromise their beliefs, no matter what happens to them in life.

The hero archetype's morals are the only thing they truly believe in and care about. This allows them to face any challenges life brings with strength and confidence. They can do so because of self-belief. As long as you believe in your self-worth and respect yourself, you can overcome any situation and achieve anything.

A hero is a powerful person who knows how to act in any situation and can make the right decisions with no second thought, as he/she does not hesitate to sacrifice himself/herself to achieve his/her purpose, which is to find out how to live and die per his/her values, beliefs, philosophy and beliefs on life, etc.

The hero uses a big part of its libido as a favor to set goals. It knows to make plans to reach out at the right time. The hero shows us questions about how we are leading our lives; have we been led, or are we leaders?

The hero is a conqueror, a warrior facing significant causes. It has a disposition, long-term vision, and power of action. The hero archetype is a key to championship success, heroes, and great warriors.

The best ones are not born; they're made from the best possible elements that we find in people and from hard work and discipline to achieve their greatness and the mission of their life. To be champions and conquerors, fighting for what they want in life, and winning, even when all seems lost, is what makes a person a hero archetype.

The most important thing about becoming a champion and conquering is to believe in yourself and dare to try to do something that seems impossible; then, it will be easier for you to reach the goal.

It shows the need for humility, our skills, and conquers because as a true hero. It looks for a better world collectivity and not just itself alone.

Light: if you choose to live this archetype fully, you'll develop behavior like:

- ✓ Direction
- ✓ Force
- ✓ Success
- ✓ Power of realization
- ✓ Doesn't get intimidated by obstacles
- ✓ Resilience
- ✓ Dynamism
- ✓ Firmness in attitudes
- ✓ Deserved Triumph
- ✓ Positioning
- ✓ Travels succeeded
- ✓ Honorable
- ✓ Willing to live to the limit and overcome
- ✓ Leadership
- ✓ Claws
- ✓ Sensuality
- ✓ Willpower
- ✓ Action

Shadow: if you resist living this archetype, you'll develop behavior like:

- ✓ Egocentrism
- ✓ Imprudence
- ✓ Conquer and divide people
- ✓ Inflexibility
- ✓ Discord
- ✓ Exaggerated ambition
- ✓ Proudness
- ✓ Stay on the defensive, see enemies everywhere
- ✓ Cause conflicts everywhere
- ✓ Bellicose
- ✓ Aggressive
- ✓ Competitive

If the Hero archetype influences you, you might have a successful vocational profession in areas such as:

- Military
- Sales
- Nursing
- Physical Education
- Politics
- Athletics
- Hospitality
- Translation
- Interpretation
- Aviation
- Sign Language
- Firefighter
- Police
- Safeguard

Powerful symbols are Horses, Car, Sword, Helmet, and Shield.

Tarot Arcana is the Card VII Le Chariot – The Chariot, The Empress

18. The Mother

Main virtues are fertility, nutrition,
generosity, love, and compassion.

Influential myths are Demeter (Greek), Ceres (Roman), Gaya (Greek), Gaia (Greek), Oya (Yoruba)

Influential Personalities are Mother Mary Teresa of Calcutta (missionary), Virgin Mary (Catholicism leader), Clarissa Pinkola Estes (writer), Amy Carmichael (missionary), Elisabeth Elliot (author and speaker), Nefertari (Egyptian queen), and Cleopatra VII (Egyptian queen).

Cultural influences are Mother (movie), Mermaids (movie), Cleopatra (movie), The Crown (series), Changeling (movie), American Beauty (movie), Stepmom (movie), and Brave (Cartoon movie).

The mother archetype represents the feminine power and realization of the material world. Symbolize the capacity to love unconditionally.

The mother archetype is a compassionate, patient, nurturing, wise, strong, powerful, and generous woman who brings positive energy into relationships. She helps you find your inner strength so that you can be free from the fear-based emotional patterns of survival, control, and domination, which keep us bound in the physical realm of the body-mind, and from our spiritual essence, our soul or higher self in which we are connected with all things through unconditional love, compassion, oneness, and truth as part of our Divine Self.

Love is the biggest creative force in the universe; it gives the power of a new life to the mother.

The archetype brings fertility into the world. It can sow the new like a baby—for example, an idea, project, or artistic expression. While conceiving a concept is relatively easy, nurturing an idea into reality requires a mother's tender affection and resilient determination for the idea to turn into a successful project.

The mother carries the energy of abundance and prosperity.

That's why everything it touches gets purified and blooms. It represents the moment to reap what was planted. It is the beginning of a new season that will be filled with growth, prosperity, happiness, and the most abundant blessings you can imagine in your life! With this comes the ability to manifest even more prosperity for yourself and everyone around you – because you are part of the plan and the process!

Other characteristics of this archetype are the capacity for nutrition and offering something someone needs to grow, develop, and strengthen. Our planet, for example, is a great mother - it nourishes sus makes us feel happy with what we need to live.

The mother represents generosity. The biggest part of its energy is used to serve those who love, especially children and family, by biological blood or heart.

The mother is an archetype full of compassionate feelings. It recognizes the emotional state of others in their need for pain-alleviation, and it shows kindness to people who are in pain.

Compassion allows the mother to be an excellent caregiver, capable of donating its time, knowledge, and energy to those in need. It can do anything to protect and defend its children. The mother archetype always decides to sacrifice its own life for children if necessary.

Light: if you choose to live this archetype fully, you'll develop behavior like:

- ✓ Creativity nourishes the world with its creations.
- ✓ Strong maternal instinct, unconditional love
- ✓ Altruistic, care about family well-being and others more than itself
- ✓ Helpful and generous
- ✓ Nourish its children, support, protect, and sustains
- ✓ Likes to be acknowledged for its efforts to loved ones
- ✓ Gets lots of tasks done at the same time, with perfection
- ✓ Confidence

✓ Trustful
✓ Dignity
✓ Loyalty, according to its principles
✓ Feels full when it can nourish the loved ones and anticipate loved needs
✓ Disposition to overcome boundaries
✓ Loves the life, great charism, and seduction power, always get what it wants
✓ Easy problems solutions, especially problems from others
✓ Extrovert

Shadow: if you resist living this archetype, you'll develop behavior like:

✓ Difficult times to say no, and put limits
✓ Absent
✓ Become dominant, and hard to live together
✓ Feels depression when its services are no longer necessary
✓ Stop value and care about yourself because getting used to caring only for others
✓ Suffering from not setting goals and unrealistic expectations
✓ Perfectionism and jealously
✓ Become resentful when your efforts are no longer acknowledged

If the Mother Archetype influences you, you might have a successful vocational profession in areas such as:

- Caregiver
- Pediatric Medicine
- Therapy
- Early Childhood Education
- Social Assistant

- Nursing
- Chef
- Landscape
- Management
- Human Resources
- Esthetic
- Public Relations
- Nutritionist
- Charity
- Missiology
- Secretariat
- Any field involving love, compassion, and nutrition

Powerful symbols are Pregnant Woman, Stork, Breasts, Ladybird, Garden, Wheat camp, and Female Lion.

Tarot Arcana is the Card III L'Impératrice – The Empress

19. The Sage

Main virtues are wisdom and solitude.
"Ye shall know the truth, and the truth shall make you free."

-John 8:32

The sage is a Specialist, Detective, Analytics, Oracle, Philosopher, Searcher, Advisor, Thinker, Professional, Planner, Mentor, Teacher, Contemplative, and Erudite. The sage archetype is known to be a master of life and death, the two are often linked together, and one can easily assume that they have some insight into what lies beyond the veil of this world and how to make it through on the other side.

Level 1: Always on the lookout for the truth, objectivity, desire, and reliance on experts.

Level 2: Skeptic, thoughtful, innovator, critic, and specialist.

Level 3: Wisdom, confidence, and master.

Influential myths are Chronos (Greek), Solomon (Hebrew), Obaluaye (Yoruba), Amun (Egyptian), and Saturn (Roman).

Influential personalities are Socrates (Greek philosopher), Plato (philosopher), Aristotle (philosopher), Stephen William Hawking (physicist), Albert Einstein (scientist), Max Planck (physicist), Nicolas Tesla (inventor), Oprah Gail Winfrey (communicator), Sadhguru Aggi Vasudev (communicator), and Gautama Buddha (spiritual leader), Dalai Lama (spiritual leader).

Cultural influences are Herlock Homes (character), The X-Files (series), The Big Bang Theory (series), The Theory of Everything (movie), The Imitation Game (movie), Dungeons & Dragons (cartoon movie), What the Bleep Do We Know!? (documentary), Agora (movie), Peaceful Warrior (movie), Back to the Future (movie), Time (song) from Pink Floyd, and Echoes (song) by Pink Floyd.

Influential Brands are CNN, The New York Times, Barnes & Noble, Google, and Harvard University.

Offering expertise or information to clients encourages the clients to think. The belief is based on a new scientific advance or esoteric knowledge—the brand quality supported by verifiable data.

The sage archetype is a symbol of wisdom, solitude, and silence. It represents the search for the truth, referencing reality, nature, and looking for your true "self" and identity. While the master believes, the sage searches - the sage represents a forever search.

Sage is about seeing the world from a different perspective, the ultimate understanding that there are many perspectives to the same thing and everyone has their unique way of seeing it, yet together they create something more beautiful than any of them could have on their own, and the universal truth in the human experience.

The sage looks to inner depth and reflects on the past as humility to reframe it. It's always in the self-acknowledgment process through its experiences as it wants to walk independently. This is also a source of wisdom that can be transmitted to other people to find their way with life experience to help others be more independent from the path they took on their journey to know themselves and others.

Serendipity, autonomy, and patience - it walks on individuation and looks for being itself. Based on their experiences, the sage believes in their past as the best teacher. They understand that everything in life is an apprenticeship or a human being's improvement; that's why it doesn't carry repentance.

The sage is introspective and prefers to isolate itself to think and reflect than be surrounded by people. It lives a solitude, glory to be alone. They discover lucid and depth of its wisdom in silent moments that transcends understanding. They know how to enjoy moments of isolation to develop ideas and projects. The sage always balances everything it lived, learns through mistakes, doesn't cling to them, and moves on.

For the rest of our lives, we must learn, balance, and grow from our mistakes to be wiser than before and become better people who are not weighed down by regrets or wasted energy thinking about things that don't matter anymore but rather make us stronger and more capable beings, thus helping us to move on and live life fully, with a little less pain and without any regrets whatsoever!

Light: if you choose to live this archetype fully, you'll develop behavior like:

- ✓ Loves to study - objective, observer
- ✓ Looks for self-identity
- ✓ Searches for the truth
- ✓ Understands life and its meaning
- ✓ Doesn't get involved socially. Looks for escape from agitated people and noises, to reflect, think, meditate, and transform
- ✓ Experiences promote wisdom
- ✓ Good balance; good sense
- ✓ Extensive knowledge of many things and knowing how to use them properly

✓ Each mistake offers a new opportunity to learn and do different
✓ Understands boundaries and persists in improvement

Shadow: if you resist living this archetype, you'll develop behavior like:

✓ Intolerant
✓ Perfectionist
✓ Arrogant
✓ Fanatic
✓ Cold-hearted; detached
✓ Create rules for everybody
✓ Excessive critics of others
✓ Feel guilty, ashamed
✓ Feeling repentance and might go into depression
✓ Might self-charge for past actions
✓ Disposition to isolation and loneliness
✓ Harbor ideas that might bring fear of movement. Don't set goals; don't make them happen

If the Sage archetype influences you, you might have a successful vocational profession in areas such as:

- Philosophy
- Museology
- Archeology
- Librarian
- Research
- Laboratory
- Science
- Pedagogy
- Astronomy
- Priesthood
- Music
- Writer

- Medicine
- History
- Occultism
- Esoterism
- Antique Dealer

Powerful symbols are the Owl, Book, Clock, Hourglass, Glasses, and Lamp.

Tarot Arcane is the Card IX L'hermite – The Hermit

20. The Master

Main virtues are mastery, authority, and discipline.

Influential myths are Chiron (Greek), Centaur (Greek), Krishna (Hindu), and Babalorixa (Yoruba).

Personalities influences are Jesus of Nazareth (religious leader), Gautama Buddha (spiritual leader), Adi Yogi Shiva (yoga founder), Pope (Catholic leader), and Osho (religious leader).

Cultural Influences are the young pope (series), Angels and demons (movie), Samsara (documentary), Little Buddha, Kung Fu (series), and Kundun (film).

The Master archetype represents intelligence, self-dominance, spiritual power, and faith in something bigger than us. It's an archetype of search and teaching.

The archetype is a leader who sets an example for others to follow, whether through service or by leading others. It also means someone who teaches about a specific skill or set of skills such as leadership, meditation, etc. This is a great archetype to work with if you're looking to get your personal life in order!

The master archetype invites us to spiritual enlightenment, to know the sacred existence within us, in everything, and human beings act according to this acknowledgment. We are all part of one another, and each of us reflects the other; we can learn from our mistakes and failures and move forward on the path to greater understanding and compassion.

The master represents the beginning of everything, guidance that shows us a life objective. Stimulates us to look for ideal, a meaning beyond the material mundane.

It shows us the need to catch divine love and canalize this love into our daily actions. It can refer to a spiritual guide, a father, a teacher, or a priesthood, but the definition of the name is master because self-mastery comes first. First search, learn and develop, then share its wisdom with others.

The master archetype is receptive to the sky and active to the earth. All inspiration received from above is transferred to those who are down. It represents the main point of two polarities: what it is above and what is below. What is on the right and what is on the left? It lives in the middle, in the center.

To be a master archetype means you have no ego or desire for recognition and respect from others. Instead, you live as your highest self by living from the heart with humility and love for all beings and life itself. It is a form of sacrifice as you give up your needs and desires and focus only on giving back to those around you, both spiritually and physically.

The master archetype trusts what was taught, and it loves to advise and shows the right way for solutions to others based on its own experiences. The master has a vocational gift to incarnate a divine unity and do its best to teach, but it wouldn't be possible without disciples who believe in its teachings.

Light: if you choose to live this archetype fully, you'll develop behavior like:

- ✓ Pleasure to teach
- ✓ Rule-follower; whatever social or religious rules
- ✓ Looks for improvement to reach out for better social and professional relationships
- ✓ Looks for wisdom from humans or divine
- ✓ Contacts with life's sacred

- ✓ Great personal and presence power
- ✓ Balanced
- ✓ Lovely; knows when to put limits
- ✓ Excellent advisor
- ✓ Mental clarity; intuition ally

Shadow: if you resist living this archetype, you'll develop behavior like:

- ✓ Fanaticism
- ✓ Attachment to power
- ✓ Dogmatism
- ✓ Believe that your truth is unique and existent
- ✓ Egocentrism
- ✓ Exaggerated self-importance
- ✓ Intolerance
- ✓ False Moralism
- ✓ Stiffness
- ✓ Desire to be followed by the others
- ✓ Need to receive attention and approval from others

If the master archetype influences you, you might have a successful vocational profession in areas such as:

- Pedagogy
- Literature
- Philosophy
- Teacher
- Professor
- Linguistic
- History
- Psychology
- Journalism
- Archeology
- Medicine

- Social Service
- Odontology
- Priesthood
- Occultism
- Oratory

Powerful Symbols are Harp, Gold Cup, Ring, pope Miter, Chiron, and Gold Cross.

Tarot Arcana is the Card V Le Pape – The Hierophant

21. The Leader

Main virtues are leadership, determination, and protection.

The Leader archetype is called Boss, Aristocrats, Mother/Father, Politician, Responsible Citizenship, Managers, and King/Queen.

Level 1: Commits to responsibility as per its conditions.

Level 2: Exercises Leadership in family, group, organization, or workplace.

Level 3: Becomes the leader of community, performance, or speaks up within an area or society.

Influential myths are Zeus (Greek), Amun-Ra (Egyptian), Indra (Hindu), Oko (Yoruba), and Jupiter (Roman).

Personality's influences are George Washington (ex-president), Abraham Lincoln (ex-president), Napoleon Bonaparte (politician), Angela Dorothea Merkel (chancellor), Gaius Julius Caesar (statesman), Akhenaten (Egyptian pharaoh), Nefertari (Egyptian queen), Cleopatra (Egyptian queen), Barack Obama (ex-president), Bill Gates (businessman), Margaret Hilda Thatcher (prime minister), and Sebastião José de Carvalho e Melo (statesman).

Cultural influences are The Crown (series), House of Cards (series), Game of Thrones (series), Elizabeth (movie), Darkest Hour (movie), We Are the Champions (song) by Queen, Beautiful Boy Darling Boy (song) by John Lennon, Tears in Heaven (song) Eric Clapton, Father and Son (song) by Cat Stevens, Who Are You (song) by The Who, The Lion King (cartoon movie), The Wolf of Wall Street (movie), The Godfather (movie), King's Speech (movie), and Suits.

Influential Brands are Microsoft, American Express, Citibank, and IMB.

The leader archetype offers products and services with the highest level of prestige from powerful people, services that assist people in becoming organized, and products with a lifetime guarantee. The leader archetypes are regulatory and protect functioning organizations. Brands want to stand out from the crowd and become the industry leader in activity camps.

The leader archetype represents conscience leadership; there's nothing with superiority or power. The leader is a group soul that understands people's needs better than anyone else. The archetype is the way to become a leader with unlimited wisdom as its essence.

They can guide others and take charge of the situation because of the personal experience and knowledge they hold in their mind and heart. They can teach the right way and correct mistakes through communication or demonstration of the right thing to do and then inspire the rest of the team members to follow them.

Everyone is a leader of their potential. Leadership is not a gift, but a connection state with oneself and others, guided through characteristics of the essence: creativity, intelligence, love, power, and organization (order). The essence makes us know our life purpose; we can see it in our dreams and aspirations or our feelings, emotions, and intuitions when we are on self-development, growth, learning, and personal transformation.

The leader represents a personality of a good ruler, with authority, self-sufficiency, discipline, and power of action. Essential characteristics to rule. It has a great ability to implement ideas and make them come true in the world for collective well-being. It comes from paternity, the capacity to sustain and protect those dependent.

The leader archetype is a necessity of financial establishment, for its kingdom gets to prosper. For that reason, it takes responsibility for its material life and those who are ruled. When this archetype is alive, we feel that we have control of our lives and feel comfortable with the material aspects of the relationship (money, car, etc.).

This archetype is the guardian angel to the king's heart, and its mission is to keep his love flowing with money for all its needs – as long as the king doesn't give them a voice (through greed).

The leader archetype is characterized by the ability to deal with life's adversities with remarkable resilience and balance, without letting itself down with circumstances. The leader is determined, knows what they want, and has great self-confidence.

They don't just go along with the flow. They make their way through everything that comes their way! The leader also has an excellent sense of timing and knows when to act and when to retreat into a state of calm to gain insight and perspective on the situation and/or the best way to move forward based on this information (self-knowledge).

A leader is always prepared for the worst-case scenario. Therefore, they are always aware of all the possible options available to them and are capable of making the right decisions under any given circumstance.

Light: if you choose to live this archetype fully, you'll develop behavior like:

- ✓ Leadership abilities
- ✓ Financial planning
- ✓ Strategizing
- ✓ Responsibility to commitment toward success or failure
- ✓ Create and develop a prosperous business

- ✓ Practice knowledge
- ✓ Personal Power
- ✓ Accountability
- ✓ Adaptation capacity
- ✓ Skills to get people together
- ✓ Communication abilities
- ✓ Uses personal power to prosper everything around it like family, company, job, project, and community

Shadow: if you resist living this archetype, you'll develop behavior like:

- ✓ Arrogance
- ✓ Aggressive
- ✓ Inflexibility
- ✓ Bad listener
- ✓ Close-minded
- ✓ Fear of uncertainty
- ✓ Selfishness
- ✓ Manipulation
- ✓ Intolerance
- ✓ Lack of trust
- ✓ Controlling
- ✓ Spiteful
- ✓ Tyrant

If the leader archetype influences you, you might have a successful vocational profession in areas such as:

- Entrepreneur
- Manager
- Business Administration
- Economy
- Math
- Law
- Diplomacy

- Engineering
- Physics
- Systems Analyst
- Politic
- Military or Police
- Corporate
- Mechanics
- Sales
- Brokerage

Powerful symbols are Eagle, Lion, Coin, Throne, Suit and necktie, Scepter, and Crown.

Tarot arcana is the Card IIII L'Empereur – The Emperor

22. The Lover

Main virtues are passion, union, and free will.

The Lover archetype is also known as Partner, Friend, Matchmaker, Enthusiast, Specialist, Spouse, Harmonizer, and Sensualist. They help people find and give love.

Level 1: Look for formidable sex or great romance.

Level 2: Seek its vision of happiness and commit to someone loved.

Level 3: Spiritual love, self-acceptation, and ecstasy experience.

Influential myths are Eros (Greek), Cupid (Greek), Aphrodite (Greek), Venus (Roman), Freyja (Norse), and Oshun (Yoruba).

Personality's influences are Marilyn Monroe (actress), Elizabeth Taylor (actress), William Shakespeare (writer), Pedro Chagas Freitas (writer), Beyoncé (singer), and John Mayer (singer).

Cultural influences are Fifty Shades of Grey (trilogy movie),

Cinderella (character), Titanic (movie), Romeo and Juliet (characters), Pretty Woman (movie), The Notebook (movie), Blue is the Warmest Color (movie), Ghost (movie), Brokeback Mountain (movie), Mulan (cartoon movie), Little Mermaid (cartoon movie), Beauty and the Beast (cartoon movie).

Influential Brands are Jaguar, Bumble, Victoria's Secrets, and Chanel.

The lover archetype can be products that help people find love and friendship. It can be products and services promoting beauty, communication, and intimacy between people or associated with sexuality or romance. To be produced and sold as intimate organizational culture and elegant, different from massive hierarchies.

The lover is an archetype of passion, union, and choices. The lover impulses us to make something that we love, find and live with greater passion, someone, idea, project, or professional status. The lover often feels alone in the pursuit of their ideal.

The lover idealizes romantic love. When the archetype falls in love, they go depths into this feeling. The lover will take risks for their partner, protect them, and sacrifice everything to be with them – even if they don't know what's going on. They will follow their love interest blindly and trust that person to look after them. They'll have an intense bond with the other person that makes them feel incredibly connected.

The lover archetype carries a deep affective aspiration and wants to love and be loved. It knows how to deal with love and adore/receive love in the same proportion. Their love transcends any human condition and is above everything for the lover. It is capable of loving another because it loves itself.

True love never tries to possess another; it flows from us every time, and anything can make us stop loving. Love is eternal, unifies everything even in the distance, and is key to soul fulfillment. The lover is naturally affectionate, kind, charismatic, and sociable.

Those who live this archetype have empathy for others, understand and put themselves in someone else's position, and feel what they feel because emotional feelings strongly influence them. They are highly adaptable and flexible to different situations and conditions in life. They can make decisions and take action and show strong determination and persistence to achieve their goals even if they have been blocked or defeated on the way to get there once or many times before achieving them.

The lover archetypes are sensitive to other people's feelings and understand that not all of them can be happy all of the time. That is why they try to find a balance between the good things and bad things and between happiness and sadness, anger and love, etc.

Another characteristic of a lover archetype represents free will, our power of choice, and decision-making. Free will is a gift that humans receive to lead a life in a conscience way, not for external determination imposed. Decisions are made for fear of losing someone and losing love opportunity. However, this archetype shows us that mistakes are not caused by bad choices but by making choices and not standing up.

It is not good to live "on the wall" in the universe because life has priorities. Deciding with the ego is difficult because ego vision dictates that we must give up another when choosing one side. It is that moment when fear, doubt, and conflict come out. However, when we choose using our essence, we understand that each choice represents one renounce, though this is not a problem. The essence lives in unity as if everything is connected, and anything is our element.

When we do something good using free will, our option is what makes us and others grow. Love is a choice that we make at any time, one good choice that results in a win for everyone in the end.

Light: if you choose to live this archetype fully, you'll develop behavior like:

- ✓ Kind and gentle
- ✓ Enthusiastic

✓ Empathetic
✓ Doing what you like
✓ Find happiness within the union with the lover
✓ Always loved
✓ Creates bonds easily
✓ Unconditional self-acceptance
✓ Worries about other people's happiness
✓ Putting other's needs above self
✓ Care for and nurture people you love
✓ Brighten up every place you go
✓ Sociable and amiable

Shadow: if you resist living this archetype, you'll develop behavior like:

✓ Jealousy and possessiveness
✓ Envy
✓ Loneliness
✓ Sex compulsion
✓ Pornography addiction
✓ Losing focus and opportunities
✓ Hard time controlling emotions, developing anxiety and depression
✓ Attention seeking
✓ Losing identity

If the lover archetype influences you, you might have successful vocational professions in areas such as:

• Decoration
• Dance
• Fashion
• Animation
• Sexology
• Art
• Sculpturing

- Music/Music Therapy
- Literature
- Landscape
- Scenic Arts
- Architecture
- Masseuse
- Chronotherapy
- Antique Dealer

Powerful symbols are Cupid, Heart, Red Rose, Red Apple, Strawberry, Bow and Arrow, and Alliance Rings.

Tarot arcana is the Card VI L'Amovrevx – The Lovers

Chapter 4

Animals Archetypes

Have you ever asked yourself how wild animals never domesticated fall in love with a couple of humans? This is evolution. People like Kevin Richardson, for example, are great friends with them. Anyone who obtains an animal's heart vibrates at a higher level of consciousness.

In Judaic tradition, the myth of Adam and Eve, known as the first man and woman, had a wonderful relationship with the whole that was called God. Before the fall of man, they had control of the entire natural world, including the animals, since their vibration was God's frequency. It is a frequency called love.

Once they had experienced the tree of knowledge, they started feeling shadow and light, known as good and evil. It's important to understand that most Biblical stories are metaphoric; sometimes, it was hard for Hebrews to understand Jesus because most of His teachings were based on parables, metaphoric stories, and tales. For example, the tree is a symbol and has a meaning. Don't worry, I will explain more about the tree in chapter 11.

Some businesses use animals to symbolize power in their brand, which is an excellent marketing strategy for selling items. It doesn't have to be an animal symbol; just a sentence, affirmation, or proverb inspired by the specific animal will be enough to take the message to your unconscious mind.

In this process, you are not looking for an answer in words; rather, your subconscious mind is responding to whatever comes through on the other side of that door, and it may lead you to many different responses—as well as a new thought or perspective that has never occurred to you before!

There are a lot of different animals to be inspired, and lots of them share different frequencies. To help you understand this, I'll show you the main animal's archetype characteristics and examples of how they influence people's behavior.

1. Eagle

"It is necessary to have the boldness of the eagle that flies without fear and, even without destiny, fears nothing."

Without a doubt, the Eagle is a powerful symbol inspired by many myths and legends. It's the most controversial archetype globally; some people avoid it, and others admire it. The reality is that the Eagle is present as an archetypal animal of power in the lives of entrepreneurs, politicians, large corporations, and businessmen.

The Eagle was worshiped and reverenced millennia ago, an incontestable powerful symbol of success in humans 'collective consciousness.

In Greek myth, Zeus transformed himself into an Eagle to control the thunders. The Sumerians believed that God showed Himself as an Eagle. The indigenous believed that eagles could cross the sun - that is why they fly higher, representing solar energy. In Shamanism, the Eagle is a strong animal that can dislocate other spiritual realms and swiftly link to higher awareness stages. It is related to the father sky and sacred sun power, developing a remarkable aptitude for spiritual transcendence. For that reason, the shamanism followers bless people using Eagle's feather.

Eagle's archetypal impacts stimulated dopamine levels in the brain, resulting in emotions of personal strength and confidence. The Eagle is the archetype that does not want to be governed; instead, it wishes to rule. As a result, it is only ideal for a boss, businessman/woman, or any other leadership position.

If you're solely an employee, I would not recommend placing an eagle on your office table. The bosses know what their staff is attempting to do with the Eagle. Business professionals are well-versed in marketing stereotypes and their consequences. However, this does not preclude someone from using the Eagle in their own house, bedroom, or wallet; the Eagle is an excellent sign of fortune. It is no accident that the president is the only one who requires an Eagle as the archetypal animal of authority.

Anyone who wants to activate and raise the Eagle on its conscience must be prepared. A high level of dopamine might bring anxiety. If there is a trauma or emotional problem to be solved, be prepared to sleep late and wake up early in the morning because this symbol makes anyone become a "workaholic."

They are masters of survival; they alter their techniques to feed themselves in difficult times. They are also adept at renewing skin if they wish to live longer, demonstrating a fantastic representation of the transformation process.

As a family, eagle couples can live for 20 years, if not forever, even after having eaglets and seeing them grow into adults. The male eagle is the provider, while the female eagle is the organizer.

The eagles are quite strict in their eaglet discipline; occasionally, they do not offer food to the eaglets to learn to live on their own for the three weeks before they leave the nest. This is ample time for them to make errors and learn from them until they are self-sufficient. The Eagle signifies freedom, which was previously described in the Bible as a liberator and overcomer in Prophet Isaiah Chapter 40, verse 31.

The Eagle teaches us to focus on our goals instead of giving up or running away. It shows us that we must improve our techniques, skills, and gifts to reach higher places. It wants you not to feel sorry for yourself. On the contrary, it wants you to admire yourself. It wants you to become your savior - Don't look for a hero, be your hero. Think big because God does. The eagle does not live in anticipation; rather, the eagle lives in actuality. "Expectation is the mother of frustration," according to one of Eagle's proverbs.

Light:

- ✓ Foresight
- ✓ Wisdom
- ✓ Strategy
- ✓ Confidence
- ✓ Personal Force
- ✓ Leadership
- ✓ Personal Power
- ✓ Freedom
- ✓ Boosted Self-esteem
- ✓ Courage
- ✓ Independence
- ✓ Discipline
- ✓ Detachment
- ✓ Self-growth
- ✓ Success
- ✓ Prosperity
- ✓ Self-motivation
- ✓ Perception
- ✓ Focus
- ✓ Monogamy
- ✓ Strong Yang

Shadow:

- ✓ Irritability as Eagle is a predator
- ✓ Selfishness
- ✓ Loneliness
- ✓ Competition
- ✓ Territorialism

✓ Proudness

2. Hawk

Also known as Falcon. The Hawk, like the Eagle, is influenced by numerous successful businesses, entrepreneurs, and investors. It is the fastest bird of prey, with flights reaching speeds of up to 136 miles per hour due to the aerodynamics of its body, which allows for simple dislocation in the air when matched with its flexible wings.

In many cultures, The Hawk is associated with solar energy - an important symbol for building physical and intellectual moral plans and achieving supremacy in the face of life's hurdles and troubles.

The Egyptian God, Horus, the divinity representing the sky, personified itself as a Hawk. Horus 'eyes are linked to Hawk's eyes, which resonates with a Hawk's far-sightedness, similar to Eagle's vision, which is why Horus 'moniker was bestowed as "the all-seeing eye of God."

In Shamanism, the Hawk is a messenger. It is considered an animal of responsibility. If he has far view capacity, he can predict the future to envision life's path.

In business, the Hawk archetype signifies quick money wins and money spends. A stellar example is the Middle East, particularly the United Arab Emirates. As an archetypal animal, the hawk symbolizes power; the Middle East is a business-growing region.

It's a tremendous perceptual archetype. The Hawk always knows if a threat or risk is approaching. He teaches us to recognize people's intentions before they approach, whether they are good or harmful, and you feel secure to say yes or no without hesitation. He's also a group animal who works through plans, making him the perfect archetype for a military profession. Hawk has a lot of ideas, opinions, and objectives.

The peregrine Falcon is a hawk that does not establish a nest or territory; its main activity is migration. Your urge to shift nation, state, or location will grow without fear. Hawk is an excellent mentor if you want to find your life's purpose, make changes, and succeed. You may be able to attract business partners, lucrative contracts, and profitable investments.

Although the Hawk and the Eagle resemble, they are distinct. For example, the Eagle likes to be first and wants to stay on top. The Eagle will not tolerate a lesser position. In contrast to Hawk, it's acceptable to be in second place or even lower; it's an archetype that makes you feel content as long as you fulfill your goals.

Jeffrey Bezos, the owner of Amazon, was a very successful entrepreneur motivated by the peregrine Falcon. Amazon grew quickly, like an explosion!

Light:

- ✓ Speed, ability to get work done fast
- ✓ Keen vision
- ✓ Remote viewing
- ✓ Organizer
- ✓ Self-esteem
- ✓ Life's purpose
- ✓ Prosperity in every area
- ✓ Focus
- ✓ Confidence
- ✓ Procrastination
- ✓ Strategist
- ✓ Self-love
- ✓ Personal magnetism
- ✓ Trusting
- ✓ Agility
- ✓ Smartest
- ✓ Independence
- ✓ Decision Capacity

✓ Observer
✓ Analyze
✓ Good memory
✓ Realization power
✓ Eagerness to win
✓ Monogamy
✓ Dopamine
✓ Intense Yang

Shadow:

✓ Perfectionism
✓ Stressed
✓ Ego
✓ Excessive focus on goals and objective

3. Owl

"Be wary of the appearance, she goes around deceiving those who don't see the essence."

-Alberto Freitas

Most people are seeking the archetype of the Owl. It is a potent symbol of the Sage archetype. The Owl has a lot to teach us; it's a terrific symbol of knowledge that shines light into the darkness.

Owl awakens curiosity due to its hunting capacity and astuteness; as a nocturnal animal, the Owl is always conscience and observing. Like Eagles and Hawks, the Owl has 360° vision and can see every angle perfectly in the darkness. It dares to attack snakes and can hunt silently and discreetly without being detected. It has exceptional eyesight and hearing; it can listen kilometers away and hunt using its ears.

Because Owl is a nocturnal animal in some cultures, she was associated with the moon, woman energy, prophecies, wisdom, magic, omens, and mysticism. It's no coincidence that the Owl has appeared in Harry Potter series as an archetypal symbol of power.

In Greek mythology, Athena was the wisdom deity, and the owl was her favorite bird. Some historians believe that Owl can discern the truth, assisting Athenas in detecting "invisible" elements that may reverse the historical curse with a single judgment. Athenas was associated with the Roman goddess, Minerva, also represented by an Owl.

In the Hindu myth, a god called Lakshmi is often introduced with a white Owl on her side. Some tribes of North American indigenous called Owl the "Eagle of the night."

The Owl denotes knowledge in Shamanism. They summon Owl energy to investigate conscience plans, seek answers to complicated circumstances, and boost awareness of natural signals, particularly nocturnal mysteries.

Owls are a great archetype for those who love reading, searching, studying, and applying for college exams. The Owl is best suited for advising rather than business; excessive research may prevent you from taking action; this is not a good archetype for getting things done.

Owls may teach us that there is no distinction between spiritual and material understanding. To exist in this world, we need both wisdom and knowledge; at the end of the day, both are one; if the cosmos is mental, everything is awareness.

Owls teach us to pay closer attention to the world around us, to see beyond and behind problems. Listening to others is preferable to talking; the revelation occurs when the words are delivered. Have courage as shyness can be harmful at times. When you make a mistake with boldness, it is readily corrected. Be faithful to your friends, your relationship, your dreams, and yourself. Don't get involved in fights or gossip since it leaves you susceptible to the ill-intentions of others.

Light:

✓ Intuition
✓ Wisdom and Knowledge
✓ Protective Mother
✓ Self-esteem
✓ Confidence
✓ Trust
✓ Power
✓ Perception
✓ Focus
✓ Concentration
✓ Loyalty
✓ Presence
✓ Strategist
✓ Clarify
✓ Clairvoyance
✓ Sensibility
✓ Easy learner
✓ Sigils actions
✓ Drives away envy and destructive criticism
✓ Intelligence
✓ Monogamy
✓ Dopamine produce
✓ Strong Yin

Shadow:

✓ Self-sabotage
✓ Lack of accountability
✓ Authoritarian. You may act like a mother to others, dictating what they should or shouldn't do. Disrespecting others' free choice.
✓ Insomnia
✓ Lethargic
✓ Non-cooperative
✓ Over-commitment
✓ Unproductive
✓ Over-analyze

4. Bee

The bee is a great prosperity archetype! But not just any bee emits wealth frequency; bees have a variety of biological roles, such as dimorphism and diverse behavioral features.

There are two bee types:

1. Drone bee – The function is to mate with the queen bee and ensure species production, which is the purpose of existence. After that, a tragic consequence occurs: he is abandoned by other bees because he is no longer helpful.

2. Worker bee – They are bees that labor for the beehive and are infertile. Their primary function is to transport pollen, and nectar, feed the queen bee, drone bee, and larva, mend what needs to be fixed, clean up the hive, and build new cells in the hive to store honey or shelter the queen bee eggs.

As an archetype, the bee must represent order, cooperation, nobility, discipline, organization, and hard work in a self-contained community. The bees are excellent at defending themselves against an opponent, even when they are not prepared for an attack. Wasps, for example, are the main bee's nemesis; they may kill anything in their path, including bee larvae, bees, and even the queen bee. When wasps appear, bees have two choices: stay in the hive and starve to death, or leave the hive searching for food and be attacked by wasps. Both paths, of course, lead to a dead end, which is why they fight! The bees developed a secret weapon to win the battle by forming a "ball" with 500 bees around the enemy and shaking their wings to raise the temperature inside the hive as high as possible, reaching 116.6 degrees Fahrenheit, which is fatal to wasps. In contrast, the bees can withstand temperatures up to 118.4 degrees Fahrenheit.

Bees were thought to have been produced by deity Ra's tears. Hence they were associated with solar energy and the purifying process with the fire element in Egyptian civilization.

Bees were associated with Demeter, goddess of agriculture and harvest in Greek society, and it was also believed that evil people would reincarnate as bees.

The bee, with its honey, represents sweetness and kindness

in Christianity, yet the bee's barbed stinger depicts divine justice.

Bees are also represented in Hinduism, with the Kamadeva God wielding a bow with a bee-made thread.

Bees symbolize communication and cooperation in Shamanism. The Shaman uses their energy to bring groups together, strengthen each tribe group, and improve communication and ability to express themselves.

The frequency of happiness is emitted by bees, who work together with joy to serve one another and provide all that nature requires to grow things, particularly flowers. They instill in us the belief that no matter what we are working towards, we are the greatest and most deserving. They work as a family and look after one another as if the problem were theirs. They are the team that says "mess with one, mess with all" and "we are all in this together."

Light:

- ✓ Cooperation
- ✓ Sociability
- ✓ Libido
- ✓ Altruism
- ✓ Solidarity
- ✓ Contribution
- ✓ Devotion
- ✓ Respect
- ✓ Protect and serve
- ✓ Loyalty
- ✓ Effort and Determination
- ✓ Organization and planning
- ✓ Attention
- ✓ Prosperity in group
- ✓ Abundance
- ✓ Work from home
- ✓ Team worker
- ✓ Synergy and empathy

✓ Minimum efforts
✓ Yin and yang balance

Shadow:

✓ Obsessive devotion that makes you blind
✓ Focus only on the work (Drone and queen don't work)
✓ Defensive instinct might attract bad situations (when they sting, they die)
✓ Attachment to material things

5. Hummingbird

The frequency of universal love is derived from the hummingbird, a little bird that can hover in mid-air and fly backward. Their wings flap ninety times per second, with younger hummingbird wings flapping up to 200 times per second and a cardiac rate of 1,200 beats per minute. A hummingbird's heart accounts for about 20% of the bird's total weight.

The hummingbird is a powerful emblem of pure love, happiness, feelings, good fortune, lightness, grace, and delicacy in Shamanism. In any scenario, it was connected with finding sweetness, delighted to enjoy the pleasant things that life had to offer by collecting flower nectar. The hummingbird enables the Shaman to resignify unpleasant experiences by tasting the nectar of pure love, tapping into vital energy, and mending communal and emotional wounds.

The hummingbird encourages us to live in the now and appreciates our daily lives' beauty and magic. It co considers all humans as well as nature. Keep an eye out for our global grace. It symbolizes beauty, harmony, truth, and force for the Amerindians.

The heart chakra is related to the hummingbird, which is linked to blood, nerves, blood vessels, and the circulatory system. The emotional system, hope, trust, surrender, self-acceptance, inspiration, compassion, and saying yes to life are all activated by this chakra. The hummingbird is a powerful archetype for inner transformation and healing.

It is known as the love archetype, capable of releasing all emotional suffering and attracting blissful and enjoyable times.

Light:

✓ Universal love vibration
✓ Emotional healer
✓ Sensibility
✓ Happiness
✓ Intuition
✓ Self-esteem
✓ Self-love
✓ Delicacy
✓ Humility
✓ Compassion
✓ Tranquility
✓ Expression of love
✓ Mutual attraction

Shadow:

✓ Anxiety
✓ Exaggeration predisposition
✓ Agitation
✓ Restlessness
✓ Going through intense emotional cleansing and purification processes
✓ Competitiveness with similar energy
✓ Selfish
✓ Territorial

6. Butterfly

"Living long is not living 100 years; living long is living every minute," says the butterfly archetype.

The most controversial and contradictory archetype of all symbols, the butterfly, causes profound transformations in people. Some people fear it, while others embrace it.

The butterfly was thought to be a "Divine Messenger" by certain ancient civilizations. It is associated with the air element in Shamanism, which is a sign of metamorphosis and change.

It's crucial to understand that the butterfly represents the final step of change, from egg to larva to cocoon to butterfly.

To determine whether you are ready for your final evolutionary phase, you must interpret each stage of the butterfly's evolution symbolically. Every single butterfly emerged from its cocoon. Every butterfly cocoon contained a larval stage. Each larva began as a butterfly egg.

Stage 1 - egg: This is the stage of immaturity when you need to be on your guard, manage all of your information, and understand your desires, ideas, and thoughts.

Stage 2 - larva: Sounds like the moment you decided to assert yourself in the world. You're making decisions and choices, investigating the outside world, learning new things, and grasping reality. You're building your personalities and conception.

Stage 3 - cocoon: Sounds like the moment you recognize your patterns and external influences, begin the reflective process, devote your focus to personal growth, and seek self-acknowledgment. Inner mobility and resourcefulness in the creation of personal initiatives represent the necessity to take action to achieve your goals.

Stage 4 - butterfly: Rebirth of the butterfly signifies that you are now ready to fulfill your destiny. Represents the right to reap the benefits of self-transformation, objectives, realizations, and the ability to live out your aspirations.

Life teaches us that change is a possibility. Life itself offers an infinite number of alternatives. The butterfly, for example, is a symbol of transformation and renewal. Stop and pay attention when you come across beings like that. The human spirit is linked to the butterfly.

Both plants and butterflies are fleeing for their lives. As a defense against hungry caterpillars, plants produce toxins, which caterpillars have discovered a way to fight. Plant poisons are internalized and digested by some caterpillars and butterflies as a form of self-defense against predators.

Butterflies are naturally exposed to various obstacles, and every living thing, including butterflies, has a defense mechanism.

Dissatisfaction and restlessness are indications from our spirits that transition is approaching, similar to how a caterpillar stops eating a few days before entering the chrysalis.

The caterpillar begins to hunt for a suitable location to transform. The former form vanishes as soon as it enters the chrysalis, and the new one takes its place. Metamorphosis is the most critical stage of transformation. By analogy, the moment of self-knowledge is the process of being with oneself inside the cocoon. It's the key to understanding the butterfly archetype.

We have a great deal to learn from its movements and expressions, which are as varied as they are powerful: The way it opens and closes its wings; how it moves through space; how it lands when it gets there; even how it eats, sleep and mates! In other words, the true nature of your soul can be revealed only in the course of your journey back home—the journey to self-acceptance, to your unique sense of purpose, to the realization that you're not just part of the world but also a part of yourself.

Have you heard of the butterfly effect motion before? Most likely in the film. According to the hypothesis, minor actions such as flapping a butterfly's wings can result in large circles, which can cause multiple changes in the climatic pattern, leading to the conclusion that a hurricane is the cause of the butterfly flap. Whatever the case may be, we can't deny that modest actions can have a big impact.

As an archetype, the butterfly reminds us to learn from our mistakes. Consider how many opportunities you missed in the previous year. How much energy did you waste on something that would have been better spent elsewhere? The butterfly is a reminder of the importance of learning and growth from all experiences; whether they be good or bad, positive or negative, large or small, or whatever it may be for you personally, this year is no different! The butterfly symbolizes transformation because it changes color from black to blue, then green, yellow, orange, red, and back to black again as it transforms into its adult form.

A butterfly enjoys every moment of her existence. It notices when life provides the answers it seeks. When it emerges from the cocoon, the butterfly is a powerful symbol of liberation. The journey to full maturity requires some struggle and adversity, but it is well worth the effort, for there is no greater feeling than being free. It flies high to freedom and new experiences.

You are what you eat, and a caterpillar will continue to consume plants until its stomach can no longer accommodate it. Its nutrition may change when it transforms into a butterfly, but pollen or nectar is the most usual. This shows that your needs, wants, and desires will vary as you evolve. However, certain things that served as your core will remain significant to your being. So, as we go through life, we will experience highs and lows, but these core values of our being will be there all along. The caterpillar and the butterfly are symbols for different parts of ourselves, which can be applied to any stage in our lives.

Light:

- ✓ Vibration of change
- ✓ Renovation
- ✓ Transmutation
- ✓ Freedom
- ✓ Lightness
- ✓ Spiritual development
- ✓ Artistic expression
- ✓ Intuition
- ✓ Self-Esteem
- ✓ Self-love

✓ Solitude
✓ Detachment
✓ Accelerated self-transformation process
✓ Life's mission

Shadow:

✓ Loneliness
✓ Accelerate and unstoppable changes (house, car, job, partner, places, companies)
✓ Intensified process of deconstructing limiting beliefs
✓ Long-term relationships difficulties
✓ Continuous trial of getting out from Comfort Zone

The activation of this archetype is not recommendable for a long time.

7. Raven

Raven, known as a mystic symbol, has been extensively explored in literature and other arts, including the Game of Thrones series, particularly as the core topic of fantasy and horror fiction.

As an archetype, it is usually associated with supernatural abilities that enable the bearer to see or hear what others cannot, often having some kind of "vision" of the future (the ability to foretell events). In addition to its mystical connotations, many authors have also used the raven to symbolize freedom, especially when set free from the past. Mythology and Literature Edit in ancient Rome, the word 'Corvus 'was used to describe a variety of birds, such as ravens, crows, and magpies.

The American writer, Edgar Allan Poe, became one of the most iconic authors of dark romanticism when he wrote the poem the 'Raven.'

The origin of the raven's enigmatic narrative is associated

with his scavenging tendencies (eating carcasses), the ability to imitate other animals 'noises, and the fact that the black color is connected with darkness, obscurity, and evil.

In a logical sense, the Raven and Crown are symbols of cleanliness since they transform and clean the environment. The ravens, in this case, have cleansed the souls of their enemies after they were put to death by decapitation, while the crowns signify that the king has been crowned and the people recognize him as their leader.

For example, when a therapist promotes healing for a patient, he is touching the patient's vibrational field, removing putrefied energies, and transmuting dense negative energy patterns into positive and beneficial energies. You are healing and giving peace to your patient.

Similarly, the raven is the medicine of magic. It helps with ceremonies. The ancient native chiefs say that the crow simultaneously sees the past, the present, and the future.

The bird has a lot of knowledge in itself, but also it brings wisdom from other creatures or people who are wise, like the owl, the snake, the bear, the wolf, the eagle, the rabbit, etc. The Raven is an intelligent creature, very clever, smart, and cunning, which can easily get food even if there is no food around, as he can follow a scent and find a hidden source of water, such as the puddles left behind after heavy rain.

Old civilizations and myths believe that the raven, like many birds, symbolizes protection and regeneration and emanates good energy. It was said to be able to foretell future events and also could bring bad omens and portents for those who disturbed its nest or its flight in an area where it nested or flew.

The Raven is one of the three birds of Odin's household: The Eagle, and the Raven, as he called them (Thorvaldr). As they are not only connected with Odin but also the whole of Norse mythology, they are often depicted together, especially the two which fly through the air above his throne on Yggdrasil, the World Tree, as it is called by the Norns.

In Japanese myths, Yatagarasu, known as Crow-God, specifically symbolizes guidance. It represents one of the most common characteristics of Gods Chi (wisdom), (benevolence), and Yuu (value).

Yatagarasu means "crow" in English and "white crow" or "black crow" due to their spiritual powers and knowledge gained from the gods, according to the myth. They can recognize the character traits of people that would be beneficial for them by seeing if the person was good at reading or writing or if they were good at doing things such as fishing, farming, etc. This type of bird also could read human hearts and minds, being able to see through walls and know what people were thinking about, so they were seen as wise with an excellent sense of judgment.

The Yatagarasu is interpreted as a powerful navigator, capable of orienting themselves easily even in unfamiliar lands.

Hugin and Munin are two ravens in Norse mythology. Hugin, which means thinking, and Munin, which means memory, are both Odin god messengers who fly all across Midgard, the kingdom of humans (Earth), gathering information and delivering it to the father of the gods.

Raven is also associated with wizardry in some cultures. Witches use the capacity of Raven's premonition to foresee the future and communicate to spiritual forces from other dimensions. The raven is strongly connected to the world of the dead and liven.

In Shamanism, certain indigenous tribes believe Ravens are divine beings and insightful counselors and protectors or shields against negative energies. The Raven used to be the animal of choice for shamans or people with shapeshifting abilities.

As your spirit guide, the raven will show you how to connect to the mysteries of life and develop your ability to perceive subtleties in energetic changes in yourself and your environment. Raven can see through illusions, especially when it comes to right and wrong, inside and outside.

The raven, as an archetype, immerses itself in light and

shadow, seeing both inner and outer realities. The crow's primal path is about being mindful of opinions and actions. It should be about willingness to put what you say into action. Balance your past, present, and future in the now.

The raven soars into the mysteries of night and daylight with equal ease. Visible and invisible are complementary manifestations within the apparent opposites that do not separate. When we break out of the convenient illusion of duality, we come closer to expanding consciousness towards wholeness. We realize that only from understanding the shadows can we rise to pure light.

The most obvious manifestation is seen in the world at large, which is ruled by its polarities: light/dark, male/female, good/bad, up/down, etc. The same holds true for personal relationships and individual psychology, including mental health problems such as depression, bipolar disorder, schizophrenia, anxiety, addiction, phobias, obsessive-compulsive disorder, and more. These opposites are so prevalent because they're just another form of duality, a false way of thinking based on our current level of awareness.

Light:

- ✓ Magic of life and mystery of creation
- ✓ Wisdom
- ✓ Alchemy
- ✓ Prophetic vision
- ✓ Intuition
- ✓ Destiny
- ✓ Personal transformation
- ✓ Intelligence
- ✓ High prospects
- ✓ Audacity and fearlessness
- ✓ Flexibility
- ✓ Adaptability

Shadow:

✓ Trickster
✓ Manipulation

8. Spider

Excellent creator, the spider weaves her web with care and zeal because she knows your livelihood will be generated there. She is confident that other insets will get stuck in her web.

As an archetype, it embodies persistence and knowledge of one's relationship with the entirety of creation. The spider symbolizes the infinite possibilities of creativity, the concept that everything is related, and that the smallest movement may swing the entire Divine Web and impact your own life and collective reality.

It encourages the use of intuition combined with creativity to create necessary conditions for spiritual evolution and progress. The Spider teaches that "it's not strength, it's the way," as she can thrive in any location and situation thanks to her formidable ability to adapt.

This ability stems from her capacity to recognize the right moment to act and be ready when an opportunity arises, which we all have in common. The Web - a metaphor used by the Spider to describe how our soul, or rather the Self, can connect with the physical world through different levels and perspectives on life, using our body as a tool to express itself in a certain form.

In many cultures, Spider is known as the Universe weaver. By weaving her web, the spider can give life to new worlds that are interlaced with each other.

In the same way that the spider is, some beings in this world have a similar personality and role of being called "weavers," and some who have their specialties to weave the webs for them in their lives, such as teachers, coaches, mentors, friends, and relatives, etc. Like Spider, the Universe Weaver is one among those weaves that create our dreams into reality. They are the ones who guide us on the right path. They help us learn from our mistakes and experience new things in life.

In Hinduism, the Spider is the main symbol of the Goddess Maya, the Goddess of Illusion and Dreams.

In the positive pole, the web symbolizes protection, firmness, security, adaptability, creativity, personal effort, the home, work, and construction. It can be interpreted as a trap, illusion, falsehood, and danger at the negative pole. It all depends on the observer.

In Shamanism, the Spider is considered a power being revered as the "Weaver of the Universe." Dreamcatchers, created by the Lakota, were inspired by the Spider's web. According to Lakota legend, the Iktomi, a deity of Wisdom - who manifested himself as a spider - taught that the Dreamcatcher catches and sticks good ideas while negative ones pass through the center, filtering the mind with good thoughts.

The Spider teaches us that the physical world, as we see it, is just the apparent world, a web of illusions and that it is necessary to look beyond the horizon of what is apparent or visible. The Spider says there are two ways: "Through your eyes" and "Beyond your eyes."

Our mind must be purified to achieve that state where the "I" disappears and one is in the pure consciousness itself, without any reference point – and then one can see everything clearly – with complete freedom from desire or fear – even if you are dying! We need to understand our body's true nature and purpose, what it truly wants to do, and how it works.

The spider's body is fashioned like an eight and contains eight legs, which allow it to exhibit endless possibilities for existence. It is associated with the four winds of change and the four directions (each direction being associated with four bodies: spiritual, emotional, physical, and mental), for a total of eight. Infinity is represented by the number 8.

The spider calls us to look at our wheel of life. Are we balanced between all aspects of our life? Or are we trapped in our mental and emotional state in the web of illusion, and the weaver's spindle stopped turning?

The spider's work is done, and she waits for her next prey to come near the web so it can be caught in its snare. So it goes on until death ends the dance with one final struggle to free itself from the trap of being bound by its web of lies, delusions, and false beliefs that were spun out of control because of a single mistake of omission or commission in the past. If you decide on your life, then first look to see what decisions have already been made, and second look to see how those decisions affect your present condition and future possibilities.

The wheel of life is like a dream catcher woven by a spider's thread! Will our life be the manifestation of our dreams or our nightmares?

The spider shows us that we can change at any time; we can weave new threads and new paths in our lives. The spider says that reality is just a stage of creation, and we, the creators of our theater, drama, or film, say that it is nothing more than that... a film, an illusion of the mind.

If we don't use our creative ability to create our life, it gets stuck, tangled up, destructive and frustrating. We put the brakes on our dreams, and we resent it. That resentment turns you into a black widow and consumes you from the inside. You become as dry as insects in a web and become a spider's dinner.

The spider always invites you to connect with your creative energy. Sow, to bear fruit, and sowing is to use the infinite potential of a seed... it is to create! It's time for you to take control of your life, and become the architect of the future, your own story, and your destiny.

Be the best version of yourself, build confidence and faith in yourself, and live in a way that reflects who you are as an authentic human being.

Connect to the infinite possibilities of manifestation of the universe, see beyond the web of illusion that is appearance and look for new alternatives to the present path.

Be aware of your feelings to gain a clear understanding of

what you are truly experiencing and why, so you can change them if necessary and avoid situations that will cause you to feel bad or unhappy again due to your unconscious patterns of thinking and feeling that cause you to believe them to be true despite the lack of evidence to support those beliefs.

Bring dreams to reality, create a new web, catch your dreams, and weave your own life. Create! Weave!

Light:

- ✓ Creativity and adaptability
- ✓ Determination and patience
- ✓ Internal home changes
- ✓ Solitude
- ✓ Sensibility, gracefulness, and keen perception
- ✓ Strong intuition
- ✓ Prosperity with fewer efforts
- ✓ Opportunity Magnet (insects go to the web)
- ✓ Power of realization and dreams manifestations
- ✓ Your home becomes a prosperity fountain

Shadow:

- ✓ Needs home to prosper
- ✓ Insensibility to affection
- ✓ Unstable relationships
- ✓ Poor resource management (multiple opportunities can lead to time shortage)
- ✓ Loneliness and isolation
- ✓ Tendency to manipulate and deceive to achieve their goals
- ✓ After installing your fountain of prosperity (Web), it tends to stay in the comfort zone

9. Cat

Spiritual vision, reiki, independence, and sensuality

Cats are our guardians in the unseen world, just as dogs are guardians in the physical world. Cats can transmute the negative energies of the environment in which they live and of the people they live with.

When our feline friend stays too much in a certain place, he probably perceives the negative vibe of the place. This is an indication that the energy of this environment needs to be improved. Cats can sense the aura of their surroundings.

The cat is a symbolically rich animal, possibly one of the most prevalent archetypes in everyday life, splitting the podium with dogs. These small domestic cats are reputed to have natural psychic abilities such as spiritual vision, energy transmutation, and reiki. This is often attributed to their ability to be in tune with nature, their close relationship to the Earth, and their ability to communicate telepathically through the olfactory sense.

Thanks to their nocturnal habits, it is not a coincidence; cats were associated by many ancient civilizations with lunar energy, natural magic, and the mysteries of spirituality and life, especially in Celtic, Nordic, and Persian cultures. In other cultures, some people believe that cats see other dimensions. Sometimes they stop to contemplate what we don't see.

In Ancient Egypt, cats were worshiped and treated as deities incarnate, as they were believed to be manifestations (or personifications) of the Goddess Bastet, the goddess of Fertility. They received special care and treatment, and when they died, they were mummified and buried in special places of greater honor and nobility. They believed that cats could ward off any evil.

In Buddhism, the cat presents an ambivalent Symbology. Early Buddhists revered the cat for his ability to concentrate and his detached lifestyle. However, some tales say that when the Buddha died, cats were the only animals on the planet that were not moved or showed condolences. In this sense, the cat also represents the negative polarity of detachment: insensitivity, lack of empathy, neutrality, and total indifference.

The symbol has a negative connotation because of the negativity associated with its meaning.

In Japanese culture, the cat appears as Maneki-Neko, also known as the "lucky cat!"

According to Japanese beliefs, each paw raised has a meaning beyond luck. For example, the right paw attracts abundant money, and the left paw is specific for attracting customers and business.

In Shamanism, the cat is considered the 'Animal of Independence and Curiosity. 'Shamans say their energy can be called upon to explore the mysteries of life without fear, guilt, or shame, simply by letting go of being judged and expanding their knowledge, being in wholeness and peace of mind.

There is a popular belief that cats can see spirits, recognize energy portals, and identify places with dense energy. They are the perfect tool for magical work since they have been associated with witches for centuries as guardians of their homes, protectors from evil spirits, and messengers to the gods who watch over us all.

Cats may also be good luck charms because their association with witchcraft is so strong in Western culture that it has become part of our collective subconscious. In some Asian cultures, however, cats are considered unlucky because they have been considered sacred animals (kitsune). This difference in belief is probably related to different views of nature and life in these two cultures.

Cat is a very interesting archetype, as it is an animal that combines his very high sensuality with his psychic, spiritual and mystical nature. Many people have had very strong interactions with their cats. The cat also seems to be able to "get into your head" and can be the medium through which you receive messages and information from spirit guides, angels, and other entities of all types and sizes. Although we don't know exactly how this occurs, something is happening between our cats and us that we may not understand and cannot explain.

Cats are famous for their inherent symbolism. Uniquely among all animals, the cat is more easily symbolized by coat color than breed.

- A black cat represents protection and magic and has the special ability to absorb negative energy even more than other cats. We know that black cats are culturally associated with bad luck because of their persecution in the Middle Ages. However, the black cat receives much more favorable treatment in other cultures. The truth is that the black cat has a greater predisposition to have a quiet, shy, and, at the same time, affectionate personality. If you ever adopt a black cat, you will be able to confirm that he has something special and unique, a personality that is even more sensitive than other cats.
- Orange cat has strong Yang, masculine energy, representing the energy of the Sun, and active, creative power. They attract money and prosperity and help have a clear focus in life.
- White cat has strong healing power. Associated with the energy of the Moon, they recharge positive energy, restore balance, and relieve stress and tension.
- Gray cat color brings stability, tranquility, and peace. This color in cats also influences their affection and love. They bring effective balance, luck, sensuality, and happiness.
- A golden cat is considered wise and brings serenity and wisdom, enlightenment, mental clarity, and material and interior wealth. If you have cats and they usually lie to you, don't move away; they know well what they are doing. This is their way of absorbing any negative energy you may have, thereby rebalancing and energizing your astral field.

  As said before, cats bring positive cosmic energy, is reiki by nature, and attract harmony to a home. Of course, they bring lots of love and cuddles too. They have a relaxing effect that calms the mind and thus helps to avoid health problems related to stress, anxiety, and depression.

- Bicolor cat colors emanate positive energies that vibrate to strengthen friendship, understanding, and respect. They promote friendship, wisdom, and the ability to understand.
- Tricolor cats have three color energy, which has the strength of female power and represents the triple goddess. They attract luck and protection toward the home.
- Tabby cat attracts luck, positive energy, and optimism, helping overcome even the most delicate situations with lightness and joy.

Whatever the color, a cat is a being of love. Always adopt responsibly and remember that an adopted animal is dependent on you for life, like any family member.

Even without talking, cats can be many times more effective at helping a person going through a difficult time than anyone else they interact with. Because they are seen as wise beings on a spiritual level, cats guide their owners and help them overcome challenges through the telepathic communication established within. They really don't need to talk because they know when to cuddle, amuse their owner, or just be by their side, which is what we need someone to do most of the time.

Light:

- ✓ High self-esteem
- ✓ Self-love
- ✓ Personal Hygiene
- ✓ Sensuality
- ✓ Libido
- ✓ Beauty and Elegance
- ✓ Natural charm
- ✓ Personal magnetism

✓ Easy going
✓ Confidence
✓ Freedom
✓ Self-acceptation
✓ Ability to meditate and mindfulness of being
✓ Tranquility, peace, and lightness
✓ Fullness and completeness
✓ Solitude
✓ Detachment and ease of letting go
✓ Independence
✓ Sensibility
✓ Keen intuition
✓ Psychic abilities
✓ Spiritual development

Shadow:

✓ Laziness
✓ Comfort zone
✓ Conformism
✓ Apathy and emotionally cold
✓ Indifference
✓ Predominantly lonely
✓ Neutrality
✓ Submission and unconscious attachment
✓ Spending too much time creates a desire for attention and love

10. Dog

Trust, loyalty, and partnership

Known as man's best friend, dogs have fulfilled the role of true guardians and protectors, standing at the front of the gates and entrances of ancient tribes and civilizations, warning of any surprise attack throughout history.

It is not a coincidence that dogs have a keen sense of smell, and their hearing is sharp, which gives them the ability to warn of possible danger or invasion.

Several mystical gifts are associated with canine beings. It is believed that they can see spirits, feel people's energy, and protect the environment from spiritual attacks.

Dogs are great companions and teach human beings about love, as they are unconditionally devoted to their owners. Dogs are excellent observers; through concentration and focus, they are always attentive to receive information from their owners, and their subconscious "copies" the owner's personality.

They symbolize fidelity, trust, loyalty, companionship, vigilance, protection, courage, fun, and sociability.

The dog was both a household and a hunting animal in Ancient Egypt. It is related to the God Anubis, the Dead, and the Spiritual Passage in its iconography. For the Egyptians, the dog represented protection, as well as the task of guarding holy doorways and guiding the deceased to the spirit realm.

Cerberus, the three-headed hound, occurs in Greek Mythology as a symbol of protection against the hidden knowledge of death and resurrection. He is in charge of protecting the path that conducts the deceased to the spirit world. It also occurs as a hunting sign for the Greeks.

In Mesoamerican folklore, the dog is also charged with guiding souls to the spiritual plane, which is why dogs 'bodies were buried next to human bodies.

In Shamanism, the dog is the 'Animal of Loyalty, 'shamans evoke its energy to help others express genuine compassion and forgiveness, increase intuition and energetic perception, and stimulate courage.

In Ancient China, the dog was considered an auspicious animal whose symbolism is part of Chinese Astrology today. The dog is one of the 12 signs of the Chinese horoscope.

- Loyal, trustworthy, protective, and generous.
- Primate and defend your affections.

- Outraged by and opposes injustices.
- They are supportive and empathetic.
- Good understanding and forgives easily.

The initial impression we normally receive when we view a picture of a dog is one of affection, devotion, loyalty, pleasure, innocence, sympathy, and altruism since canines bring these traits with them.

Because the dog archetype reminds us of the characteristics of this animal, most individuals have a positive mental and emotional image of this entity.

Light:

✓ Loyalty
✓ Companionship
✓ Confidence
✓ Courage
✓ Valor
✓ Playful
✓ Affection
✓ Kindness
✓ Friendship
✓ Compassion
✓ Sociability
✓ Humility
✓ Intuition
✓ Sensitivity
✓ Devotion to others
✓ Universal love vibration
✓ Reduction of stress and anxiety
✓ Oxytocin production

Shadow:

✓ Enhanced sexual instinct (except if using castrated dog's archetypes, in which case it is even worse, as it lowers the natural libido)
✓ Relationships are just friendships
✓ Too playful
✓ Compassion and submission
✓ Difficulty dealing with dense and negative energies.

11. Horse

"A mind controlled with the reins of conscience reaches the supreme state."

The horse symbolizes the archetype of physical and mental strength. This is one of those symbols that can be associated with various meanings, as many cultures have used it in their rituals to bring them closer to nature's spirit and power.

In the beginning, when the first horse was born from the cosmic egg (Aryavarta) in the form of a golden horse, it represents the power of thought, or the mind's capacity to understand and control the world through will, self-knowledge, and wisdom. In some ancient mythologies, horses have been considered divine creatures: they are often associated with royalty, gods, or heroes, and sometimes they even stand for a deity as an individual animal instead of a herd.

This animal has been with us since ancient times, participating and contributing to the development of humanity.

In the history of humanity, we know that many events were remarkable. One of them, which is seldom mentioned, was the time when man learned to tame horses. Before taking them on distant trips, great effort was needed to cross long paths. The displacement was slow and sometimes unfeasible. When the horse was tamed, humanity leveraged its evolutionary process as fast as it mastered fire.

Some tribes called the horse the "Sacred Dog" or "Big Dog."

There is a proverb from indigenous Americans: *"To Steal horses is stealing power."*

In Shamanism, the horse is considered a "Spiritual Force, Freedom, and Clairvoyance." The horse represents compassion and humility. Rain or shine, he will serve the man. The horse also symbolizes 'Trust. 'It can take time, but when it becomes attuned to a human, he is very affectionate, patient, and tolerant.

Some researchers point to the horse as the first totemic archetype represented by ancient civilizations, even more than an eagle.

Horses have a spiritual debt to humanity. Consequently, the power of motor vehicles is evaluated in "horsepower," extolling the notion of the partnership of horse and man's intelligence.

The horse archetype means strength, vitality, mind control, and cooperation, which takes a person on a wave of instincts. It is often in the shape of a stallion or an older male, with a powerful aura and a deep voice. Yet, it has a gentler nature than any other archetypal animal energy level—though when aroused, it can be aggressive, stubborn, and obstinate.

The horse is known for being loyal and honorable and having great endurance and stamina, but also for its tendency to take advantage of the weak and vulnerable; this makes it prone to being domineering and abusive.

On the shadow side, a horse is subject to panic, like all instinctive creatures lacking a higher consciousness to tame them. The animal's nature is to run in terror from a danger it doesn't know. A panicked horse will run blindly in whatever direction it feels is an escape from danger; sometimes, it will even run off and trample its owner underfoot if it feels threatened.

Anyway, the horse archetype brings us the idea of self-control over our forces and impulses. It becomes easier to get to the target when you direct your mind and control it.

By analogy, if you see the image of the Centaur, the mythology shows a creature half man and half horse, which exactly symbolizes the idea of man controlling his animal instincts. So it is not an allusion to a particular animal; but rather represents the idea that people who can control their sexual drive and lust have a greater chance of being able to tame the animal within themselves, i.e., they become more civilized in nature by having less of this base instinctual drive in them than other people do.

Know yourself as a conductor of your own life. Knowing your intellect (soul) as the coachman and the mind (emotions) simply as the reins, and the senses, like horses. When your being is united with your mind and senses, you have clarity of the facts that happen to you.

From the same point of view, Plato sees man as a being made up of parts, yet there is only one true self.

Just to illustrate, the carriage represents the body. Horses again become our feelings, emotions, desires, and sensations. A certain driver or coachman represents our intellect and the egoist mind.

The coachman holds the reins, doing his job of controlling our emotions, heading in the direction the master tells him to go. The master is the real you, and he is the passenger inside the carriage too.

If our body is fully integrated and operating at a certain level of consciousness, communication between the master and the driver becomes clearer. As we move along through life, the mind/body connection will continue to deepen, allowing for more clarity in our decision-making processes regarding all things pertaining to our well-being, including career decisions and relationships with others.

Activating horse archetype is following the model of:

Strength: The strength listed here is mental - the greatest human challenge. Use mental strength rather than physical strength.

Vitality: Have courage; it will take you far.

Evolution: In principle, let your mind open to the new and accept new ideas and points of view.

Mind Control: Control your mind, or it will control you.

Achievement Strength: It's no use just dreaming; you need to be an achiever.

The horse archetype is the best model for managers, directors, supervisors, and any other areas of higher position in the company. The horse represents leadership while respecting hierarchies or his superior.

Light:

- ✓ Fearlessness
- ✓ Expressive instinct
- ✓ Vitality
- ✓ Physical and spiritual strength
- ✓ Will to live
- ✓ Self-motivation
- ✓ Work performance
- ✓ Useful to others
- ✓ Patience
- ✓ Humility
- ✓ Compassion
- ✓ Wisdom
- ✓ Elevated self-confidence
- ✓ Independence
- ✓ Sexual vigor/ Boosted libido
- ✓ Resistance
- ✓ Resilience
- ✓ Sensitivity
- ✓ Energetic
- ✓ Dopamine release
- ✓ Proactivity

Shadow:

- ✓ Enhanced sexual desire
- ✓ Workaholic
- ✓ Compassion and submission
- ✓ Relationships take time to build trust
- ✓ Cannot deal with dense and negative energies.

12. Wolf

Learning, cooperation, and union

Surely, you've heard of the wolf archetype mainly because of its ability to live in groups. However, this archetype goes far beyond team spirit.

First, wolves are extremely adaptable animals. They are practically found all over the world. That is, they can live in entirely different environments.

Secondly, they are loyal, and companions live in packs of up to 8 members, with well-established hierarchies where there is an Alpha couple, a Beta couple, and others of lower rank.

The beta couple's role is to care for the alphas 'offspring in their absence. In this way, the care and protection of the group are maintained.

The wolf is an extremely interesting animal. It is known that wolves live in packs (the Pack) and treat each other like family. Wolves are monogamous animals; when they find and recognize their "soulmate," they unite and go until the end of life. They are extremely affectionate with their puppies.

At times, the wolf leaves the pack to allow himself to learn by himself: he explores territories and develops his hunting skills. When he returns, he shares his acquired knowledge with the pack and the cubs, taking them to new places. Another striking feature is the howl, used to join or alert the pack.

The wolves are swift and have a keen sense of smell. They are quite observant of where they are treading and have a good sense of the area in which they are. They are pretty territorial.

By virtue of all this organization, the wolves avoid physical confrontation with each other as a form of respect for the pack. In contrast, they are full of personality within the family. They prefer psychological warfare to physical confrontations.

In conclusion, the wolves 'hierarchical positions are based much more on posture, personality, and attitude than on size or physical strength.

In Shamanism, the wolf is the 'Teacher. 'It is a 'Power Animal 'that stimulates the "teacher that exists within each of us," guiding the mission of teaching children to live in harmony and understand the mysteries of life. In ceremonies, shamans invoked 'Wolf Spirits 'to help eliminate negative thoughts, heal, improve relationships, honor a couple's union, and stimulate the desire to learn new things.

For psychoanalysis, the wolf hunting at night symbolizes constant contact with the 'Shadows. 'The howl at the moon manifests a desire to get in touch with new ideas hidden from the unconscious mind. The moon represents psychic energy and the unconscious: a place where the secrets to reaching wisdom and knowledge are kept.

Activating the wolf archetype results in the following example:

Adaptation: Can adequately interact with the different demands of life's changes.

Friendship: Knows how to live in harmony with the group and is concerned with all members 'well-being.

Wit: Quickly perceives the situation of the environment and knows everything around it. Always watchful.

Intelligence: Knows how to act at the right time and with discretion. Uses the rational mind.

Courage: Not afraid of new responsibilities and new positions.

Independence: Knows how to act and defend themselves.

Leadership: Can organize, motivate, and lead a group or self.

Light:

- ✓ Loyalty
- ✓ Companionship
- ✓ Wisdom
- ✓ Creative vision

✓ Desire for learning
✓ Ease of teaching
✓ Healthy relationship
✓ Lovely
✓ Cooperation
✓ Unity
✓ Inner child
✓ Facing the shadows
✓ Gets out of the comfort zone
✓ Cleansing negativity

Shadow:

✓ Aversion to other social groups (the pack is restricted)
✓ Work on family issues
✓ Awakens nocturnal habits
✓ Assigns himself the responsibility to instruct, protect and help others
✓ Strong attachment to relationships

13. Tiger

Energy, strength, communication, and agility

It is essential to know that the tiger is a very independent animal in nature, so in the realm of animal archetypes, the tiger archetype also brings you a lot of independence, especially emotional.

Tigers are strong physically, but their strength comes from their spirit and willpower and not just their physicality alone; it comes from their mind, heart, soul, and will – the internal strength that they have to face their environment with courage and confidence without any fear or doubt, which makes them stronger than others even though they are weaker than some people in terms of physical might and size; because their inner strength gives them power, authority, and dignity.

The tiger is a slow-approaching animal that carefully prepares to seize the best moment to attack. His run reaches eighty kilometers per hour. The tiger possesses immense muscular strength; he can run long distances to catch his prey. The tiger studies his prey and enemies. His hearing is extraordinary, his sense of smell is keen, and his vision is six times that of a human being.

In India, the tiger is represented as serving as a seat for Shiva, the Sky Father, meaning that Shiva dominated the forces of nature. In East Asia, the tiger symbolizes royalty, fearlessness, and anger. For Buddhists, the tiger symbolizes spiritual strength, faith, unconditional trust, disciplined conscience, gentleness, and modesty.

In the Chinese horoscope, the tiger is a 'Yang' sign (masculine, sky, fire), characterized by impulsiveness, unpredictability, generosity, and affection. For the Japanese samurai, it was an emblem that symbolized balance, strength, and royalty. For Koreans, the tiger is considered the king of animals.

In Neo shamanism, the tiger is considered the 'Power Animal' that brings wisdom to take advantage of a unique opportunity, acting as a "Messenger of the Now" that warns: "pay attention to the Present!"

The tiger, as an archetype, comes with an aspect of inner strength and courage to continue your life journey. They use their challenge as a catalyst to help grow and expand themselves than getting overwhelmed by the situation.

In the same way that tigers are strong and courageous, they remain steadfast in their survival despite the scars of their battles. They do not let any enemy get a hold of them; they can be found roaming around with no fear of anything or anyone, whether man, beast, or even death itself; they are truly fearless and majestic creatures of the jungle.

Tigers are constantly tested on their astute for food, as nature itself demands it of them. So, they use whatever weapons they have available, such as the ability to camouflage and walk without making noise, sight, and smell. They know how to create ambushes; tigers know how to impose themselves.

In this sense, the tiger archetype evokes this cunning within you. And that cunning is the awareness of your qualities and virtues that give you the power to effect changes without resorting to aggression.

When it's said "you are a tiger," it is not that you're going out there and killing people, but rather that you're using your power of will to create a situation that allows you to be a more effective person in life. The most powerful thing about this particular archetype is that it is a reminder to ourselves that we have the ability to change our lives for the better—we just need to tap into it and follow through with it.

This is an animal that has a beautiful and subtle power of communication. The tiger releases scents to communicate to others that it continues to reign in its territory. The tiger really sends messages, warnings, and hints.

In this way, the tiger warns other enemies and the surrounding females. This is one of the characteristics of the tiger archetype, knowing how to communicate and leave your messages clearly.

The tiger can intimidate and be strong with a look or a snarl because of their physical strength and the power of their claws and teeth, which are very sharp and dangerous weapons for the prey they hunt.

Alternatively, the tiger knows how to act silently when it comes to hunting his food; thanks to his padded paws, it manages to catch his prey without making any noise. The tiger archetype warns you not to go around telling everyone your goals and plans.

The tiger's symbol represents power and strength through beauty and elegance and their ability to conquer by stealth and mystery rather than force or violence alone. The color red is associated with the element fire, representing the energy and speed of the tiger, as well as the courage and strength that can overcome any obstacle. The white tiger symbolizes the balance between darkness and light

Tigers mate more than 50 times a day. Be that as it may, when activating this archetype, an awakening component of libido occurs in your brain, making you feel more powerful and sexier.

When tigers are defeated in a dispute, they bow before the loser, then withdraw. They are humble and accept defeat. In a fight, they know how to lose. The tiger archetype teaches acceptance gracefully after giving something your best shot. It shows there is no shame in losing. The tiger possesses great power that comes from its ferocity.

Therefore, as the tiger has great internalization, you will have more contact with your inner world using the tiger archetype. You can only use this power when it is in balance with other parts of yourself and the whole so that you do not fall into egoism or selfishness (in which case the tiger becomes an enemy) or into self-sacrifice (when it is used against yourself). The tiger symbolizes great energy, strength, and courage—these qualities all become active when integrated in a balanced way.

Tiger, as your mentor, is following advice like having courage, seeking wisdom, developing wit, and moving towards your goals. If you need courage or go after a project, use it, use the great power of observation, cultivate humility, and know how to recognize your mistake.

If you need wit, seek out wisdom, practice using wit and humor, be willing to look at yourself honestly and see your mistakes, then laugh at them and move on, use self-discipline, keep pushing forward, and make sure you're doing what you want to do rather than what you feel like you should do.

Light:

- ✓ Courage
- ✓ Determination
- ✓ Caution
- ✓ Speed
- ✓ Intelligence
- ✓ Wit
- ✓ Focus
- ✓ Force

✓ Self-esteem
✓ Self-love
✓ Presence
✓ Caution
✓ Resistance
✓ Heads up
✓ Intuition
✓ Frequency of action and movement
✓ Predominant Yang energy.

Shadow:

✓ Awakens nocturnal habits
✓ Rage
✓ Fury
✓ Irritation
✓ Stress
✓ Attachment to goals until achieved (workaholic)

14. Lion

Alpha, empowerment, and leadership

The lion is a big feline regarded as the "King of the Jungle" and "Guardian of the Underground World." It is associated with the Sun, representing the virtues: power, royalty, authority, youth, resurrection, security, protection, and justice. It can also represent lust and pride.

The lion has been a symbol of strength, courage, and bravery for much of history, especially in Ancient Egypt. They were worshipped as symbols of power and fertility and were associated with Osiris, the God of Life. Lions have often served as a symbol of majesty and leadership among ancient rulers from India (where they were considered sacred) to Africa (where they were used for hunting purposes). The lion's reputation as an aggressive, territorial hunter and the fact that lions are large predators made them a popular figure throughout history and across cultures.

At first, the lion archetype is seen with negative characteristics. It can be seen as a representation of accommodation, as females (lionesses) go hunting to bring food and support the family. In the same way, a lion is seen as the archetype of the individualist because it is the females (lionesses) who hunt, but the one who feeds before everyone else is the lion.

This can be contrasted with a tiger which, although also an individualist, feeds in a pack with others of its kind for protection and safety from predators; they are social animals that need each other to survive.

The lion archetypes have a strong sense of personal sovereignty. They are fiercely independent, with little patience for anyone who tries to hold them back from getting what they want in life (even if that means pushing others away). They can become bossy, stubborn, or even mean at times, but they will usually do anything to get what they need (as long as it doesn't harm others). A person born with this archetype may be fearless, but they can also be careless and reckless.

The lion only awakens his combative hunting instinct and goes into action when he is in critical situations, desperate, and very hungry.

However, it is important to say that before the lion reaches the "King" phase, he will have to go a long way and face great challenges. On the other hand, they are full of hope for a new future. The next step is when the Lion reaches the King stage; it is his strength that has been recognized and his ability to change his behavior, and his willingness to listen to others to make changes that help society (change).

The lion earns the title "King of the Jungle" because he has natural predators and is concerned with defending his harem of lionesses while maintaining his power. That is because his sovereignty is constantly challenged by other lions who are strong, experienced fighters who want to rise to power.

This is how the world works at a large scale: there will be a lot of competition, and a few people will win out over others in certain areas of their life; the same can happen in business – it's all about fighting for supremacy and establishing your kingdom over others 'lands!

In cases of kingdom loss, the herd is subjected to heinous brutality by the homicidal lion. The king is expelled, and the cubs are also mistreated and slaughtered. Furthermore, the lionesses will not accept a lion king who is not virile and powerful enough to mate and guard the cubs.

Therefore, to reach his post as the king, the lion needs to develop strength, leadership, courage, determination, and self-esteem.

In astrology, the lion is the fifth sign of the zodiac, its ruling star is the Sun, and its element is fire. The Lion in your chart is about being courageous and defending yourself against threats, whether real or perceived, from enemies or others who might wish you harm, such as jealous rivals or those who envy you for your success.

In Shamanism, the lion has been considered the 'Animal of Leadership.' His energy can be used to encourage, increase sexual potency, raise self-esteem, and give strength and vitality. He is also considered a protector of the sacred feminine, representing both male and female energies in balance within the body, mind, and spirit, which allows him to be an ally for both sexes when needed most! His role is one that many shamans would like us to take on – we should all have at least some knowledge and understanding of how the Lion affects our lives and the rest of nature!

In Egyptian mythology, the lion was an ancient symbol of resurrection and protection used in funeral rites. It is a symbol of the soul or spirit and appears on tomb paintings and funerary papyri in the form of a lion's head with wings at the top of the body, representing "the sun" and "life."

Lions appear in many cultures as symbols of power, majesty, nobility, and strength. In Africa, lions have been used as royal regalia since antiquity and continue to be associated with royalty today. The lion has long held a place of high esteem among the Chinese, who associate it with strength and bravery.

In Christianity, there is a passage in the Bible that Jesus is called the Lion of the tribe of Judah in revelation 5:5. In other words, He is seen as the king who will rule over all of his people and reign with them forevermore in Revelation Chapter 5 verse 5, "The King will be taken from Zion; the scepter will not depart from Jerusalem, until Shiloh comes, and to whom shall he be opposed? Or who shall oppose him?"

Isaiah 9:6 Jesus was born on the throne of David, and His kingdom was established right here on earth! The kingdom of God will one day be established at the very end of this age in heaven, and it will never end, for it is eternal! This is why the Bible says that Jesus was sent to establish this kingdom of God on earth, and then it will be taken from here.

In psychoanalysis, the lion represents strength and authority, being a symbol that represents a perverted social drive. When it appears in dreams, the personality is confronted with strong, passionate desires and affections that become stronger than the ego itself.

The lion archetype teaches you how to be:

Insightful: They use their instincts to face danger.

Wise: They are bold, but they know when to back off.

Intelligent: They learn quickly from all experiences.

Determined: Always ready to go a little further.

Aware/Alert: They sniff and pay attention to everything around them.

Cunning: Steal food from other animals.

Keen: Willingness to learn what is needed.

Focus and Concentrate: Be attentive always.

Decisive: Know when to act and when to give up.

Strategic: Knows how to work in a team and strategically.

Opportunist: Don't let the opportunity pass you by.

Light:

- ✓ Increased libido
- ✓ Alpha male
- ✓ Self-confidence
- ✓ Self-affirmation
- ✓ Self-esteem
- ✓ Presence
- ✓ Empowerment
- ✓ Sexual potency
- ✓ Force
- ✓ Resistance
- ✓ Leadership

Shadow:

- ✓ Pride
- ✓ Vanity
- ✓ Selfishness
- ✓ Laziness
- ✓ Territorialism
- ✓ Comfort Zone
- ✓ Dependence on a partner

15. Lionesses

*Divine Feminity, courage, self-control,
force, wisdom, and intelligence*

The most important lionesses 'archetype influence is transforming your heart and gaining courage. True courage does not consist in controlling others.

It is a quality of the inner life that changes us as human beings when it comes from our soul or spiritual self (the lioness within). Consequently, we need to take care to let the light shine through us and be open and honest with ourselves so that our inner world can transform into what we desire it to become for us, rather than remain stagnant and limited to the roles we have chosen to adopt based on the conditioning we received growing up and the expectations of others.

The lioness archetype comes to overcome your inner fears, master your own emotions, and find an inner balance.

The more you embody the lioness within, the stronger your power becomes as a woman in this world. You become brave, powerful, independent, courageous, and confident– you stand your ground with authority and don't back down when challenged by others or yourself! The lioness archetype female has strong convictions, she stands up for what she believes in, and she can be pretty stubborn when it comes to being right.

First, it is essential to say that internalizing an archetype is necessary to educate oneself in the silence of observation. Always observe first with a quiet (non-judgmental) heart and mind. When you have finished observing enough, you will be able to understand the archetype.

If the lion is the king of the jungles, the lionesses are the queens, and they reign equally in their territory. The queen that makes her children warriors. That same queen is a great commander and a powerful hunter. She is the one who goes after the food to support the family.

Likewise, it is the lioness who has the function of keeping the pride together and appeasing the brutal, colossal, violent, and unpredictable king, the lion.

The lioness archetype is a 'No Time to Mourn!'

Survival takes precedence. The lioness understands that they do not live in a paradise and must be powerful and cunning since "good girls" do not inherit the kingdom of nature. They are strong enough to withstand a family that, despite its unity, is not especially dependable.

They must be cunning to have the cubs safely. The lioness often needs to move away from the pride as the other lions are not kind to cubs and often kill them.

The lioness turns her anger into wisdom. After all, there is no time to grieve. We are attacked by suffering when we take things personally by clinging to anger and power.

We should not be surprised when we get the suffering we

seek because our anger was already in the wrong place! Our ego-centered mind is like a little child who wants everything it needs for its gratification, without any thought of what is best for everyone else—including the self that creates that anger in the first place! Our egos are like children with big stomachs who think they can eat anything! The lioness is wise enough to realize that she has to care for herself, as well as for others.

There are so many threats all around you that you can't afford to let your guard down at any time. Lionesses are wise; the envy of hyenas makes lionesses increasingly improve their skills.

There is no time for fear. However, it is necessary to know your abilities well and not hurt yourself with the weapons of envy. The lioness archetype brings this wisdom. The envious encourage people, even more, to remove difficulties and see where their gaps are. And they're right in a way that can lead us down the wrong path of self-pitying misery if we don't get the point – but if we do, we can be guided along the right path to happiness and fulfillment!

The Lioness Archetype Lions are fierce protectors of their pride; they will fight to defend what they love at all costs because that is who they are and what they want to be in this world and beyond. The lioness has a strong sense of responsibility and will be loyal to those close to her.

The lioness and lion archetypes mean controlling your emotions and, from the same point of view, letting go of the need to control the outside world and starting to control yourself and your actions.

If you're a natural-born leader, you're also naturally emotional. Still, your inner world is calm because your emotions keep your thoughts focused on what you want to accomplish and how you can make it happen, rather than worrying about what others think or fearing for them if they don't approve of what you do or don't do, and so on. In reality, emotionally regulated individuals (as many leaders are) obtain what they desire more often than those who aren't since they are emotionally wiser and have higher self-control and discipline.

Like the lion, the lioness is associated with the Sun, and so her virtues are royalty, authority, youth, resurrection, security, protection, and justice. At the negative pole, it represents lust and pride.

The lioness hunts to feed her linnets and her mate; she always keeps her family in mind. For this reason, In Neo shamanism, the lioness represents the 'Healing of the Sacred Feminine' and the 'Awakening of the Warrior Woman.' She goes after what she needs without depending on her partner, faces any challenging situation, and helps the collective. The lioness's energy encourages women and brings willpower, attitude, leadership, courage, and fearlessness.

The lioness archetype influences you to become:

Insightful: They use their instincts to face and perceive danger.

Wise: Transforms pain into wisdom.

Intelligent: They learn quickly from all experiences.

Determined: Pursue their goals.

Attentive/Alert: They sniff and pay attention to everything.

Keen: Willingness to learn what is needed.

Focus and Concentrate: Always very attentive.

Decisive: Know when to act and when to give up.

Strategic: They know how to work in a team and strategically.

Opportunist: Don't let the opportunity pass you by.

Cooperative: Always cooperate for the well-being of the group.

Light:

- ✓ Alpha female
- ✓ Initiative
- ✓ Empowerment
- ✓ Ability to perform
- ✓ Determination
- ✓ Self-confidence

✓ Self-esteem
✓ Sexual potency/libido
✓ Force
✓ Resistance
✓ Leadership

Shadow:

✓ Pride
✓ Vanity
✓ Ego conflicts
✓ The family depends on you

16. Black Panther

Black panthers are more solitary, fierce, and territorial than jaguars or tigers. They are excellent swimmers and climbers as they can sprint (at higher speed near the end of the race). They have over 400 voluntary muscles that can be used when needed. They can walk in absolute silence without being noticed.

Symbolically, Black Panthers translate the idea of the ability to transform their reality by having complete control over their own body.

Their fur is sensitive and picks up subtle vibrations, so the Black Panther is associated with sexuality and the need to pay attention to feelings.

The panther was associated with desire and power, represented in tattoos as a symbol of bravery and courage. In antiquity, panthers were associated with lunar energy. Later, they became a symbol of feminine energy and symbolized night, death, and rebirth.

In Shamanism, the panther is the medicinal totem of Mental Healing and Sexuality. In some ceremonies, the Shaman invokes the panther's spirit to transmute villagers 'fear and encourage them to face their shadows. The panther is also said to have the power to drive away evil spirits attempting to harm the village or Shaman during a ceremony.

It's not uncommon for shamanic practitioners from all over the globe to keep pumas, leopards, jaguars, and other wild cats as pets. The panther is also invoked to heal sexual trauma and enhance sexual vigor. It has been used as a shamanic tool for healing sexually transmitted diseases such as syphilis, gonorrhea, and herpes simplex, as well as HIV/AIDS.

One of the other qualities of Black Panther as an archetype is its ability to work under pressure and the ability to multitask. It can do many things at once and not worry about which task is important because all are equally necessary for life's journey.

However, this archetype also works with our shadow side, helping to deal with traumas, blocks, and knots rooted in our subconscious. This means that some of these energies can be challenging to manage and may need a different approach to balance or heal them fully through integration and cathartic release.

We approach these issues through cathartic processes such as journaling, exercise, yoga, and spiritual practices like meditation, visualization, and chanting mantras that heal and balance us internally from a deep level within ourselves. As a result, we can tap into the power of the Black Panther and transform our lives into a place where we no longer need to be afraid or struggle with our emotions anymore but rather live them in their fullness and beauty.

The archetype of the Black Panther is about taking a stand, not letting go, and having enough strength to keep going even if it's at times dangerous, difficult, and painful to do so (see here for more on the power of the Black Panther archetype). It is often associated with the warrior archetype, but its characteristics make it unique.

The Black Panther may have difficulty expressing feelings, but this does not mean that they do not have them or that they never get angry with people who have hurt them (as well as those who have helped). They do not usually show it outwardly or use their anger for anything more than a defensive tactic, which can make it hard to recognize, let alone understand what the true source of the anger is or how to address the issue that has caused it in the first place, if possible.

The Black Panther archetype will help the person overcome their shadows so that they have a happier, fuller, and more balanced life.

Michael Jackson was one of the most famous pop music celebrities influenced by Black Panther when he performed in the movie clip black or white (1991).

Light:

- ✓ Independence
- ✓ Detachment from the house
- ✓ Courage
- ✓ Self-esteem
- ✓ Self-confidence
- ✓ Value
- ✓ Fearlessness
- ✓ Solitude
- ✓ Focus
- ✓ Self-control
- ✓ Subject
- ✓ Force
- ✓ Sexual vigor
- ✓ Well-resolved sexuality
- ✓ Presence
- ✓ Attention
- ✓ Silence
- ✓ Action power

Shadow:

- ✓ Irritation
- ✓ Difficulty in socializing
- ✓ Dealing with dark aspects of the unconscious
- ✓ Emerging sexual impulses

17. Bear

Introspection and access to the unconscious

The bear is an animal of great contrast. He loves the sweet taste of honey and the succulent meat of fish, but, if need be, he will attack fiercely with its overwhelming force. The bear can be represented as a gentle and noble creature and a fierce and brutal animal. The bear lives with its mother until it becomes an adult, then goes on a lonely path.

If you are seeking to develop your wisdom mind, this is one of the best animals for you to choose as your archetype because the bear has a strong nature that resembles human's; he enjoys his life in freedom and takes a long time to reach his goal, just like humans do when they live a peaceful life and take their time to work out what is truly important in life

Celtic people and some European cultures used the bear to symbolize war. The Germans considered it a symbol of bravery. In the Old Testament, the bear was associated with bad influences. In Jungian psychology, the bear represents the danger caused by the uncontrollable contents of the unconscious. Because of this, the bear is often associated with an attribute of a cruel and rude man.

Jung also found that bears were common in the world of dreams, and they are frequently used to represent the subconscious mind, which contains our personal and emotional issues and fears.

In Shamanism, the bear is the 'Animal Totem of Introspection and Physical Healing. 'As an animal that hibernates for a long time in a cave, the bear is associated with contact with the dream world and is invoked by shamans for physical healing, understanding dreams and visions, and traveling on the 'Spiritual Plane.'

While the bear hibernates and dreams in his cave, he is looking for answers to his questions and solutions to his problems. The symbolism of the 'Bear Cave 'reflects returning to the womb of Mother Earth. This also suggests a strong feminine, nurturing, and protective aspect.

In India, caves are associated with the Brahman, which symbolizes the pineal gland. The bear wakes up in spring; this transition symbolizes finding his inner truth and can now thrive on life's pleasures: fish, nuts, and honey.

The bear teaches us about the value of introspection and withdrawal. In the silence of autumn, the dry leaves slowly fall, and we can meditate on our imperfections, look within, and identify all the attachments that hinder our spiritual progress.

We can also learn to focus on what we have rather than what we lack, which is a useful lesson for this time of year as well! The bear symbolizes strength and determination; it is fearless because it does not fear its power but instead uses it to protect itself.

The bear invites us to seek our answers to use in times of greatest difficulty and trial, welcome our vulnerabilities and find our inner strength. From death, we are only reborn into a new cycle.

We can only face ourselves as we truly are and live in a way that will enable us to get through this life with honor and dignity by learning from the lessons of our past failures and victories alike. The bear invites us to see ourselves as we are, with no shame and no regrets, and learn from them for future challenges without judgment or anger. This journey is a long one, and if we are lucky, it might take us a lifetime but what matters most is how we live during those moments when it feels like it's all over. And there is nothing we can't be.

The bear invites us to open our hearts and minds to explore the universe's wisdom and make the most of every moment on earth. Bears may seem solitary animals, but they travel in groups, especially during mating season.

The bear totem symbolizes the physical vigor and grandeur of the warrior archetype and brings sensitivity and intuition. The bear knows how to balance his great strength and fearlessness with an extremely welcoming, sweet, and receptive side to the other. Strength and sweetness; rest and movement coexist in perfect harmony on the Bear Trail.

Let's respect the moment to reflect on the privacy of our cave before deciding. By delving into solitude, we learn to enjoy our own company. We feed on the strength of Mother Earth and find the way back to spiritual wholeness, where all healing manifests. We die, and then we are reborn.

May we contemplate the eloquent wisdom of silence with serenity and confidence, certain that the greatest challenges the physical experience offers us are those that hide within ourselves.

Light:

- ✓ Force
- ✓ Resistance
- ✓ Intuition
- ✓ Conscience
- ✓ Self-perception
- ✓ Redo
- ✓ Understanding of deep issues
- ✓ Access to the unconscious
- ✓ Astral travel ability
- ✓ Courage
- ✓ Sweetness
- ✓ Ease of teaching children
- ✓ Self-love
- ✓ Family love
- ✓ Building lasting relationships
- ✓ Fidelity
- ✓ Love vibration
- ✓ Action strength and prosperity in warm seasons

Shadow:

- ✓ Somnolence
- ✓ Dealing with unconscious patterns

✓ Reactivity and irritation under pressure
✓ Attachment to home
✓ Gluttony
✓ Weight gain
✓ Deprivation in cold seasons
✓ Unwillingness to work in cold seasons

18. Moose

The moose is the largest of the deer animals. Only males have a huge antler or horn up to two meters wide, with different shapes. This is undoubtedly one of their most famous features, making them easy to identify. In addition, during the period of heat, males compete to copulate with a female.

Large-scale horned animals are regarded as symbols of fertility. The horns are also a sign of abundance (association with the archetype of the cornucopia: extreme wealth and abundance), hospitality, generosity, peace, and hope.

The Hebrews commonly referred to the horn as "the Horn of Plenty" due to its association with abundance and fertility and the belief that it could bring abundant food, drink, and prosperity.

In antiquity, people considered the horn a weapon of attack and defense, a symbol of physical strength and superhuman power.

In ancient Egypt, the horns served many gods as a headdress connected to the crown. The simple people considered them as a summary of the terror surrounding the supernatural. The Horned God was not just a symbol or a cult, but it was also one of the three main deities that ruled over all of Egypt and the whole world; the other two were Osiris and Isis.

In ancient Mesopotamian art, deities are adorned with the crown of horns as a symbol of their super-earthly power.

In Babylonia, the degree of importance of the gods was identified by the number of horns attributed to them.

The moose is a sign of wealth in Canada, and it appears on

coins. Having a stuffed Elk head is an honor for many hunters because it is a tough animal to shoot and "brings fortune."

The moose is regarded as the totem of self-esteem and confidence in Shamanism and is evoked by the Shaman in situations requiring the Shaman to define priorities, express confidence to others, engage publically, and delegate/manage a group.

The Shaman can also utilize moose as a guide, using its power to help the Shaman through times of crisis or despair when the Shaman is lost or confused about what to do next, how to cope with challenges inside oneself, or how to go on in life.

Light:

- ✓ Self-confidence
- ✓ Self-love
- ✓ High self-esteem
- ✓ Opposite sex attraction
- ✓ Self-empowerment
- ✓ Robustness
- ✓ Status
- ✓ Harmony
- ✓ Stamina
- ✓ Resistance
- ✓ Force
- ✓ Prosperity
- ✓ Fertility
- ✓ Leadership
- ✓ Decisive
- ✓ Firm

Shadow:

- ✓ Narcissism
- ✓ Pride
- ✓ Lust
- ✓ Vying for attention from the opposite sex

✓ Not adept at monogamy

19. Dolphin

Genuine joy

From the Greek Delphi, the dolphin is regarded as a messenger of love and a conductor of souls from beyond, signifying redemption due to his intelligence and speed. Furthermore, in Christianity, the dolphin is the church's emblem and is thus directed by Christ's love.

Legend has it that the Greek goddess of love (Aphrodite) took the form of a dolphin, becoming the "woman of the sea." In mythology, dolphins were often portrayed as wise and intelligent creatures with extraordinary senses — so much so, in fact, that they were thought to be divine entities who could communicate with humans and predict their future fates using complex language systems known as cetacean codes and dialects.

In addition, the dolphin is seen as a very intelligent animal, the great master of navigation who sometimes appears with an anchor or pitchfork, representing Poseidon. In the meantime, sailors and fishermen believe that dolphins are guide animals and protectors of sea voyages. This made the dolphins an ideal candidate for ancient sailors to consult during storms and navigational difficulties.

The dolphin became an animal totem of the 'Sacred Breath of Life 'in Neo shamanism. When the dolphin breathes on the surface, he dives again (as deep as possible) to be silent and connect within himself. This is a good practice because if you remain in your mind during meditation, you are still connected to your world and what you don't know.

The dolphin teaches that we must release emotions by controlling our breathing. Before diving into our inner world, we must breathe, releasing our repressed emotions to tune into the Higher Self.

For Shamans, the dolphin is the animal medicine of alignment, harmonic relationships, purity, joy, and unconditional love.

In short, the dolphin symbolizes love, water, salvation, protection, purity, harmony, freedom, transformation, wisdom, joy, prudence, and even divination.

Light:

- ✓ Sociability
- ✓ Intelligence
- ✓ Eloquence
- ✓ Acceptance
- ✓ pure joy
- ✓ Connection with your Life Mission
- ✓ Happiness
- ✓ Benevolence
- ✓ Sensitivity, depth
- ✓ Lightness and fluidity
- ✓ Harmony
- ✓ Fun
- ✓ Tranquility
- ✓ Friendship
- ✓ Self-love
- ✓ Healing relationships
- ✓ Helps cure depression
- ✓ Elimination of negative feelings
- ✓ Reduced self-sabotage
- ✓ Unlocking your life for the love you so much seek
- ✓ Open prosperity

20. Snake

*"Behold, I send you forth as sheep in the midst of wolves be
ye therefore wise as serpents, and harmless as doves."*

-Matthew 10:16

Snakes are animals that have always been very misunderstood. As much as they inspire terror in many people, they certainly also have a lot to teach us.

Observing the snakes from a safe distance, we can perceive the elegance, courage, and mysticism that surrounds them. Their movements are discreet, and their curves are insinuating with colors that reflect the beauty of nature. Snakes survive anywhere on the planet; just like wolves, snakes are adaptable beings.

Snakes lack maternal instincts and leave their eggs in the nest to thrive independently. That's correct; everything is against a snake from the minute the eggs are hatched.

Snakes see the world in a different way than humans. Snakes do not perceive objects with their eyes since they have poor vision. On the other hand, they utilize their tongue to detect their environment, i.e., they employ their senses to hunt and comprehend their surroundings.

Snakes are extremely sensitive and can detect any circumstance in the air. Snakes are extremely observant thanks to their great sense since they can hit the target even in complete darkness. Their sensitivity is exceptional.

Another powerful sense that comes into play is the heat the snake feels through two organs called the loreal pit. These organs show the snake what the environment it is in is like.

Snakes grow during the course of their lives. Their skin, on the other hand, does not grow together. Thus they must renew themselves. As a result of their discomfort, snakes alter their skin from time to time.

The serpent is connected to the symbolism of death and rebirth. Those who walk with this animal totem are invited to change their skin constantly, leaving behind harmful habits, old patterns, conditioning, and limiting beliefs.

By crawling with the snake into our depths, we can access

and contemplate our darkest aspects that need to be transmuted. Light, after all, cannot exist without understanding the shadow.

For the Shipibo people, the Universe was created by Ronin, the Cosmic Serpent. From the meeting of the sound of the Serpent's song with the absolute primordial silence, there was an explosion that integrated light and darkness. The native peoples treat this animal with great reverence, seeing in the snake the power of renewal and contemplation of the secrets of the invisible world. With it, our biggest fears are placed right before our eyes.

The snake is the guardian of the mysteries and the very representation of healing. It brings with it the power of sexual energy, cosmic force in its raw form, the awakening of Kundalini, and our hidden abilities.

The snake was connected with the Hindu deities Shiva, Vishnu, and Ganesh. The snake symbolizes the kundalini power located at the base of the spine. When awakened via meditation and specific exercises, the snake ascends through the seven chakras, bringing profound awareness, enlightenment, extrasensory, psychic, and omniscience.

In Tantric philosophy, the serpent is a living entity that dwells in each human being, and it is said that there are 365,000 serpents within the body of every human being. The snake or kundalini (Sanskrit: cakra) has been identified as one of three basic principles, along with etheric energy and prana, which comprise the body's subtle bio field (or life force). It is also described as the inner ruler of consciousness and cosmic energy associated with Shiva, Vishnu, and sometimes Brahma.

In Greek mythology, Hercules, a demigod hero, fought the Lernaean Hydra, a creature with a dragon's body and nine serpent heads. The snake also appears in the symbol of Asclepius, the God of Medicine and Healing, entwined in his staff, representing rebirth, fertility, and healing power. Today it is the symbol of Medicine.

The snake brings us the poison and the cure itself. The feminine force born that dies is reborn. In its crawling, it leaves a trail of transmutation and revives the flame of our inner healer.

In Shamanism, the snake is the animal totem of Healing and Regeneration. Shamans use Cobra Energy to assist physical, emotional, and psychic healing processes. It can also be evoked for moments of adaptation and overcoming. Cobra is a versatile animal with many uses in Shamanism, Magical work, and daily life! It symbolizes regeneration, wisdom, love, power, transformation, and protection of self and others.

In Egypt, Ouroboros is a mystical symbol representing the concept of eternity through the figure of a serpent that bites its tail. The symbol contains the ideas of movement, continuity, self-fertilization, and, consequently, the eternal return.

The snake was a great symbol of the queen Nefertari and Cleopatra; you will see how snakes influenced Egyptian queens in chapter 10.

Light:

- ✓ Strategist
- ✓ Sensuality
- ✓ Healer
- ✓ Strong Yang
- ✓ Energetic Transmutation
- ✓ Personal Power
- ✓ Intuition
- ✓ Fertility
- ✓ Sexuality
- ✓ Rebirth
- ✓ Renovation
- ✓ Renewal
- ✓ Resurgence
- ✓ Spiritual Elevation

Shadow:

- ✓ Destruction
- ✓ Aggressiveness
- ✓ Treason
- ✓ Manipulation
- ✓ Insensibility
- ✓ Frozen heart (snake has cold skin)
- ✓ Death

21. Octopus

Flexibility, creativity, defense, mystery, power, knowledge, strategist, potential, and illusion.

Octopus 'symbolism reminds us that you must camouflage yourself and go unnoticed to get what you want. In other words, keep doing what you're doing, but be inconspicuous. Wait until the last possible moment, when your target is within grasp, before revealing your intentions—strongly expressed in the Spectre movie.

The octopus may indicate the desire to be someone you are not. Of course, there are moments when you need to be outgoing and expose yourself to achieve your goals, but there are other occasions when you need to remain invisible.

Occasionally, you'll even have to imitate people to blend in.

What's more, the octopus symbolism lets you know that you can move through whatever barriers keep you away from your goals.

Other closely related values to this animal are the world of energies, secrets, and consciousness. The octopus can offer valuable lessons to those willing to seek and find them. The octopus is also linked to mystery, it is a water creature, so it is related to this element. In relation to water, the octopus 'symbolism involves purity, the psyche, emotion, movement, fluidity, intuition, creativity, and flexibility.

Agile and flexible, the octopus is the master of disguise. Its energy is linked to the camouflage of our goals to avoid harmful interference that can come from the outside world. To achieve what you seek, it is recommended that you maintain discretion and preserve the privacy of your findings. The flexibility of the octopus can help you escape from a variety of toxic situations and people with great cunning and subtlety. Octopus teaches us to respect our sacred space.

Its eight tentacles represent universal abundance and teach us to understand the limitless, the flow without beginning or end. The end is just the closest point to some beginning, just as the apex of darkness is the point that marks the beginning of the day. Octopus invites you to contemplate these cycles naturally, to live the flow. Closing a cycle is always an opportunity for re-birth, an auspicious moment for self-observation.

One of the totems that invite you to explore the depths of its inner ocean is the octopus. It will follow you to the most abyssal area of your universe, where your emotions, fears, and limiting beliefs are hidden. This is your chance to let go of anxiety and dig deep within yourself, tracing the origins of attitudes and habits that do not speak to your core and instead impede your progress.

Light:

- ✓ Adaptability
- ✓ Complexity
- ✓ Creativity
- ✓ Cycles
- ✓ Defense
- ✓ Diversity
- ✓ Evasion
- ✓ Expansion
- ✓ Flexibility
- ✓ Focus
- ✓ Illusion
- ✓ Insatiability
- ✓ Intelligence

- ✓ Knowledge
- ✓ Magic
- ✓ Movements
- ✓ Mystery
- ✓ Obstacles to come
- ✓ Potential
- ✓ Power
- ✓ Strategy
- ✓ Unpredictability

Shadow:

- ✓ Manipulative
- ✓ Aggressiveness
- ✓ Isolation

Chapter 5

Financial Prosperity

A variety of archetypes might influence people's motivations to gain money. Archetypes that attract money, opportunity, luck, and excellent investment outcomes; occasionally, an invention is required; anybody who believes in the law of attraction and has learned to let go may easily materialize results.

This principle, which originated thousands of years ago, says that everything we desire comes from within us. Still, it's a process we must work on continuously to have our wishes fulfilled. However, before one can become rich, one must learn how to use archetypal symbols or, in other words, to understand their meaning, which will determine one's future success. You might say that it depends on how you use them.

The symbols will help you as an impulse to reach your goals, bringing inspiration and guiding you on what to do in a certain way.

When someone is influenced by an archetype representing prosperity, ideas come naturally from their mind. This person's thoughts tend to be full of good things. For example, if you want to become a great investor, the archetype knows exactly what must be done, including timelines.

If you need 150 days to learn everything about money, put your knowledge into action until you reach the rank of millionaires - the archetype knows it. Otherwise, if you choose to procrastinate, the result won't be in 150 days anymore. They would be in 151, 152, 153, 154 days, and so on.

Ultimately, you will understand that everything you learned you've already known. The archetype was just an impulse to turn something created in another dimension manifest into reality. Your task is not only to learn how the universe works but also to make it work for you!

Only one thought is necessary. Once you think about becoming a businessman or woman, you'll never get rest or find true happiness until you get it.

That is the secret of the archetype. It is not something that has to be played for fun or something that can be used. Contrary, archetypes influence you and use you. You don't play them as a tool - but as a part of yourself.

It is like a magic spell that uses your personality and emotions to create the whole experience of playing a character within the game – instead of creating a character out of a book or a movie with the help of another person. The archetype is your inner self, your core characteristics, the very things that define you as an individual – so it is already inside you when you are born. You will never change it even if you tried to do so consciously or unconsciously during your life.

Now, archetypes aren't limited to animals or personality traits; archetypes are also symbolized through food products. These foods are very much like our character, and when we eat those foods, we become the corresponding person in our lives.

1. Wheat

Abundance, multiplication, nutrition, cosmic mother, mother nature, planting, harvesting, loyalty, self-domination

Wheat is part of the primary and essential food of the world population and therefore brings the energy of multiplication, prosperity, and nutrition on a large scale.

In the parable of weeds, the bible describes wheat as part of the kingdom of heaven. It can be interpreted as the labor that produces good fruits, and weeds are those who try to corrupt production.

Wheat produces the fruit of love, joy, and peace. Weed produces hatred, depression, and disturbance. Wheat bears long-term fruits, kindness, and goodness, while weeds produce impatience, malice, and perversity. Wheat produces the fruit of faithfulness, humility, and self-control, while weeds produce infidelity.

If we are born with a particular personality type, it is like having an inherent personality pattern that has already been programmed in our body. We may not be aware of this, but this programming goes on every time we breathe. In order to change your life, you have to begin to alter the way you think.

If you are on a path that will bring about balance, it is important to understand the two archetypes to know how to cultivate them effectively. When they arise within us, we need to know how to use them to help grow in our inner wisdom and healing process and be more effective at manifesting what we desire in our lives by making decisions with love instead of fear or anger in mind and heart.

We have to know that there are times when it's okay just to let things go because even if we "win" sometimes, we still win anyway (and if we lose, we still lose). We cannot control what comes up for each individual, but we can choose how we react to the events that present themselves.

Wheat tells us that anything we produce must be beneficial to others because the outcome of excellent or terrible work is linked to how we feel.

Wheat also teaches us to learn how to deal with the weeds while we are producing. This is part of spiritual evolution; help without complaining even when someone tries to harm us.

In Christianity, wheat symbolizes rebirth. This act of being "born again" is connected to the fact that to generate "life," when it falls into the earth, wheat must first die and then generate the food responsible for maintaining life.

The Egyptians believed in rebirth as well. When someone dies, some wheat is placed in their tomb to ensure that they can be resurrected in the hereafter.

Wheat is a great representation of abundance, prosperity, and happiness. Wheat represents abundance because it can grow without water or soil and can be found in many countries with little rainfall and no fertile soil for crops to thrive (for example, Japan).

Wheat also symbolizes fertility as it grows from seed into a stalk, then into ears, and finally, seeds are produced (reproducing). This process helps the wheat grow and increase, thus giving life to all around it (hence the phrase "a blessing"). This is what makes the wheat so very beneficial and powerful! So if you are looking for prosperity, abundance, or just simply happiness, look no further than this beautiful grain.

2. Seed

"Jesus told them another parable: The kingdom of heaven is like a man who sowed good seed in his field."

- Matthew 13:24

The seed is also found in the parable of the weeds; the wheat is a result of a good seed planted on the sand.

The seed is a very powerful symbol, it can bring life into the world, and where there is life, and there is abundance, opportunities, and prosperity for the good of others. The seed is not physical but rather a spiritual one, which brings forth its fruit in time.

The seed comes to live inside us through love, joy, peace, patience, kindness, goodness, faithfulness, gentleness, self-control against selfish ambition against resentment, arrogance, and all forms of envy. We are to do unto others as they would have done unto them if they were here in their place. It can bring new fruits, and from these fruits comes more seed.

The seed as an archetype represents a new life project. It can be anything, a new child, new work, new business, new house, new dreams, etc.

The seed as an archetype is unlimited prosperity. Self-sabotage is the only way it may become a stumbling block in someone's life.

It is said that no one can truly be free if he cannot get out of his way. Self-sabotage will not allow this to happen for you, at least not without some struggle on your part first, but let us say that you have done your best to overcome yourself by following the principles of The Law of Attraction in your daily life: To manifest anything new in your life, you must focus on the steps required to create that outcome rather than just focusing on what you want.

The seed teaches us to be open to new experiences, to let go of pain, taboos, prejudice, and self-sabotage. The only person who can stymie your personal development is you. If the spirit is boundless, then our progress must be unlimited as well.

Some seeds include a tree within them. For example, if you take apple seeds and plant them in the sand according to all available guidelines, they have a high chance of becoming an apple tree—the same is true for other fruit trees.

Most of the seeds produce some plants when we are watering them. It's like the seeds are sleeping, and if we want to awaken them, we must stimulate them using the water. The most important thing is to have patience and not get impatient because it takes time for a plant to grow into an adult, so give it time to develop the roots, and leaves will come later due to this growth process. As for the role of water as an archetype...I'll explain more about it in chapter 11.

Once this seed awakens, it will only be with you from then on. What does this mean? You must be like fertile soil for the seed to grow; you must lapidate your being, raise your frequency by choosing, love over fear, be cheerful, active, and working rather than being distraught; this is a choice.

The sprout is delicate; if it is stepped on or abandoned, it dies while having immense potential to expand. What should we do? Take care of it, nourish it with light, love, and everything good inside us. We should continue to perform these things until it matures into a robust adult tree.

Our love and nurturing effort are seen once the tree matures; some trees produce flowers, which scent the atmosphere and fruits until harvest time.

The seeds also need patience because they take time to sprout once sown. The time of the trees is not our time. It means no anxiety because they will never get anywhere if they keep jumping from one project to the next. It is vital to select what you truly desire and stay until you see results, immerse yourself in the subject until you know it so well that you can dominate the field, and no one knows better than you. Finally, the seeds remind us that to reap the benefits of our labor; we must first sow seeds.

3. Fortuna

Luck, prosperity, success, change, wheel of life, cycles, destiny, positive changes.

Fortuna, the root of its name, "fero," may be of Latin origin and means "to bring, win or receive." It is also known as the "luck herb" because it was once used to ensure a good harvest for farmers and good fortune in their endeavors through luck charms and spells and other magical uses. Fortuna was one of the seven planetary deities associated with the planet Mercury (the Roman god of commerce). In ancient Rome, Fortuna had a temple on Capitoline Hill. The image of Fortuna Primigenia, the "Greater Fortune" deity worshipped by the Romans before the reign of Augustus, was housed there.

Another possibility would be the derivation of the Etruscan Goddess Veltha or Voltumna, whose name is connected to ideas of turning and the alternation of seasons. The Romans associated her with the concept of fortune and fate and believed her to be responsible for all aspects of life, including good and evil luck, prosperity, death, and war.

Fortuna, behind the wheel leading the journey, also directs us to chance, instability, sudden surprises, and unforeseen events. The challenges presented by her often lay bare our pride and whims, summoning the need for resilience and faith.

We can interpret the combination of random circumstances that present themselves on the way as good or bad luck. When the Wheel of Fortune turns, we don't know where it will land, but we always hope and expect that it will stop at the exact point where it will bring us the good news!

Fortuna was a very popular Goddess in ancient Rome, worshiped with various domestic or public attributes according to the type of circumstance and luck one wanted to achieve. There are records of personal amulets, jewelry, paintings, and statues related to her. Whether honored as a personal Goddess, of mothers, of soldiers, prosperity, or destiny of the Roman Empire, it turns out that Fortuna had many temples and oracle centers in her honor.

We can highlight the great temple of Praeneste, today, Palestrina, located about 20 km southeast of Rome, and the oracle in Antium, the current city of Anzio on the west coast of Italy.

In her most common representation, Fortuna appears holding the cornucopia, a sort of "horn of abundance" from which all good things flow, symbolizing the aspect of the Goddess that bestows prosperity and good luck. She also carries the rudder of a ship in her hands, which portrays her governance over our destinies and events. Sometimes Fortuna is revealed to be blind, indicating that her blessings reach everyone without distinction or that she distributes her graces according to luck.

Fortuna teaches us to be open to the new, breaking old paradigm for transformation. Fortuna does not separate spiritual and material; she unifies them. There are no differences; everything is one.

Despite the challenges, the wheel's turning always presents us with the possibility of transformations and opening new phases in our lives. Experiencing the Wheel of Fortune also involves the contradictions inside us, learning to laugh at our faults, admit weaknesses and trust ourselves to destiny. The 'wheel 'refers here to the concept that everything has a beginning and an end, to the idea that there is no such thing as an eternal "now," but instead only moments in time where we are 'here.'

The colors are fundamental as part of Fortuna's representation: Green for prosperity; blue for tranquility; red for strength and success; yellow for communication and creativity; gold for good luck; purple for spirituality.

4. Gold

Wealth, light, eternity, wisdom, prosperity,
perfection, and purification.

Gold is considered one of the most valuable metals in the world. It represents financial prosperity, abundance, and money attraction. Gold is a noble metal with high density and low hardness. It also stands out for its good electrical conductivity, value, and chemical inertia.

Archaeological studies reveal that in the year 4000 BC, gold was already being worked in Mesopotamia. Subsequently, the techniques for obtaining metal and manufacturing objects were transmitted to all the civilizations of the Eastern Mediterranean, with emphasis on the Egyptians.

The civilizations of the Aztecs and Mayas on the American continent also knew and worked with gold, which they considered a precious metal.

Gold has been used as a currency since 3000 BC. However, it was not until the end of the 18th century that it acquired universal monetary status.

The majority of gold produced globally is used by nations to mint money and, more importantly, for bank reserves to ensure balance in international economic transactions. It is believed that this location receives more than half of all global gold output.

Gold can even be used in treating arthritis, as a soluble salt, with intramuscular administration.

Gold is a chemical element of the Periodic Table represented by the symbol Au, whose atomic number is 79 and belongs to the transition metals. It is one of the first metals manipulated by man since it is found pure in nature.

As a noble metal, gold is one of the most coveted metals and is widely used to make jewelry, coins, and ornamental objects in the form of an alloy with other metals.

Nicolau Flamel was the first alchemist to transform lead into gold; the bookseller would have discovered the formula for wealth and immortality. Some believe he is alive, at 688 years old.

Records from the 14th century show that Flamel owned a bookshop in Paris. His great passion was alchemy, the set of medieval chemical practices and knowledge. Legend has it that his life was changed because of a mysterious ancient Hebrew manuscript of Abraham the Jew, not the Abraham of the Bible, but a 14th-century wizard. After 21 years of trying, the bookseller would have been able to decipher the work with the help of an old Spanish Kabbalist.

The "transformation" of lead into gold did not occur on the first try. First, Flamel turned lead into another metal. Then he transmuted the metal into silver, and finally, silver into gold.

Connecting with gold frequency as an archetype, we discover that we must go through a process to become of tremendous value. What makes us as precious as gold?

Human life is divided into five strategic sectors: the physical (which relates to your health and energy level), the mental, the spiritual, the relationships, and the financial. When one of them gets out of balance, the others start to give problems too.

The gold can bring this balance to anyone's life.

The gold is resistant. The very first impression is the feeling of self-control. It also shines and has yellow color representing energy and the sun and can transmit happiness to everyone.

5. King Midas

Wealth, money attraction, and opportunities

Once upon a time, there was a great sage named Silenus who was the father of the deity Dionysus 'creation. Because this sage enjoyed drinking, he was always drunk. They even claim that he was inebriated when he gave the world his best teachings.

He drank too much one day and slept at the tree's base. When the peasants saw this tree, they decided to transport it to King Midas 'castle. Because King Midas was a close friend of the deity Dionysus, he decided to host Silenus.

Silenus spends many days in the castle, drinking and eating the best. After ten days in the castle, Midas (the King) took Silenus back to Dionysus, who was extremely happy with the care and hospitality given to Silenus by Midas.

Dionysus then decides to present the king with a wish. Midas could ask for absolutely anything, and without overthinking, he asked Dionysus for the power to turn everything he touched into gold.

As it was a gift, Dionysus soon grants Midas 'request. The King, all excited, touched a stone he found on the floor of the kingdom, and that stone turned to gold. He proceeded to touch everything he saw in front of him, reiterating his newest power.

When he touched his daughter, she turned to gold. The King loses his mind and goes after Dionysus to beg that this spell be reversed. As Dionysus was someone of extreme generosity, he told the King to stay calm and bathe in the Pactolus River to heal.

The first argument is that King Midas made a completely rash decision without considering any probable outcomes. He made a decision based only on his gains, but he failed to consider the potential consequences of his action—a lack of balance and contemplation.

Another very interesting point is that when we want something and focus on it, the tendency is for that thing to come true. Desire, combined with thought and feeling, has a lot of power in our lives.

When we turn these forces into action, we have a lot of power to accomplish whatever we want in our lives.

Dionysus tried to warn Midas, yet he was firm in his decision. Midas managed to get rid of his problem because of Dionysus 'benevolence, but the losses he had had no way to recover.

Midas desired power but could not sustain it and blamed it on wealth as if the gold had been responsible for the disaster in his life, not himself. A big shadow was created over wealth unnecessarily.

Anyone with a great life balance can become a pioneer in making money if influenced by Midas. They are the archetype of great investors and other successful people. For example, when a journalist interviewed wrestler Honda Rousey, she stated that her mother once told her that whatever she touches turns to gold and that one of her victories was opening up chances for women in the UFC, which took a short period but a lot of hard work and dedication.

6. Diamond

Rare, value, wealth, truth, purity, perfection, hardness,
maturity, immortality, cleanliness, energy, the sun.

The name diamond derives from the Greek Adamas and means "invencible," an association made for its durability.

Its unparalleled hardness makes this gemstone a fitting symbol of durability and constancy; its clarity is related to the notions of sincerity and innocence. The diamond also represents life, light, shine, and the sun.

The diamond is also a symbol of invincible spiritual power and the stone of commitment between couples, expressing fidelity.

The hardness of the diamond, its power to scratch and cut, is especially emphasized in Tantric Buddhism, where the vajra (ray and diamond) is the symbol of invincible and unalterable spiritual power. According to the etymology of the Tibetan dodge equivalent, "the queen of stones."

In Tantric Buddhism, the diamond symbolizes the invincible spiritual power, the unalterable, and the immutable.

Buddha appears on a diamond throne radiated by the light emanating from the stones, symbolizing strength, truth, and perfection.

In Western European traditions, the diamond works by warding off ghosts, evil spirits, nightmares, sorcerers, and night terrors.

In this sense, diamond is also associated with the sun's luminosity and is related to cleaning the environment and energy.

In Indian alchemy, the diamond is considered the philosopher's stone symbolizing immortality. Widely used in meditations, diamonds are believed to absorb emotions and cleanse the soul.

During the Renaissance, the diamond symbolized equality of soul, the integrity of character, faith, courage, and freedom of the spirit from any fear.

Diamonds are carbon crystals that have been subjected to extreme pressure and heat. So don't dismiss it as merely a good luck charm. As an archetype, the diamond conveys all of its information, including the process that made it as beautiful and precious as we know it. As a result, the diamond is a highly powerful surge of knowledge that will propel you to numerous catharsis.

Diamond also adds remarkable quality to the growing process. The ability to improve, debugging the taste, deliberating on options, soul purification, spiritual purification, and debugging with information

Cultural traditions such as the Tibetan philosophy of the "Diamond Way" see the diamond as a symbol of human progress. As the diamond passes from coal to the brilliant and enduring jewel, the human being can become refined even from humble beginnings. This philosophy is symbolic, but many cultures still believe today that diamonds empower the wearer.

Diamonds have also been associated with good health and represent long life and good heart health.

In crystal therapy, diamond crystals help unite the mind and body, helping them work together to cleanse and restore your mind, body, and soul.

Diamond crystals are the perfect antidote if you are feeling lost or confused. They help clear your aura of negative thoughts and bring back love and light.

While diamond crystals do not change your emotions, they heighten them and function as a mirror of your emotional state. Thus it is crucial to utilize them with this in mind since they boost both good and negative energies.

Almost everyone is familiar with transparent (white) diamonds, but there are colored diamonds as well. A diamond gets its color through trace elements that interact with carbon atoms during the formation process. Different chemical elements create a different hue. Diamond colors are associated with different meanings and symbolism. They are as follows:

- Red, symbolize courage and are extremely rare and valuable.
- Orange, one of the rarest colored diamonds, is formed with boron's chemical presence. These diamonds represent energy and enthusiasm.
- Yellow symbolizes happiness and friendship. Formed with nitrogen, yellow diamonds, sometimes called gold diamonds, are among the most common fancy colored diamonds and are a good alternative for an engagement ring.
- Pink symbolizes romance, joy, and creativity. They are very rare and very beautiful.
- Blue symbolizes royalty and power. They are very rare, and if you choose to give a blue diamond, this represents respect and love for the recipient.

- Brown symbolizes humility and grounding, as its color emulates the earth below us. Brown diamonds form in the presence of nitrogen and are believed to denote internal strength and balance.
- Black symbolizes eternal and unchanging love. They are also associated with action, energy, and passion.

7. Pyramid

Prosperity, energy, death, rebirth, power,
magnetism, and Healing.

The pyramid is one of the oldest and most important symbols in some cultures. Its meaning is often connected to death or initiation, origins, and knowledge. It symbolizes ascension, elevation, and the power of life over death.

The pyramid symbol combines with the triangle, one of the most powerful geometric symbols.

The Egyptians were the pioneers in the construction of the pyramids. Subsequently, they emerged in pre-Columbian America as an instrument to honor the gods and carry out secret rituals in other parts of the world. These monuments have always been related to mysticism and the belief that they have supernatural powers.

The way it is built, where all points converge to a single point, tells us a lot about the meaning of the pyramid. The square base symbolizes matter, and the form and the elevations on each side symbolize the idea, the spiritual dimension.

Another interpretation is that the base symbolizes nature, and its four angles represent truth, intelligence, silence, and depth.

There are pyramids both in Mesoamerica and in China, Egypt, and Bosnia. In the classical world, there are also examples, such as the pyramid of Cestus in Rome.

The pyramid was considered a special figure esoterically because traditionally, it can attract energy, increase vitality, fight bad vibrations, attract prosperity, and is related to healing themes, among others.

The therapeutic pyramids, for example, are dependent on the material from which they must be created and the function for which they will be employed. Thus, copper ones are useful for meditation, as they are the ones that stimulate most self-knowledge and intuition.

Brass ones have a vibration to generate regeneration, re-birth, and transformation. Crystal ones have high energy power and are used for all cases due to their wide properties. The aluminum ones act more effectively in dense matter and vibrate in resonance with material, earthly things.

The silver ones should be used in magnetic conflicts between people, serving as a balance between opposing forces. The gold ones act more deeply as amplifiers of our magnetic vibratory field, making it balanced and automatically eliminating the harmful forms of energy that can penetrate our vital layer.

8. Apple

Energy, magnetism, prosperity, sensuality, seduction, love, desire, sexuality, fecundity, youth, freedom, magic, immortality, and spirituality.

When you cut the apple in half, can you notice the identification, even if subliminal, with the image of a vulva? It is a potent symbol of beauty, reception, sexuality, and reproduction, supporting the association with nature's feminine polarity and Eve. However, this is not the only issue I want to discuss. If you cut an apple horizontally, you'll be able to see Flaming Star that symbolizes luck, protection, and prosperity.

The legendary scientist, Isaac Newton, was an astronomer, alchemist, natural philosopher, and theologian. However, he is best known as a physicist and mathematician. When Isaac was resting under the shade of an apple tree, an apple fell on his head, causing him to receive insights and enter a process of phenomenal introspection, leading to the formulation of the theory and the Law of Gravity. According to certain symbology scholars, the apple was connected with creativity, learning, and understanding because of this incident.

You probably know the company Apple. It is one of the most significant technology companies globally, manufacturing various electronic devices (iPhone, iPad, iPod, Mac). Apple is reputed to be "the brand of the bitten apple." The bitten apple is a very powerful archetype because of the symbolism of the apple. It conveys the desire for experimentation and the desire to consume, to taste.

It also alludes to the biblical account of Adam and Eve, albeit the apple isn't mentioned precisely because it's a symbolic story. And because it is a metaphorical narrative, there is a reason why the apple is such a powerful emblem of wisdom in Eden Garden. It has a negative connotation: sin, wickedness, temptation. However, it may also be viewed as freedom in search of wisdom, youth, and the learning process. Nevertheless, in general, this biblical tale depicts humanity's hunger for answers, knowledge, and evolution.

The Golden Apple is another well-known archetype; in Greek mythology, they are fruits of the Tree of Life Garden of the Hesperides spring Goddesses, signifying the Fertilizing Spirit of Nature, and confer immortality to those who eat them.

Hercules picked three apples from the Tree of Life on one of his quests. Another famous tale about the Golden Snitch has the Goddess Eris of Discord as its protagonist. Because she was not invited to celebrate the wedding of Peleus and Thetis, she created a golden apple. She wrote "the fairest" on its skin, tossing it between Aphrodite, Athena, and Hera. There, discord was made, and the final consequence was the Trojan War.

You've probably heard the expression "apple of discord" (something that can generate confusion), which originates from this story of Eris.

The last well-spoken archetype is the wet apple! Great archetype to drive sales! It works because this archetype is irresistible. To begin, it should be noted that water has a link with the emotional part of the human being and a sensitive connection with their dreams. It reflects both the body and the psyche and provides richness and flow. In this sense, this archetype, in addition to delivering the apple's symbolism, engages the person's emotional side rather than his rational side. This is an unconscious occurrence that may be leveraged to increase sales.

The apple also has a red tint; in psychology, red is related to strong emotions such as love, passion, and rage; it stimulates oxytocin, a powerful hormone in the brain that promotes self-esteem and vitality.

9. Cornucopia

Multiplication, wealth, prosperity, production

It represents unlimited abundance. It's also used during the Thanksgiving holiday.

The cornucopia is a horn that comes out countless different things unlimitedly—an inexhaustible and unlimited source of positivity.

Several foods also vibrate in the frequency of prosperity (pumpkin, corn, various seeds, wheat, grapes, flowers, fruits, sunflower, etc.)

The cornucopia vibrates in the frequency of abundance, opulence, and multiplication. It is also a phallic symbol that represents the Sacred Masculine (strength, action, power) which is the energy that makes prosperity manifest. However, its interior symbolizes the uterus - thus representing the Goddess, which, when filled with food, symbolizes the generosity of the fertile land, representing the sacred feminine.

The cornucopia is connected to an infinity of possibilities, the frequency of prosperity. It's also an archetype that is open for the new, breaking paradigm, transmutation processing, and self-knowledge and sets you free from negative beliefs about money, health, relationships, values, etc.

It gives us an impulse to produce or get into action. It's an excellent archetype for whoever wants to stop procrastinating and move, create, produce, work, and realize dreams.

The Fortuna goddess is represented holding a cornucopia sharing its wealth to bless everyone. The cornucopia also brings the frequency of charity. Once you are blessed, you will be multiplied, blessing others.

Chapter 6

Relationship

Man is a social being who needs the others to survive and evolve. A live-in relationship allows us to contrast the choices, situations, and experiences necessary for spiritual evolution. However, the sad picture of humanity is that most people suffer from a lack of love in their lives.

Some don't love, others don't express the love they feel, others do not allow themselves to be loved, and many confuse love with possession. It is no surprise there are billions of people in virtual lives paralyzed because of ignorance or willful infraction of the universal laws that govern relationships.

Every person emanates a vibrating field resulting from thoughts and feelings that attract, by electromagnetism, people with the same vibration.

Failed romantic relationships tend to repeat themselves indefinitely throughout life because they are based on a particular personal vibration pattern.

Archetypes can help with that problem by changing thoughts, feelings, and frequency. It's possible to notice that archetypes can influence our whole life in every aspect, including love relationships.

Relationships have become very complicated, especially in 21 century, also called the modern world. Why? Basically, we live under the Heisenberg principle of uncertainty; quantum physics says the position (momentum) of a particle is given, and the less precisely can one say its momentum (position). This is what is happening in relationships today: We have different positions of (momentum). That means one person is in position or stopped, and another is in momentum; she has speed or movement.

You meet someone and have a relationship for a while because he has paused. He has the position, while another has speed and momentum. It doesn't matter if he is a man or a woman; there is momentum and position. To put it simply, when one person is walking, and another has stopped, their frequency will eventually no longer match due to various things such as values, paradigms, interests, and so on. Whoever is growing goes away. Consequently, the relationships become uncertain as an uncertain principle.

For example, if one person vibrates at 80% speed and another at 50% speed, and both wish to have a nice conversation, the person at the higher seed must drop his frequency and slow down to meet the other person's vibration.

Because each person's pace and velocity differ, the phrase "only death separates us" has become rather difficult in the modern world. It's difficult for both to grow simultaneously and maintain momentum when two individuals grow together. One factor is the paradigm. If one lives in the old and another in the new one, there is a significant frequency difference.

That would normally be simpler if men and women had equal self-growth if the paradigm was the same. Some people look to make all things work. Unfortunately, this is impossible. We have a great and healthy brain and intelligence from the cosmos. All we need is to know how to use it to make things work.

The archetype is not a miracle thing; it is information. The brain receives information and commands every time we are exposed to TV shows, social media, announcements, or any other means of communication device. What are you listening to? What are you watching?

The frequency will vary and change every time since archetypes are everywhere. Any information your brain receives unconsciously will be there for the rest of your life. You might carry it into another life. This is quantum physics...not Esoterism, not magic. It is pure physics.

The results would be spectacular if no one put up resistance when impacted by archetypes and overcame traumas, taboos, prejudice, blockage, self-sabotage, paradigm, and comfort zone. Instead, an open mind is required to experience results. Quantum physics is the science that produces outcomes; otherwise, we would not have cellphones, the internet, satellites, nuclear weapons, etc.

Results are easy to obtain from the universe because the universe has laws, rules, and protocols to be followed. We have laws in the economy, psychology, chemistry, sociology, civil rights, etc. Everything has rules to keep the system organized. Likewise, laws of relationships are not on the list.

What is a feeling or emotion? We call it a byproduct of chemistry. Everything you feel and behave is a result of the neurotransmitter's chemistry. You have dopamine, serotonin, endorphin, and more. All these chemical elements combine to build the love formula. The rule that no one wants to hear is that creating this formula takes time and patience. Can you prepare a delicious dinner dish in 5 minutes? No, right? It takes time, about 40 minutes or an hour. That's the rule. The same rules are applied in relationships.

We are biological computers that produce a chemical substance that communicates between neurons, neurotransmitters, and hormones. This formula creates neuro-association. It means you are associated with a hero when donation centers announce, "Did you save a life today?" Whoever works in the marketing area understands that commercials or announcements of the product or service must be indirect. For example, if you have a beauty brand, you will never ask consumers to buy your product. Instead, you must talk about your product and how good it is to convince people to buy it.

Relationships work in the same way. If you want to make a

love formula for another, you need time and chemistry. Without it, there is no base. That's why most relationships don't work. There is no chemistry or base built.

I hear many people remark, "Chemistry in the first sign." Without a doubt! Because this is an unconscious relationship, when one person catches a wave function from another, both vibrate at the same frequency. It indicates whether you have a chance, whether they are pleasant, sympathetic, etc. This is a positive indicator but is only the beginning. Sometimes it takes 15 seconds to determine whether something is worthy or not, and sometimes a 15-minute conversation can determine a person's worthiness.

The love formula takes time to build. The time can range from two months, six months, two years, ten years, or infinity. Some people separate after 40 years of marriage. Why? Because 40 years weren't enough time to establish the love formula.

To build love chemistry, it is necessary to form chemical brain associations like dopamine, serotonin, endorphin, etc. Many factors, like affirmation, encouragement, admiration, and confessions, provoke stimulus. Otherwise, pushing, fighting, envy, and bad remarks merely deplete the formula, resulting in fewer dopamine, oxytocin, endorphins, and so on. As you increase the formula gradually, the formula must also go down gradually. That's why nobody stops loving the other so fast; it takes time.

In an environment where everyone knows everyone else, the love formula may never establish properly. For example, a school; Gina likes Mike - Mike likes Nicole - Nicole likes Ryan - Ryan likes Kate, and so on.

When you start a discussion, it takes time for atomic processes and molecules to combine and become something new, which we might name love. This time cannot be tallied in a nightclub in 10, 30, or 45 minutes; it is simply impossible! What happens if there's no patience to form chemistry? Only sexual

attraction would exist. There's no chemistry, no brain information; that's why it takes a short period.

We need months to form this chemistry if we want something with probability, position, and momentum. Typically, one
of the couples is in motion, so who is in motion is devoted to
taking charge of building this chemistry. The paradigm is the
only issue that might lead to someone failing to recognize or ignore these truths.

Anyone searching something about relationships and finding archetypes and neurotransmitters methods to form chemicals of love might say, "This is impossible." Of course, it is
because of the paradigm or belief system. Otherwise, an open-
minded person might try.

Technology is part of most people's lives, and archetypes
also work in social networks, but how to identify if someone you
just met online is worthy? I can use my experience as an example. When I share my social network with someone, such as on
Facebook or Instagram, he will see different pictures of me.
From playing guitar to wearing a bikini on the beach or a party
dress, taking a simple self-picture, etc. I will know precisely the
kind of lady he likes from the picture he likes on my social media.

Some relationship advisers and coaches say the most important to find if someone is worthy or not is to pay attention to
hobbies, personality, and values. It doesn't matter which music,
movie, or books they like. Most people don't perceive that they
are all connected because music, movie, and books express
themselves as archetypes. People listen to music and watch
movies they identify with; I explain it in chapter 8.

Some archetypes are strong love symbols that influence you
to become the conqueror of hearts.

1. Heart

Spiritual love, passion, partnership, vitality,
intuition, and expansion.

The heart symbology is strongly, unconsciously connected to love. There are many heart forms like winged heart, heart with a key, heart pierced with an arrow, Sacred Jesus heart, Aztec heart, and others with different colors popular in the social network emoji.

The heart represents rebirth and the beginning of life in Greek mythology. When Zeus devoured Zagreus 'heart, he gave birth to his son, Dionisius.

The heart of the dead was weighed in the judgment hall in Egypt; this organ was the seat of knowledge linked with Ma'at, the Goddess of truth.

Since 15 thousand years before Christ, the heart was already portrayed in a mammoth figure painted in a cave located in Spain.

Observe the various vital functions that can be attributed to this organ, such as the energy necessary for the maintenance of life and the maintenance of blood circulation.

Some people perceive that when they are in love, a magnet is manifested in a short time, attracting people's attention and energy. It happens because they vibrate more, and everyone around us can feel it unconsciously.

2. Cupid

Love attraction, passion, love energy,
beauty, regaining old relationships.

Eros, the Roman God of love, is also known as Cupid. This archetype is often represented by a winged boy or youth with golden curly hair and wings, holding a bow and arrow. Those hit by Cupid's arrows will have their hearts united and fall in love. His bow and arrow represent the impulse of love. When the target is reached, the manifestation of love inevitably takes place.

Cupid is one of the main symbols of love, passion, and eroticism. Without Eros, no electrons move. He is the electromagnetic force field of love.

Many images of him blindfolded symbolize love's origin, where he loves everyone without restrictions. Its wings represent lightness and from which love flows in the air. Eros is what permeates everything. It is the love force of the Universe. When Eros propelled everything, life began. He is behind every archetype.

Eros (representing love) met Psyche (representing the soul), a beautiful and simple mortal who received numerous courts, making the Goddess of beauty Aphrodite envious. Psyche reflects the ego, or personality, in certain ways. She is the one who eventually caused Eros to move. The meeting of Eros and Psyche is the meeting of love with our spirit, our soul.

The God Eros, Cupid, lived a great love with the Goddess Psyche - the couple represents Love.

The most common Cupid signal is when a family member or friend tries to introduce you to someone special.

3. Red Rose

Seduction, Passion, Love, Romance, and Secret.

The rose opens the heart chakra. Then, concerns relating to the emotional portion will be addressed, such as love, sympathy, romance, and relief. All flowers have beauty and fragrances that make them unique. On the other hand, the rose has an even stronger and more distinct personality, owing to its symbolism.

When roses are a means of gift, the representation goes far beyond love and passion. After all, this traditional flower represents devotion and respect for the loved one as well. The meaning of a red rose inspires people to gift it to loved ones. It is quite common to associate roses with women and their sensuality, including mothers. After all, as said before, this plant is perfect to represent respect too.

In Greek mythology, the rose was a symbol of Aphrodite and Venus.

In Egyptian civilization, Cleopatra threw red roses across her bedroom rug when she was with Mark Antony.

The rose is an excellent archetype for attracting or maintaining a relationship. It's one of the most universally-liked flowers globally, and it symbolizes love and devotion — qualities we all desire in a partner.

4. Flamingo Pair

Soulmate, love attraction, harmony, affection, loyalty, sympathy, happiness, beauty, open heart, fraternity, enlightenment, and welfare.

The flamingo is a large, pinkish bird that knows and indicates light. It symbolizes the soul on the rise, which leaves darkness to find the light. The flamingo is a wading bird with a flexible, long neck, found in tropical and subtropical areas of the Americas and Africa.

Thanks to their characteristic pink plumage and tendency to stand on one leg and highly social behavior: flamingos form huge colonies alongside ponds, shores, and wetlands. In addition, the flamingo is a monogamous bird that remains with its partner until the end of its life!

It is no coincidence a couple forms a heart when they unify heads.

The Egyptians believed that the flamingo was the personification of Ra, the Sun God. Therefore, the flamingo potentiated the process of learning the lessons of the soul. In Florida, this bird represents prestige. In Hinduism, the flamingo represents spiritual enlightenment, given it is the symbol of light and is associated with the heart chakra.

In Shamanism, the flamingo was incorporated as the Animal Totem of "emotional filtering"; its energy helps maintain the balance between its spiritual mission and the heart's desires and heals family relationships.

Light:

- ✓ Love
- ✓ Beauty and elegance
- ✓ Health
- ✓ Sympathy
- ✓ Body self-control
- ✓ Self-esteem
- ✓ Lighting
- ✓ Spiritual development
- ✓ Friendship
- ✓ Cooperation
- ✓ Sociability
- ✓ Harmony with the collective
- ✓ Family union
- ✓ Fidelity
- ✓ Fraternity
- ✓ Emotional sensitivity
- ✓ Loyalty
- ✓ Companionship
- ✓ Emotional relationship

Shadow:

- ✓ Lazy
- ✓ Co-dependency
- ✓ Dealing with a relationship shadow
- ✓ Irritation from superficial, convenient, and false relationships

5. Wolf Pair

Twin flames, love, loyalty, family, harmony, fertility

A couple of wolves are significant love influencers. When they recognize each other as soulmates, they remain together forever. Even if one dies, the other doesn't relate to any other wolf.

The wolves are often thought of as an animal that brings the energy of harmony with it. Due to its characteristics, the wolf learned to find the right moment to act, managing to live peacefully even with its most significant difficulties.

The wolf symbolizes strength and perseverance in life since it can adapt to any situation without losing its sense of self-confidence and dignity and keep on being strong during the hard times in its life... In ancient times, the wolf was a sacred totem for several tribes, and it was also associated with power, nobility, and wisdom, among other important spiritual aspects of human beings. In many cultures, wolves were considered holy animals, and their presence on earth was believed to be a sign of the coming of the New Age.

Since the pack is a family environment, the wolf can be invoked to bring peace to family and professional relationships, harmonizing tensions and bringing balance. The wolf also teaches that harmony can be achieved not only through the blood family but through the bonds of friendship that are created along its journey.

The association of the wolf with fertility involves two main major factors. The first concerns their ability to walk in groups, which shows they are animals that reproduce and interact easily.

The second concerns an ancient belief. Women who had difficulty conceiving a child called on the energy of the wolf so that they could generate life and be able to create their pack. It was believed that these calls brought luck and resulted in pregnancy. Thus, wolves became symbols of fertility. Consequently, your archetype must be invoked by all those who wish to be fertile and have a child.

The wolf is a much disciplined mother, training her puppies

to feed themselves, work in groups, and be brave.

If you want to connect to wolf frequency, as mentioned in chapter 4, you need to open yourself to the new and awake what is within you, courage, friendship, etc. Feel what the wolf feels and let everything flows naturally without anxiety and precision.

Chapter 7

Flowers and plants

The impact of plants on our life is very well. They are an important part of our lives, creating oxygen, curing our illnesses with teas, relaxing our bodies with lotions, and providing stress relief. We all love the beauty they create; the leaves of the rose, the color of a sunflower, the green of a fern or a palm tree! Plants and flowers play an important role in our lives as archetypes. They are a symbol of love, power, beauty, and strength!

We investigated the plant's historic function as an herb or food when it existed and its many qualities. Herbalists, healers, and wise women who had once disappeared are now reemerging with their knowledge of how plants can heal. These people are now known as an alternative treatment, vibrational medicine, phytotherapy, and supplementary medicine, and they have their own offices and offer lectures.

Female healers are a part of humanity's old archetype. When someone is sick or in pain, an older woman arrives in all stories and myths to provide tea, prepare a compress, and give insightful advice. In truth, the elderly woman is a mythological figure of the 'healer,' 'often known as the Great Mother.

It's not about chronological age because this is an archetype shared by all women who feel compelled to be creative, curious about new information, and continually seeking deeper inner growth. Their wisdom understands that we are all "work in progress" despite our exhaustion, failures, and losses. These women's spirits are perpetually youthful, and their souls are older than time.

1. Cactus

Resistance, force, and adaptation

The cactus is a great symbol of persistence as it can survive arid and hot ecosystems, such as deserts, caatingas, and savannas. It has a resistance that few plants have. Despite its lack of attractiveness from the outside, it has a fascinating interior capable of giving several distinct advantages to itself and species that produce fruits and flowers.

The cactus in Chinese Feng Shui science is considered the guardian who protects the house. He is an environment purifier, rids the place of toxins, and provides good energy to the home. The most common cactus used for Feng Shui is the Chinese prickly pear cactus or Opuntia microdasys, a member of the Cactaceae family of flowering plants native to North America, South America, Africa, Australia, and New Zealand. This particular cactus has been found to positively affect both mental and physical wellness, with research showing that it may help improve memory, lower blood pressure, reduce stress, ease anxiety, and promote healthy skin.

For Native Americans, the cactus represents protection and resistance. He is a symbol of help in difficult situations. The yellow cactus flower also symbolizes warmth and protection. It is related to the motherly and caring spirit.

2. Dracaena Trifasciata

Protection, beauty, and strength

Dracaena trifasciata is also called "mother-in-law's tongue," "Saint George's sword," or "snake plant" because of the shape and sharp margins of its leaves that resemble snakes.

This plant is native to South Africa. African religion symbolizes the orexin's sword (or spear) known as Ogun.

In Catholicism mixed with Afro influences, Ogun is confused with Saint George, the Cappadocian saint who drew his sword to kill a dragon, according to the hagiographic version.

Inheritance of this double religious reference is the mystical fame of the plant, cultivated in a vase near the door or inside the house, the Saint George's sword would have the power to scare away brokenness and the evil eye, lightning, and thunder. It is also possible to use the Saint George's sword as an amulet to protect against accidents, especially when carried in your pocket while traveling, working at home, or in the garden.

3. Sunflower

Prosperity, success, balance, health, and happiness

The scientific name of the sunflower is Helianthus annus, which means "sunflower." It is a plant native to North America and is particularly heliotropic. That is, it rotates the stem positioning the flower in the direction of the sun during the ripening phase. When the plant's stem stops growing, the sunflower remains stationary towards the east until it dies.

The sunflower has been used as an important agricultural crop for centuries. In the United States alone, approximately 70 million acres of sunflowers are grown annually, and the annual production has increased steadily over the years. Sunflowers have many uses, including use as a food source, oilseed crop, ornamental, cover

The heliotropism of sunflowers makes these potent plants accumulators of solar energy (electromagnetic), which, together with their components, make plants valuable as food medicine. This magnificent plant gets its name because it follows the course of the sun from sunrise to dusk. There is no other plant on the planet with such strength! That alone would make it noteworthy, but the picture and the color elevate it to a level of absolute beauty!

Greek Mythology presents a legend that explains the appearance of the sunflower flower. Clytie was a nymph who was in love with Helios, the God of the Sun. When the latter fell in love with Leucothoe, Clytie began to weaken. She would sit on the cold floor, not eating or drinking, feeding only on her tears. Clytie did not look away from him for a single second while the sun was in the sky, but her face turned to the ground during the night, and she continued to cry. Her feet grew roots over time, and her face blossomed like a flower that followed the sun. This is how the genesis of the first sunflower bloom is described in Greek mythology.

The sunflower, together with the sun, enhances these therapeutic effects on our body and mind, bringing relief and more cheer. The sunflower contains a high concentration of Vitamin D3 in its seeds which is good for your health and can help treat depression and other conditions associated with low levels of vitamin D3 in the body – such as arthritis and diabetes! The sunflower also contains significant quantities of calcium, phosphorus, magnesium, manganese, iron, copper, zinc, protein, essential fatty acids, and fiber (which aids digestion). This combination makes it a great food for vegetarians and vegans! It has long been used to promote strong bones and teeth, especially in children, since they are prone to tooth decay due to a lack of vitamin C and a healthy diet.

The sunflower is a flower that follows from the rising sun to the setting sun. This plant is always lit up, looking for the sun's rays, always following it. In this way, the sunflower archetype always symbolizes enlightenment. She will always be exposed to primordial light (sun), the flame that warms and illuminates so that she will attract good energies.

In this way, she is protected from evil forces because her radiance attracts only loving people with open hearts who want to help her on her journey of awakening. Sunflowers also represent the feminine principle in a relationship; they symbolize balance, harmony, and unity between male and female energies within any given situation or environment. Understanding this energy exchange within the flowers allows us to see the interplay of masculinity and femininity in all relationships and our gender.

The shadow side of the sunflower archetype is attachment or emotional dependence. After all, the sunflower turns to each other in the absence of the sun, and so it is with humans as they turn to their friends when life gets rough (or when their friends become unavailable). But this neediness can also lead us into a trap of feeling "dependent" on toxic people in our lives. The result can be codependency, a debilitating disease that affects many relationships and often leads to despair about the future as we try to cope with how bad things are in our lives. If you already have this in your personality, you get attached very easily to people, material things, etc.

Nevertheless, developing the sunflower archetype makes it possible to establish greater personal and spiritual balance, vitality, cheer, and good mood.

4. Orchid

Wealth, purity, beauty, seduction, sensuality,
love, desire, and luxury.

Orchids are millennial flowers with a wide variety of colors and beauty, originality, and exuberance. Its existence dates from approximately 4,000 years ago. It is the most widespread flower globally, occurring naturally in almost every climate zone on land and in water; it is the second-largest family of flowering plants after the flowering grasses (Poaceae).

The orchid family consists of more than 20,000 species worldwide, with an estimated 12,500 in China and about 5,000 in Taiwan alone. Orchids have existed for a long time as a single species but then underwent extensive hybridization, creating new types that may be quite different from each other.

The orchid archetype is represented by a beautiful flower found in several varieties, presenting many different colors, shapes, sizes, and characteristics. We can easily see that this archetype is represented in several places, especially at the entrance of luxury stores and malls. It is very common for orchids to be one of the archetypes most associated with money, having their energy directly connected to abundance.

Orchids are abundant in nature and can grow in various soil types, representing wealth and abundance on earth in terms of natural resources and land. We can also associate them with business success due to their ability to bloom and reproduce quickly, giving them an advantage over other flowers in this regard. The orchid bloom symbolizes a new concept of prosperity. Orchids were formerly solely regarded as valuable commodities, not flowers: these fragile plants had been utilized as medicine and spices for thousands of years.

The orchid archetype has a vibration that acts on the crown chakra located at the top of the head. With this, we can say that the orchid energy also contributes to developing pure feelings such as love, joy, gratitude, happiness, and peace.

Orchid derives from the Greek word orkhis meaning "testicle-shaped." This denomination was attributed to Theophrastus, a Greek philosopher who verified the similarity of the roots of some orchids with human testicles. Therefore, it was believed that orchids had aphrodisiac characteristics in the Middle Ages.

The Greeks believed that the orchid was a symbol of virility. In Ancient Greece, if a young woman presented herself with orchids adorning her head, it meant that she was looking for her ideal match. If the same happened to an older woman, it was a sign of ostentation, a demonstration of the wealth and luxury in which she lived.

The Aztecs ingest a mixture of orchids and chocolate for power, vigor, and strength in medicine. The Chinese ate the flowers to cure respiratory ailments.

The different colors of orchid also represent an archetype

quality, which is as follows:

- Ludisia – White Orchid: Pure love.
- Notylia – Pink Orchid: Flower of seduction.
- Vanda Pachara – purple: Dignity and a sense of purification.
- Brassia – Yellow Orchid: Erotic love.
- Cymbidium – Black Orchid: Symbol of power and absolute authority.
- Renanthera – Red Orchid: Sexual desire.
- Phalaenopsis – Blue: Harmony, reconciliation, tranquility.

Orchids grow on trees as a support to seek the light. They are not parasitic plants, as they feed only on decaying matter that falls from trees and accumulates in their roots.

5. Lily

"Consider the lilies, how they grow: they neither toil nor spin, and yet I say to you, even Solomon in all his glory was not arrayed like one of these."

- Luke 12:27

The meaning of lilies may vary depending on the color of their petals. But, in general, the species is significantly associated with romanticism and symbolizes purity, innocence, and pure love.

The lily flower is full of magic, religiosity, and mysticism as it has a strong relationship with faith and devotion in different religions and is considered sacred. For these reasons, they are used in bridal bouquets, wedding decorations, and religious celebrations.

In Roman mythology, following the advice of the goddess of

justice, Minerva, the Goddess Juno nursed the still baby Hercules, who had been abandoned in an open field by his mother, Alcmene. The milk spilled from Juno's breast spread across the sky, forming the Milky Way and tiny drops fell to the earth, turning into the first lilies. Medieval alchemists used these flowers to manufacture perfumes and secret ointments, used to smoke rooms, preparing them for performing mystical rituals.

In the 17th century of the Christian era, lilies were used to decorate churches to honor the Virgin Mary, symbolizing virginity, purity, and holiness. In this case, the stamens and pistils, this species's male and female organs, were removed from the flowers to make the flowers truly "virgin." To this day, the lily has this symbolism and is still widely used in bridal bouquets, in the decoration of wedding ceremonies, and in religious celebrations in general.

There was also a belief that lilies helped reconcile lovers who had broken up. A simple piece of the flower bulb would suffice, which would have the power to bring the couple together again.

The flowers with the most intoxicating scent consequently emanate phenylethylamine. This substance stimulates the production of endorphins in the human body, providing a wonderful sensation of tranquility and well-being.

One of the meanings attributed to lily is 'Eternal Love. 'It was named by the Chinese, who have been cultivating it for over 3000 (three thousand) years. In China, the lily means plenty and is the flower associated with the arrival of Chinese summer. In many other parts of the world, lilies are considered the kings of flowers.

The lily is the royal flower represented in the image of the fleur-de-lis, a symbol of generation, prosperity, and race, used by French nobility and royalty in their coats of arms. Represented as fleur-de-lis, the lily symbolizes power, sovereignty, loyalty, and honor, symbolizing the purity of both body and soul.

6. Lotus

Elevation of consciousness, win over obstacles, purity, birth, rebirth, cosmic harmony, resistance, peace, beauty, wisdom, and prosperity

The lotus flower predominantly represents purity, beauty, and wisdom present in various religious beliefs.

The traditional lotus flower is represented by eight petals related to the eight space directions. As a symbol of cosmic harmony, it often appears in mandalas. It represents the yang side of the Chinese yin/yang dualism and is associated with the earth element.

The lotus flower is an aquatic flower with various meanings for Eastern countries, especially Japan, Egypt, and India. It is considered sacred and one of our planet's oldest and deepest symbols. In the teachings of Buddhism and Hinduism, the lotus flower symbolizes divine birth, spiritual growth, and purity of heart and mind. We'd have complete control over the physical body and all it contains, demonstrating that the only way to live a healthy and long life is to seek the essence.

Lotus's worship is closely connected to meditation. Therefore, meditative representation is often done in the form of a lotus. Its symmetrical shapes and beauty connect with feminine attributes.

The meaning of the lotus flower starts at its roots. The lotus blossom is a kind of water lily with roots that grow in pond and lake muck and silt. The lotus blooms magnificently as it climbs to the surface. The symbolism is powerful in this capacity to rise above the gloom and bloom in a way that is so pure, beautiful, and unique to so many people.

At night the flower petals close, and the flower plunges underwater. Before dawn, it rises from the depths again until it rises to the surface, opening its petals again. Because of this ritualism, the ancient Egyptians associated the lotus flower with the sun god Ra because the flower closes at night and opens each morning with the resurgence of the sun.

It is also the only plant that regulates its internal heat, keeping it around 35°, that is, the same temperature as the human body. Another peculiar feature is its seeds, which can stay more than 5 thousand years without water, just waiting for the ideal condition of humidity to germinate.

- Pink Lotus Flower - The pink lotus is the supreme lotus and is often associated with the highest deity, namely the Buddha himself. Although often confused with the white lotus used for other deities, the pink lotus flower symbolizes the true Buddha.
- Yellow Lotus Flower - Yellow is the color of the sun, energy, and happiness. It's a bright, cheerful color. It's like being at a party every day and associated with the intellectual part of the mind and the expression of our thoughts.
- Red Lotus Flower -The red lotus symbolizes the original nature of the heart. It symbolizes love, compassion, passion, and other emotions associated with the heart.
- Blue Lotus Flower - The blue lotus symbolizes the victory of the spirit over one's material senses. It also symbolizes wisdom, knowledge, and intelligence. It is always represented as a partially opened bud, meaning that knowledge never ends and must be continuous.
- White Lotus Flower - The white lotus symbolizes a pure body, mind, spirit, spiritual perfection, and pacification of nature itself.

In the Buddhist legend, it is reported that when Siddhartha, who would later become Buddha, took his first seven steps on earth, seven lotus flowers sprouted. Thus, each step of his represents a step in spiritual growth. Thus, each step of his represents a step in spiritual growth. To understand and apply this lesson, think of your life as a journey to enlightenment, and take each step as you go on your path to awakening by asking yourself, "What am I learning?"

The lotus flower is a sacred plant in Ancient Egypt, where it is depicted in Egypt's pyramids and ancient palaces. Another Egyptian legend says that the sun god Horus was also born from a lotus flower.

In Greek mythology, the lotus flower represents unrevealed desires. It is said to have psychedelic properties, and the residents of the island of Lotophagi are known as such because they eat lotus flowers.

The lotus flower is referenced in Homer's epic poem known as the Odyssey. In it, the hero of the narrative (Ulysses) and his companions arrive at the island Lotophagi to investigate what was there. After eating the flower, as the natives usually did, Ulysses 'companions forgot to return to the ship. After getting them back, Odysseus had to tie them up so they wouldn't run back to the island.

Lotus in medicine, like any plant, has a series of components with physiological effects. Like its preservation principles, these effects connect with spiritual attributions. The presence of narcotics in their teas induces sleepiness and probable amnesia, a type of sleep in which you sleep to your old self and are reborn without any memory of who you were (amnesia). This is, in fact, the awakening to the new, fuller, purer life.

In the field of pure physiology, users report that the consumption of infusions has helped a lot in their cases of insomnia. The lotus flower possesses some advantages: Astringent; Aphrodisiac; Anti-hemorrhagic; Anti-inflammatory; Antimicrobial; Antitussive; Cardiotonic; Hypotensive; Mucolytic.

"The most beautiful people we have known are those who have known defeat, known suffering, known struggle, known loss, and have found their way out of the depths."

- Elisabeth Kubler Ross

Later this explanation was transformed into the term resilience, the essence of the resistant personality. Resilience is defined as the ability of individuals to overcome periods of emotional pain and tremendous adversity. The lotus flower implies a wonderful metaphor of how there are people capable of bending pain and unfolding it later in the form of serenity, self-control, and persistence.

Chapter 8

Music

Everything is archetypical; as we could see in the prior chapter 3, and archetypes are present everywhere. Our perception will determine what a myth or symbol actually is. Music contributes to it as well because it consistently evokes strong emotions. I'm writing this book because of the fact that certain songs are written to help individuals and others to manipulate them.

There are numerous methods used in the music industry to create songs, codes, hits, programs, and subliminal messages. Information that you cannot consciously perceive since it is being used for unconscious technique. The fact that meditation is so effective in reducing stress is not a coincidence. What are you listening to?

Whoever follows the principles of the law of attraction makes prayers to the cosmos, meditates, uses binaural beats, etc.? They might desire a satisfying relationship, money, chances, etc. However, a lot of people claim that It doesn't work. Okay, anyone who wishes to fall in love but listens to music with sexual imagery in the lyrics may postpone the process! You emit different frequencies every time you listen to music, and the more you listen to songs that make you feel unhappy and disappointed, guess what you're attracting? There is an archetype in music that you can identify with and that can have an impact on your personality.

Now you know why some songs are at the top of the billboard; a sexual archetype in the music stimulates libido. Every type of music has an effect on the environment. The vibration that matches it is drawn to it. Joy, happiness, growth, success, health, etc. are all produced by sound archetypal patterns. Others result in negative outcomes, including disease, despair, unhappiness, unemployment, and poverty. Everything depends on how the sound makes you feel, which activates or deactivates the release of neurotransmitters.

Due to the unfavorable music that people listen to, certain shops and restaurants are losing customers. Depending on the music we hear, we can elicit the precise emotional response we desire. Since everything emits sound and vibration, sound is arguably the most potent kind of energy. And like vibes draw like vibes.

In general, when music affects us, it awakens our inner archetypes and causes intuitive, emotionally-driven responses that are independent to logic. According to Carl Gustav Jung, when an archetype is awakened, a compulsion develops that forces a reaction against all reason and volition. Songs and music can elicit a range of feelings in each of us as we listen to them. The sound of a sound composition has the power to make us cry, laugh, feel sad, miss, rejoice, and be moved. The ability to recognize and express emotions through music has a purpose and serves something within us, which allows us to consider how various archetypes might appear in various musical genres.

Electronic music, rock'n'roll, funk, jazz, and country music are distinct from one another since they all convey various emotions and ideas. As a result, every musical genre has a different effect on listeners. Additionally, there are others who are eclectic in addition to those who only listen to certain types of music and belong to particular groups. The dictionary definition of eclectic is various, variety.

People that are eclectic tend to be more well-balanced since they like a variety of musical types. Each frequency's energy and information are carried by it, and it can move through all of them. He embodies diversity as a person. Your life is filled with music, from lullabies to requiems for infants. The dream of what was born and what was lost is packed in music. They are tendencies that structure how people think, perceive the world, and behave in daily life. Archetypes "affect" how people think and behave.

In ancient Greece, it was believed that music started with the gods. The god Apollo, the patron of the arts and music, is an illustration of an archetypal portrayal of music. Even the gods themselves were spellbound by the muses' musical compositions. Musicians were regarded as the offspring of Apollo and the Muses in ancient Greece.

When Orpheus entered Hades' realm, he used his music to influence both Hades and Persephone. The lyre is a stringed instrument that Hermes is credited with creating. Dionysus and the Eleusinian mysteries were both celebrated with music. Many different mythology contain archetypal depictions. Music has influenced human history and has a profound impact on how individuals perceive the world.

Chapter 9

Male Archetypes

Myths have always played important roles in most cultures and societies. Their presence often reveals an immanent and transcendent dimension of human evolution.

In psychology, understanding the myth behind our behaviors can be of extreme value to us, identifying the plot of the collective unconscious that moves us and which may influence our actions. In this way, deconstructing the internal myth and updating it more healthily in our life contributes to our health and balance.

Every human being inherits universal images from the ancestral past, including pre-humans, animals, and gods. All have a constructive and a destructive dimension. Jung classified it into five major types in the individual's personality: – persona or mask, animus, anima, shadow, and Self.

The anima is the feminine dimension of man's masculine psyche, and the animus is the masculine side of the woman's feminine psyche.

The shadow is part of human history and an expression of the darkest, most sinister, occult psyche and lower tendencies of the collective unconscious, which can be the most powerful and dangerous of the archetypes.

The Self, the greatest of all archetypes, the higher dimension, unifying, harmonizing among the archetypes promotes the full development of the personality and its strengthening to fullness and individuation. In transpersonal psychology, this archetype is called the archetype of synthesis.

For Jung, historical personalities who reached this level of individuation with spiritual maturity would be Buddha and Jesus. Maslow calls this level transcendent self-realization or meta-realization.

Myths may thus unconsciously activate all of these layers of archetypes in our psyche or, on the other side, provide us knowledge of the underlying causes behind our behaviors, assisting us in understanding and inner transformation.

In some cultures of indigenous tribes, parents perform severe rituals for children and adolescents to reach maturity at 20 years of age. In indigenous religions, adult men with immaturity could generate disorganization throughout the region caused by fears, frustrations, uselessness, etc. Lack of results would occur, such as a lack of food, failure to execute godly ceremonies, a lack of productive resources, etc.

In civilization, the consequences of the lack of knowledge are not different. It is not required to suffer greatly to mature; knowledge is sufficient if gained through experience.

A male archetype does not just influence men; archetypes are consciousness's that can influence women just as female archetypes influence men. Jung believed that male immaturity was the result of an immature female. If we follow the logic, mothers are responsible for the information inserted into their children's brains, whether negative or positive. This can generate an imbalance.

It requires a long process of physical, mental, and spiritual self-knowledge to save archetypical ideals. These archetypal values shape the human psyche in 4 aspects: sovereign (King), protector (warrior), creativity (wizard), and loving (lover).

Any culture of patriarchy that unconsciously influences culture and results from these archetypes makes self-knowledge even more important because we learn to heal the shadows when out of balance.

So, in their genius, the ancient Greek sages created symbologies to explain male psychological types. These symbologies are the 6 Greek gods.

1. Zeus

Power, realization, warrior.

Zeus, without a doubt, is a God who brings together, as a metaphor, a great archetypal power.

It is he who leads a ten-year war of the gods against the titans, defeating his father Chronos (Time) and taking his place, sharing the conquered territories with the brothers Poseidon and Hades. For Poseidon, a telluric God, it was the seas. To Hades, the underworld. Zeus took the heavens. And although the Earth and Mount Olympus were shared regions three, it is notorious how Zeus ended up imposing his dominion over them.

Man influenced by Zeus are those mighty lords of a great empire. Indeed, it is the archetype of the domain of kings, emperors, dictators, and businessmen. They are powerful, ambitious, competitive, conscious, strategic, and successful. In addition, they always impose themselves; they are very sure of themselves and their conquests. Everything for Zeus is based on achievement, be it a romance or something professional. When it comes to relationships, they are womanizers, flirts, and love to entice, and conquer hearts in the same manner.

Zeus is the God of organization. Zeus had several wives throughout his life. However, it was with the Goddess Hera that he ruled Olympus.

He had several children with his ex-wives, the Queen of the Gods, and a number of his lovers.

Zeus also symbolizes lightning, which by analogy means intelligence, ideas, and quick thinking. He then organized the world, undid chaos, and became the lord of Olympus - the mighty king of the Gods.

Zeus is punitive; he punishes from a distance. He is powerful, proud, and conquering. He is the will-to-power archetype. Sexual practice, in turn, has exercising power. Men-Zeus have a hard time indulging in relationships with intimacy and depth.

For this reason, although Zeus poses as a great conqueror (including using artifices to deceive, seduce and even rape the woman who is the object of his desire), the sex he offers does not give his partner fullness. He is given to marriage, but he is not faithful. He is a man with a preponderance of commercial and political alliances, quickly gaining essential positions in decision-making centers. From the top of the world, the executive/politician only sees numbers and makes decisions without being aware of the human pain involved.

Zeus is insightful, not for nothing. His symbol animal is the eagle, with a comprehensive view of the whole and a keen eye for detail. Zeus-men must be careful not to feel too quickly filled with the divine right of life and death over everything and everyone. Here, there is a tendency toward megalomania, the loss of human, earthly references, and loss of contact with their emotional and physical dimension. As shadows of the worsening of this archetype, paranoia can arise (thinking that he is being persecuted, that everyone is conspiring to "dethrone him"), while he is at the mercy of sycophants (he does not realize that he is being manipulated by weakness and blindness of his own proud). The lack of contact with emotions and the physical can even accelerate a heart attack.

Light:

- ✓ Inseminator (creative agent)
- ✓ Provider (is the provider of rainfall)
- ✓ Comprehensive view with a focus on detail (eagle)
- ✓ Decisive
- ✓ Conscience (it is the God of Heaven, of Light)
- ✓ Conquer
- ✓ Warrior (directed the War on Titans and won)
- ✓ Logical reasoning (he loves his daughter, Athena, to the detriment of Ares, God of War)
- ✓ Flirt
- ✓ King (predisposition to marry and make his house his kingdom)
- ✓ Good father (took care of his children)
- ✓ Good strategist (knows how to make alliances)

Shadow:

- ✓ Punitive (lightning caster)
- ✓ Goes out of their way to see their desires fulfilled (seduction, incest, rape)
- ✓ Haughty and authoritative
- ✓ Emotionally detached
- ✓ Not a good lover (does not give in to deep and intimate involvements)
- ✓ Lack of contact with feelings and sensuality
- ✓ Unaware of the suffering his decisions cause
- ✓ Believes that the pursuit of power is his divine right, whatever the cost
- ✓ Paranoia (thinks everyone is conspiring against him)
- ✓ Vulnerable to sycophants
- ✓ By not taking care of feelings, he tends to have heart problems

2. Apollo

Harmony, order, moderation, focus, attitude

Apollo is the archetype of attitude, who observes and acts from a distance. He is one of Zeus' favorite children. There were several important stakes in the mythology and Olympus of the Gods. He is a skillful administrator; he knows how to plan, organize, and control.

Apollo carries a bow and golden arrows with him - weapons representing aim and focusing on achieving objectives. In other words, this weapon symbolizes the grand vision that makes you see the purpose and reason of situations.

Apollo was the second-most worshiped and admired God in ancient Greece. This is significant because Mars, the god of battle, was the second most revered God under the Roman Empire, but in Greece, Ares was hated and overlooked by his father, Zeus. In some ways, this quick comparison allows us to infer the profile of the Greek people, civilizing, seeing the development of the arts and laws as a sign of harmony. The Roman people, as a conqueror, versed in the arts of war, in some ways inebriated, with "blood in his eyes" to solve things his way, fearless in hand-to-hand combat.

Being the second most popular God (in Greek culture) isn't an issue for Apollo, who is quite content in his role as the one who came to reveal and carry out his father's wishes. The harmony between Zeus, the father god, and Apollo, the son god, may be witnessed by men who rise to prominent positions within a hierarchical structure and seek to support and expand the projects in which they work rather than toppling their superiors. People who vibrate in this archetype work well as a team: they prefer to be the star of a great team of stars rather than being a solitary star in the firmament of professional life.

Apollo sees far, likes clear definitions, and favors thinking over feeling. He is detail-oriented, but his vision is (paradoxically) panoramic. As a solar god, he is a sky god - therefore emotionally distant. He is not a dreamer, although he can develop a spiritual vision. Having an Apollonian mind means having feet in objective reality, knowing what you want, and having the will to achieve it.

Apollo's bow indicates a sense of the future. Apollo is also the God of prophecy. Remember the Oracle of Delphi, dedicated to him? It is said that the Oracle was dominated by a great ancient Goddess, Python, who was fought and defeated by him. For this reason, priestesses are known as pythonesses, capable of foretelling the future. Two maxims are attributed to this God: "Know thyself" and "Nothing in excess."

Light:

- ✓ He is a patron of Medicine (father of Asclepius or Aesculapius)
- ✓ Lawgiver: Great ability to put things in order
- ✓ Your bow and arrow indicate a great ability to see far and set and pursue goals

- ✓ His lyre is a symbol of harmony, of the beauty of classical music. He is the god of the arts
- ✓ He is a director, a winner. It's the sun god
- ✓ Young and "upright," he usually does very well in professions that require discipline and years of study
- ✓ Harmony, order, form, purity, moderation, and beauty are values that vibrate in this archetype
- ✓ Ability to see the future, preponderance for the prophetic field
- ✓ Predisposition to work in groups
- ✓ Prudent - prefer to avoid physical risks, acting from a distance or in the role of an observer
- ✓ In competitive situations, you don't usually hold grudges or hurt feelings
- ✓ Has practical sense

Shadow:

- ✓ Difficulty getting emotionally involved
- ✓ Not a good lover
- ✓ Your instinctual, sexual, and sensual dimension is less consciously developed
- ✓ He gets involved with sensitive, emotional, irrational women who cannot admire his qualities (objectivity, rationality), which ends up attracting relationship situations that do not have a happy ending
- ✓ It tends to classify women as "to marry" or "not to marry."
- ✓ It has the potential for hostility, although it values prudence and exercises violence and even cruelty without mercy if it is within legal limits.
- ✓ He lets out some poison arrows (toxic words, for example, hurting people through words)

3. Hermes

Knowledge of invisible and visible

Hermes was the son of Zeus (father of the gods) and Maia, a wise and shy goddess. Hermes is born from the union of Zeus (creation) with Maia (discretion and wisdom).

Hermes was a cunning, intelligent, and wise God, and he had the gift of communication. With the purpose of elevating our mentality and giving wings to our creativity to solve our difficulties, he is represented by a shepherd's cap with wings.

It is preferable to have an action plan in place as soon as you become aware of the situation so that you may work quickly and efficiently toward resolving that problem or issue, rather than waste time thinking about it for hours, days, or months without coming up with a solution.

Hermes received the Caduceus from Apollo - a staff around with two serpents intertwined and the upper part adorned with wings. This represents all the opposites of life; male and female, light and dark. At the same time, it represents the power of communication and diplomacy.

Hermes was born in a cave. The day he was born, Hermes got rid of the bands that surrounded him (release from limiting beliefs) and went out to know the world.

Hermes was a clever and gifted baby. Soon after birth, he crawled from one side of the cave to the other in a few hours and began to babble, asking his mother for light to inspect the cave's inside. As no one gave Hermes a light, he by himself hit two stones on straws and lit a flame. Nobody had done that before. In this sense, Hermes 'attitude shows that if there is no one to help us, let us do it ourselves. We should not waste our time waiting for others to do something for us.

While walking along the slopes of Mount Cyllene, Hermes saw a dead turtle. Immediately Hermes had an idea. He took the turtle's flesh, used the shell and its guts, and created a musical instrument called the lyre. Through his creativity, Hermes transformed bad luck into luck. Hermes achieved immense prosperity when he exchanged the first lyre ever created for the 50 cows stolen from his brother Apollo.

Any gift from Hermes is an opportunity since life is about what you're going to do, not what will happen. You can't control the outcome of things, but you can control your actions and re-actions. You can change everything about how you act if you have a different attitude and approach to life.

No one could match this god's trickery and agility. Hermes had wings on his feet, and his speed made him the gods 'messenger. Not only because of his speed but also because of the ease with which Hermes communicated.

Zeus made extensive use of his son, Hermes', assistance due to all of these qualities. For example, during the battle against the gigantic Typhon, all of the gods fled Olympus in panic, leaving just Hermes and Athena. Thus, it is vital to create Hermes to face anything dangerous. It is always good to find a real and effective strategy that can be used for all the challenges you may come across.

Hermes, who knew heaven and earth, went into Hades ' realm. Hermes possessed the mind, heart, and subconscious, completing all three levels. He ruled the roads, walked with incredible speed, wore other winged sandals, and didn't get lost in the night because he dominated the darkness. He knew the script perfectly.

In conclusion, life happens when we are on the move. So if you wish to speed things up, the Hermes archetype will be the guide.

Light:

- ✓ Intelligent, cunning, and inventive
- ✓ Diplomat and a great negotiator
- ✓ It is very adaptable and attentive to its survival
- ✓ Able to explore new paths

- ✓ Make the most of the present moment
- ✓ Solve problems in an unprecedented and inventive way
- ✓ Extremely creative and intuitive
- ✓ Humorous, cheerful, and fun
- ✓ He knows how to use his good luck skillfully
- ✓ Easily captures the meaning of an idea or situation
- ✓ Values of freedom and independence
- ✓ See the dangers and pitfalls along the way

Shadow:

- ✓ He has no shame in deceiving or lying to harm
- ✓ Use good luck and your intuition to harm
- ✓ Don't plan your life
- ✓ Do not reflect on your actions
- ✓ Opportunistic and irresponsible
- ✓ Agitated and anxious
- ✓ Just do what you like and what appeals to you
- ✓ It does not submit to hierarchies
- ✓ Naughty and mischievous
- ✓ Knows how to lie skillfully
- ✓ Does not follow ethics

4. Dionysius

Renaissance and enthusiasm

When you meet the archetypes, our psyche's human and divine parts become active. Dionysius can help you balance your life by strengthening your connections and enhancing your enjoyment of life's joys. Dionysus is an archetype that has held us back in our teenage years, and it's a "forever young" archetype.

Dionysus is popular among males in the modern world because it represents the adolescent who refuses to commit to anything and does not accomplish things consistently, frequently giving up along the way. He may be gloomy, and anything that produces mood swings fascinates him, whether it's music, drugs, or anything else. This stage can persist for years till maturity, and many who go through it are still perpetual youths at 30, 40, and 50.

At this point, Dionysus seems negative archetype, but this is not quite right. If you perceive the wisdom contained in the archetype and identify yourself, you can review your life and continue psychic evolution.

In fact, Dionysus 'life is the symbology of the two poles between male and female. He disguised himself as a woman to hide from Hera's wrath and spent time among women. This experience made him understand a lot about the female world and develop the intuitive part that everyone has but is more touched on in women.

About the duality of this archetype, whoever uses it integrally, without conscience, control, and balance, ends up living both extremes? One day the person is extremely good, affectionate, and pleasant, and the next day he becomes wild, violent, and aggressive. The god Dionysus is one of the last Olympian children of Zeus with a lover named Semele, Princess Theban. The goddess Hera discovers the betrayal and decides to take revenge, and her cunning and subtlety make her come up with a plan to kill Semele.

Hera went down to earth, pretending to be an older woman named Beroe, Semele's nurse. They began to converse, and soon Semele revealed that she was in love with a man claiming to be Zeus. Hera then sowed doubt in Semele's mind, advising her to seek confirmation of Zeus 'divinity from him. Hera eventually gained possession of Semele's psyche, which obeyed her commands. Later, Hera discovered the disguise and drove Dionysus crazy, who by this time had already earned his fame as the god of wine.

Accompanied by Silenus, his instructor, nymphs, pans, curettes, and satyrs, Dionysus traveled the globe. He traveled to

India and was met with hostility. To exact vengeance, he transformed the waters into wine, causing all the Indians to get inebriated and fight one another due to the drunkenness created by the wine.

The god Dionysus is that kind of person who loves to delve into the unknown and constantly clashes with our conservative, cautious, and realistic side. That young spirit is prepared to fall into the world, trusting its luck. Dionysus represents the freedom of the spirit in all spheres: art, music, poetry, theater, festivals, dance, philosophy, and many other aspects of life — in short, the creative impulse itself! The god of wine and ecstasy.

Dionysus was a god who needed to declare and conquer his divinity and place among the gods. He suffered a lot until he reached Olympus. His father Zeus urged him to ascend to Olympus, where Dionysus assumed Zeus's seat at the right of the ruler of the gods, after much traveling and victory in various trials.

Light:

- ✓ Has revolutionary habits and ideas
- ✓ Use the five senses and physical sensations well
- ✓ Understands the female soul
- ✓ Accept anyone the way they are
- ✓ He knows how to open paths
- ✓ Spirit of an eternal youth
- ✓ Attractive, fascinating, charming, and sweet
- ✓ He has a strong maternal instinct
- ✓ Go out of the way now and then
- ✓ Dating frequently

Shadow:

- ✓ Despise the prestige and power of material life
- ✓ Emotional immaturity
- ✓ Androgynous mind, male and female contents in disharmony

✓ Difficulty in having goals
✓ You can't get your emotions
✓ Has addiction tendencies
✓ Difficulty maturing
✓ Immediatism
✓ Temperamental
✓ Strong feeling of rejection

5. Poseidon

"Emotions are what make us human. And when we are taken by a strong feeling, it seems to occupy every space of our being."

Poseidon is one of the most important gods in Greek mythology. He is the god of the oceans, of the waters. This masculine archetype symbolizes the emotions and instincts that, when agitated, are impelled so that they flood the personality, drowning the rational mind. When he is angry or violent, his fury can be devastating. The word for Poseidon means "to pour." The exact meaning could be applied to the feminine aspects of this archetype: the mother, the wife, the sister. They all have the power to release watery energies.

Once Poseidon was angry, he shook the earth, destroying nature and symbolically damaging human nature. Waters and emotions are metaphorically linked. Water is our body's emotional expression of feelings such as sadness, happiness, anger, love, fear, compassion, hatred, jealousy, envy, guilt, shame, lust, greed, gluttony, etc. Accessible emotions are similar on the surface, and many don't sink in right away. On the other hand, the most primitive and bizarrely formed creatures we do not know live in the deepest portion of the ocean.

The sea represents the emotional realm of personal feelings and instincts. Certainly, all of us have been taken by strong emotions of anger and revenge, which are like powerful waves flooding our being, making our bodies tremble like an earthquake.

Our emotions have the power to wash us over and drown us or let us sail through them smoothly when tranquil.

In Greek mythology, Poseidon was the god of the sea. The Romans referred to him as Neptune. He is the third most powerful and influential god after Zeus and Hera. Poseidon visits Olympus exclusively on special occasions, such as assemblies or celebrations. He lives at the bottom of the sea in his kingdom.

According to the Greek books, he is portrayed as looking like Zeus in his appearance, strong man, virile with a beard, and using a trident. As incredible as it may seem, Poseidon was much more virile than Zeus.

Poseidon's favorite animal was the horse. He had two immortal and powerful horses, symbolizing his attempts to control his emotions and thoughts.

Poseidon's position before Zeus reveals his discontent with the ruler of Olympus 'power. There was a lottery for the split and ruling of the planet to avoid disputes and grudges. Olympus belonged to Zeus, the Sea to Poseidon, and Hell to Hades. When Zeus rescued his brothers, he was an adult, having many more attributes and experiences than the others, as Zeus grew out of Kronos rather than from within.

Poseidon was known for his fierce personality. He was always angry, moody, violent, and vindictive. When he was in that mood, he caused earthquakes and destructive waves. Emotions took over Poseidon; he exploded in his anger, shaking the planet and causing massive ripples in the sea.

For this reason, Zeus 'favorite children, Apollo and Athena, did not get along with Poseidon. Apollo and Athena were the rational gods capable of logical thinking, which are necessary attitudes protecting us from the damage caused by strong emotions. This means that when we are feeling strongly, our emotions tend to cause us to act in ways that are not necessarily in our best interests. It's easy for us to lose track of what is important to us and what is not or become confused about who we are and what we want to do in life (which has been linked to low emotional intelligence). Logical thinking helps us avoid these mistakes and ensure that we don't get lost along the way.

Poseidon was not only pleased to have won the kingdom of the seas, but he also attempted to acquire the patronage of a city. Another goddess, his niece Athena, goddess of knowledge, also applied for the post. The contest would be won by the god who provided the city with the most helpful gift.

Poseidon was the first to intervene, striking the rock with his trident, which miraculously produced a supply of salt water to aid fishermen. Only Athena was wiser, she reasoned before deciding what to gift the city. She then planted an olive tree that would benefit the community by giving the city light, art, and culture. The people quickly chose Athena, who thought the gift was more helpful than Poseidon's.

As soon as Poseidon heard the sentence, he became furious and slammed his spear on the ground, calling Athena to a hand-to-hand fight. The goddess, who had no fear in her heart, accepted the challenge by cocking her spear. They got into a fighting stance, facing each other and grinding their teeth in anger. The fight of emotion (Poseidon) against reason (Athena) began, but Zeus interfered at the exact moment, bringing diplomacy and balance to the dispute.

In the end, your life must always be led by reason most of the time. Regardless, never, under any circumstances, reject your emotions. Emotions are not destructive; they are a part of life. The only thing that separates us from animals is our ability to control them and channel them into rational actions to achieve whatever goals we have set for ourselves in life. The main problem with emotion arises when it goes beyond its proper place, like in a child who cannot distinguish between their emotional responses and objective reality.

Light:

- ✓ Great in relationships
- ✓ Creativity

- ✓ Live well in the present
- ✓ Intuition
- ✓ Make everyone happy when you are happy
- ✓ Affectionate
- ✓ Don't be intimidated by anything
- ✓ Confidence
- ✓ Merciful
- ✓ Grateful
- ✓ Loyalty
- ✓ Passionate
- ✓ Sensitive

Shadow:

- ✓ Low rationality
- ✓ Impulsive, acting before thinking
- ✓ Intolerant and ill-tempered
- ✓ Never forgets
- ✓ Does not forgive
- ✓ Does not let go
- ✓ Lose sight of goals
- ✓ Doesn't know how to observe the world
- ✓ Reckless
- ✓ Low self-esteem
- ✓ Doesn't know how to listen to others

6. Hades

"When you have internal dialogue, everything becomes possible; the most impossible projects come true."

-Carlos Castaneda

Hades is the masculine archetype of the introverted man. In other words, those who prefer to be alone, in the company of themselves. There is a vast potential strength in this archetype that is not externalized unless the person is driven by some significant motive that leads him to bring forth this latent inner force.

Hades rules and governs the inner life, which does not express itself in his emotions, appearing to be someone who has weak emotions, where there is no spontaneity in life and relationships.

Hades was the son of Cronos and Rhea and the brother of Zeus together with other gods. As a child, Hades was swallowed by Cronos, later being saved by Zeus.

Zeus took Olympus (sky), Poseidon took the sea, and Hades took hell. In Greek mythology, the analogy of hell is different from Christian hell, where it is a place of condemnation and suffering. The hell of Hades means the inner world of each of us, where all the information of our life is; it is our unconscious. All fears, ghosts, and shameful memories stay in our inner Hades in this sense. These emotions cannot be seen but can be felt in every second of your life as pressure or pain inside you, like a black hole that sucks your energy and time away from your conscious life without letting you notice it.

You are completely unaware of this black hole that takes so much out of you because you don't even know about its existence! It is very common for people to experience the hell of Hades during times of high stress when they are tired, sick, or sad.

Hades was the invisible god; his helmet guaranteed invisibility, perhaps symbolizing behavior or even the riches we all have in our minds and inside us, which we never see. Hence, you must frequently reach the lower world of the soul to get solutions and conquer the resolution to seek answers to life's questions.

Hades was in the realm of darkness and knew very well how to deal with everything that happened. The realm of the Furies, of Cerberus, of the Ghosts, of the Shadows. He was relentless with all of them.

According to legend, Hades, the Greek god of death, only appeared in the realm of Hades twice. The first was Persephone's capture, which was "approved by Zeus." And the second is said to have gone to seek Apollo to heal a wound. Therefore, to avoid the death of our emotions and victories, we need to use consciousness to bring light to a problem, an issue, and emotional pain.

The male archetype of Hades is a secluded and grieving individual. In addition, he is generally introverted and apathetic. However, in the professional world, this may be quite beneficial because this personality type has a high level of focus and a lot of inventiveness. Like Persephone, he can either become celibate or make the other person the queen of his universe when they are in a relationship.

Here's the big secret, do you talk to yourself? Do you talk about your things with your own heart? We all have an internal guide who speaks to us and shows us through insights a roadmap of a way and what we will find during the walk. We are truly lost if we do not listen to it since it is that voice within our heads that gives us guidance on how to travel from point A to point B without getting lost or confused along the way! We must learn to pay closer attention to hear the direction of our inner guide - our Higher Self, God, or higher self, whichever name you want to call it.

You are often descending into the world of Hades, the moment there is the end of a cycle, the death of a relationship, the death of a goal, the death of a way of behaving, the death of hope.

Now you understand why Hades 'hell is rich; all the diamonds are inside it. The whys of your life are all within you.

Light:

- ✓ See beyond appearances
- ✓ Have a deep inner life
- ✓ Discreet

✓ Faithful and committed to your things and people
✓ Prudent and adaptable
✓ Learn from your inner experiences
✓ Knows how to deal well with death and rebirth
✓ Gets work done
✓ Knows how to deal with life-changing processes
✓ Reflective
✓ Good advisor
✓ Empathize with people

Shadow:

✓ Weak; emotionally numb
✓ Strange, relentless, and cold
✓ Distant in relationships
✓ Low self-esteem
✓ Suffers from inferiority complex
✓ Lacks physical and emotional vitality
✓ Prefers to be alone.
✓ Does not react to everyday facts
✓ Feels rejected
✓ Doesn't have close friends, just acquaintances
✓ Always suspicious

Chapter 10

Female archetypes

Female archetypes are increasingly prominent in the modern world, especially in celebrity's lives.

Since ancient civilization, women have gone through a long and difficult journey to conquer independence. Being regarded primarily as male properties prevented the woman from exhibiting all the potential within herself due to our unconscious lack of recognition of the goddess or the Sacred feminine.

Some followers of spiritual doctrine believe that the need for women from past lives to be incarnated in a male physical body was the main cause of their results in the modern world. If we use this conception-making analogy, you will perceive that it is not surprising to see feminists and the LGBTQ+ community working together.

Archetypes can be represented or created by the human mind and come to exist in people's lives. Because the soul is preexisting, human personalities, mythologies, the deceased, the living, and those who will exist in the future may impact the physical world.

In the Jewish tradition, King Solomon wrote in the book of proverbs in Chapter 8:22-30 that says, *"The Lord possessed me at the beginning of His way, Before His works of old. I have been established from everlasting, From the beginning, before there was ever an earth. When there were no depths, I was brought forth, When there were no fountains abounding with water. Before the mountains were settled, Before the hills, I was brought forth; While as yet He had not made the earth or the fields, Or the primal dust of the world. When He prepared the heavens, I was there, When He drew a circle on the face of the deep, When He established the clouds above, When He strengthened the fountains of the deep, When He assigned to the sea its limit So that the waters would not transgress His command, When He marked out the foundations of the earth, Then I was beside Him as a master craftsman; And I was daily His delight, Rejoicing always before Him, Rejoicing in His inhabited world, and my delight was with the sons of men."*

We have an impression that Solomon was always on God's side before he came to Earth. This describes the origin of the pre-existence of archetypes as consciousness, ideas, thoughts, or any other name you want to give it.

In this theory, everything exists outside of time and space, including ideas, emotions, and beliefs, which are also consciousness in another form, like our souls before birth (but not in a religious sense). It is important to understand that this does not mean that the unconscious mind is an actual thing. Still, it means that we are all aware of it and can access its contents through hypnosis, meditation, other states of altered consciousness, and even dreams and intuition without being in a particular state of mind.

As a result, archetypes affect our feminine energy unconsciously, which we can empower. It's important to note that the masculine energy does not create these archetypes, but rather, they originate from the feminine energy and are part of her nature (and ours).

Our first experience with this is when we hear the words "the mother archetype" used in most books about the subject and seems to be the main source for people who want to learn more about it but don't know where to start or what it means.

In this chapter, I will not only express the archetypes of goddesses, but I will also make a brief analysis of some of the most outstanding women in history.

Remember that archetypes don't have sexual options because they are unified. It doesn't matter if men or women want to manifest the energy of these models in their lives because they are in all of us, and we are all part of the archetype manifestation.

1. Cleopatra

Power, seduction, leadership, businesswoman, wisdom, magnetism, courage.

A psychic Helio Couto presented her narrative through canalization. "A great opportunity was missed in the Roman Empire when Cleopatra came into this world. The opportunity to unite the Middle East and the West under a single administration ended today's rivalry. Cleopatra's greatest conquests in history were cultural interchange, peace, and human growth; she worked hard and never stopped trying to make the world better.

To start with, what do you know about Cleopatra? Who was Cleopatra? Every documentary and search you make on Google is partial to reality about her. She was more than what you might have watched in the movie production, a character interpreted by Elizabeth Taylor.

Cleopatra was a perfect woman! Any attributes you think or expect to see in someone, she had! Cleopatra was famous for the following attributes: Queen of Egypt; Expert military strategist; Ability to evaluate the most complex situation and variety of military or political situations; Capacity to understand the human mind and predict enemy action; speaking eight languages; Perfect human knowledge to choose ministries without interview or investigation.

Can you imagine how great Cleopatra's consciousness was? While traveling for business and addressing problems, Cleopatra would entrust Egypt to her ministries by taking a simple look at the individual. She had the talent of identifying a person's intention, and such intuition is not for everyone!

Cleopatra always trusted her intuition like a snake - her precious animal of power. She used to take four years out of the country; nobody had an airplane in that time.

Egypt was a prosperous country, literally the World Bank in every way, and it was tranquil with no military strength at the super potential level. Cleopatra's administration was perfect in accounting, finance, economy, regulator stocks, and importation taxes; she controlled everything.

It is almost impossible to see all these skills in one person, but Cleopatra had it all! The amount of perfection in humans is astounding! You can observe someone skilled in one area but not in another, and it is unusual to find someone with many specializations.

All of Cleopatra's work talents were Yang; what about the Yin? Her Yin side was also perfect! A great Yin and Yang in one person.

Cleopatra was dealing with something powerful at all times - the Roman Empire. If the goal is to maintain the state together, negotiations are required, as is engagement with the imperator. Otherwise, everyone disappears and becomes a colony.

Cleopatra had a lot of opponents she had to overcome to get to the imperator. She indeed got herself rolled up in the carpet and sneaked in until Gaius Julius Caesar's presence, only to obtain the chance to talk to him. Cleopatra had to pass a lot of military barriers and ensure she didn't die in the process.

Cleopatra felt hungry and thirsty, turned sweaty, and spent a long time in an extremely uncomfortable place. This action caused a great impact when the carpet was unrolled. Later, she got what she wanted the most - to talk to Julius Caesar.

Gaius Julius Caesar was a superhero, a military strategist in battle, and had a metahuman mind. Julius would write after solving problems, "I came, I saw, I conquer." Anything that could be a big problem for anyone was no problem for him.

Julius had extraordinary leadership ability and an oratory government; he created good laws to improve Roman life. Obviously, a man with such a great capacity would fall in love after meeting a perfect woman like Cleopatra. Julius Caesar was "the superman," and she was "the wonder woman."

The love between Gaius Julius Caesar and Cleopatra was genuine. However, the political factors were complicated, as they had always been until modern times. However, Gaius understood how to deal with them; his efficiency was astounding.

A great man like Gaius Julius Caesar began to inspire envy. It's like a competition where one person wins all the games until 70 people unite to ruin the great guy after all the parties, successful jobs, and good deeds he did for them. One day, Gaius went to the senate, was disarmed, and got punished.

Cleopatra was in Rome. Only God knows how she felt when she saw his bloody body. The moment she saw Julius Caesar, Cleopatra realized that Egypt was in danger as Gaius guaranteed that unification would happen. Only unification would have allowed Egypt to prosper and become the great land it was meant to be.

Egypt is what it is now because she died with it connected. Cleopatra attempted to carry on what Pharaoh Akhenaten began a long time ago when Egypt was lost for the second time.

Cleopatra had to return to Egypt and restart her plan, strengthen the country, create the fleet, and get at least one minimum defensive chance because the Roman Empire was strong. Imagine managing a wealthy land like Egypt with all malevolent eyes on it; a lot of talent was required, which Cleopatra possessed.

Gaius Julius Caesar had a trusted and loyal friend, Marcus Antonius. Marcus knew that Gaius was an amazing man, and he kept his loyalty to Gaius until his death. When Gaius died, the power was divided, and Marcus took partial government command.

Cleopatra had to talk to Marcus Antonius. She had to move and plan her trip to talk to the new Roman leader once more. If

Cleopatra wanted to see Marcus, she had to make a big impression; she would never go as a beggar; the carpet had been used for Gaius Julius, so she resolved to do something different. What did Cleopatra do?

A great ship was decorated, full of gifts. The floor was covered with 100,000 roses! That is the woman who knows how to impress and make everything flawless; as Marcus stepped on the flowers, their fragrance was released. As I said in previous chapters, the marketing tactic links the symbol with the person or product.

Can you see Cleopatra's capacity to interact with the opposite sex? She knew how to operate and manipulate a human mind in her favor, things that Plato, Freud, and Jung discovered years later. Today, we have access to this knowledge; the significance of the symbols and models that build our personality and who we are, information that Cleopatra did not have.

Consequently, Marcus Antonius fell in love with Cleopatra; she fell in love with him. These examples are the perfect experience of how to gain someone's heart. The stories we read, listen to, and watch about Cleopatra make us think that what she did was nothing less than just a seduction strategy. But if you carefully analyze her story and understand her personality, it will not make sense. Her feelings were genuine, honest, real, and pure.

Later, Cleopatra and Marcus Antonius got married. When the vile people rose against Egypt once more and destroyed their lives, it was time for Cleopatra to awaken to a new perspective of reality, Egypt, the Roman Empire, opponents, and how they thought without illusions. This capacity is the most important thing to succeed in every area of life, and she had them all.

Cleopatra tried hard to argue and motivate Marcus Antonius that he had to take the initiative without wasting time. Else he would be betrayed in many ways. But Marcus had strong Yin (emotion). He was a great guy who thought everyone was good.

It is hard for a person like Marcus to deal with politics and see how much a human being can do. That's why he hesitated in taking power, so somebody else took it. The problem was not one of democracy; he had two choices: take action or let the people of darkness take power, ending in servitude and the ruin of Egypt.

Cleopatra could conserve Egypt in the best way she could. Egypt still survives today, while the Roman Empire has fallen. She eventually succeeded in her governance of the region over which she was queen. Cleopatra aimed to work as hard as possible to bring happiness, wealth, and peace to her people, and she succeeded!

If you want a perfect example of a human, think about Cleopatra!

Because of distorted information from media like historians, movies, and writers, the myth of Cleopatra was created. Most people see Cleopatra as a seductress, deceitful, a home wrecker destroyer, etc.

Cleopatra ascended to the throne at the age of 18. She was Macedonian rather than Egyptian and was the 7th Cleopatra, a descendant of Alexander the Great. She was forced to marry two of her brothers since they were regarded as gods, and incestuous marriage was required to keep the dynasty closed.

Cleopatra ruled for 21 years as the only ruler. She did what she did, yet most people only remember Elizabeth Taylor for her beauty. Cleopatra did not have great beauty. A couple of registers of Cleopatra's pictures are not impressive, but her presence caught men's attention. Cleopatra had perfect oratory and knew everything about the art of communication. It was impossible to talk to her without being enchanted by her words. She dominated everyone with a simple conversation.

Unlike what the media and historians have stated about Cleopatra, she was not a family destroyer. Nevertheless, her being depicted as a home wrecker is not surprising given how difficult it is to accept a woman with all those traits, especially during those times. Cleopatra was a bridge builder between women and authority.

The Roman Empire devised the tactic to keep everyone diverted from the truth of what Cleopatra was promoting as a lovely woman. The Roman Empire never recognized imperators, kings, or queens; they cared about expanding their territory.

Cleopatra was a remarkable woman; she was the first woman to resolve to study the languages of her subjects. She was raised in a Greek home and had access to the renowned Alexandria library.

The snake was a strong Egyptian symbol. Legend says that when Cleopatra was buried, one snake was placed next to her.

Cleopatra's story ends with her last political act. She knew what would happen to her after Marcus Antonius's death. Cleopatra prepared a basket with two venomous snakes to poison someone. This person would die in a couple of seconds without pain. The basket stayed in the temple and was hidden in a safe place.

When Egypt was to be conquered, Cleopatra would have been held prisoner for several days before being sent to Rome as a slave woman with a chain around her neck. This could not have been acknowledged. She was Egypt's Queen, after all. If the Roman Empire was to humiliate a queen, think what they would have done to her people!

To save Egypt's dignity, Cleopatra had to make a radical decision and strategize. She lied to the guards and got into the temple, took the basket, and was consequently bitten by snakes; she died immediately. Cleopatra didn't act out of desperation or cowardice, and she died for Egypt.

You won't discover her entire tale on the internet; there's a distinction to be made between searching online and traveling into multidimensional time to witness what truly happened." (Couto, 16-Paixão, 2018).

The Bible says that nothing is impossible, but how impossible are we able to see? For example, in the movie Lucy, a woman we capable to activate other parts of the brain, reaching 100% of brain capacity, and improving her abilities to manipulate material things. Later, she gained access to remote view, which implies the capacity to see the past, present, and future. Anyone may achieve that degree, but it requires knowledge, wisdom, and well-preparedness because it is not a simple task. In the series Devs, a quantum computer is programmed to access these multidimensional times. Spiritual teachings inspired anything that scientists did or will do in the future, and one more time we noticed their strong connection.

I'm writing her story it in this book because Cleopatra as an archetype is an amazing experience. It is something that someone may sense and perceives that not everything mentioned in articles is true or tells the entire story. Cleopatra had her shadows, but her light was so bright that I believe Cleopatra like every other great leader the world has seen learned to sincerely love others, even if it meant sacrificing their lives and using all their knowledge and expertise for their benefit.

Light:

- ✓ High self-esteem
- ✓ Self-reliance and independence
- ✓ Personal empowerment
- ✓ Magnetism
- ✓ Charming and seductive
- ✓ Politically conscious
- ✓ Eloquence, oratory, sociability
- ✓ Financial management
- ✓ Financial prosperity and abundance
- ✓ The attraction of powerful men
- ✓ Intuition
- ✓ Strategist
- ✓ Yin and Yang balance
- ✓ Leadership
- ✓ Organization

Shadow:

- ✓ Authoritative, demanding
- ✓ Proudness
- ✓ Arrogance

✓ Only relates to men of power

2. Nefertiti

Influence, magnetism, personal power, influence, leadership.

Nefertiti "A Beautiful Woman Has Come."

At 12, she was betrothed to the pharaoh Amenhotep IV, known as Akhenaten. At 14, she became the youngest Egyptian queen of the 18th dynasty, whose marriage had six children. They are Meritamen, Amun-her-khepeshef, Meryre, Pareherwenemef, Henuttawy, and Meryatum. However, throughout Akhenaten's Egyptian reign, three of his daughters succumbed to the spread of a malarial plague, which was known as a "magical disease" for its devastating power. Another of the couple's daughters, Henuttawy, would die early due to accidental drowning.

This couple gained fame for the religious revolution imposed on the annihilation of polytheism, introducing only monotheism, the worship of a single God, Aton, and God Sun, the creator of the whole.

Nefertiti was not a simple Queen; she was worshipped as a "living goddess."

Even marrying early, Nefertiti and Akhenaten are examples of a marriage of collaboration and loyalty. That's because Nefertiti was always ahead of everything. She was very celebrated and had great empathy and charisma among the population, giving popularity to the cult of Aton. That's why she was worshipped as a "living goddess" and still had an active voice (very unusual at the time) in the pharaoh's decision-making.

The pharaoh and Nefertiti were mutually in love. Another unusual feature of this relationship was that both allowed themselves to be "drawn" in very intimate scenes, such as eating, playing with their daughters, and even in sexual moments.

Nefertiti was unique in the entire history of Egyptian queens. Assigned to the Pharaoh's Statute, which belonged only to the Kings, was increasingly attributed to pharaonic prerogatives. This is proven in several images where Nefertiti appeared with the pharaoh's cap and tablets.

Amarna's pictures portray the queen alone when her husband Akhenaten died, leading religious processions and even armies. These roles were designated solely for pharaohs, even though Akhenaten's successor overturned practically everything the pharaoh did during his reign. The cult of Aton became extinct, and the old gods were resumed less than five years after his death.

However, Nefertiti could not stop the religious and social crisis that plunged Egypt into a period of political instability. After only three years of power, she would have died in a situation that has never been clarified. There are reports that when Nefertiti found out that she would be killed and dragged through the streets of Egypt, she allowed herself to be bitten by a snake and died.

There is no evidence to confirm that her body was found. One more time, according to some wise mediums that travel through dimensional portals and access multiverses to space continuous-time affirmed that she was poisoned when she smelled a flower from a gift box. For example, one movie that expresses poisoned plants is No Time to Die.

Nefertiti is contemplated as the most faithful queen who ever lived. She had high Yin, so she brings the frequency of female empowerment and strong self-esteem. Like any archetype with a dominating feminine, Nefertiti attracts many men, but she prefers quality over quantity since she only accompanies those who can, not those who want to.

As seen in her story, in addition to being beautiful, Nefertiti was absurdly intelligent in commanding and directing the plans of someone superior to her. Some examples of celebrities influenced by Nefertari are Beyoncé, Rihanna, and Michael Jackson in the song Remember the Time.

Light:

- ✓ Force
- ✓ Courage
- ✓ Beauty
- ✓ Intellectuality
- ✓ Focus
- ✓ Fearlessness
- ✓ Fidelity
- ✓ Companionship
- ✓ Relationship aligned with life purpose
- ✓ Consciousness of devotion to the Universe
- ✓ Complicity
- ✓ Revolutionary
- ✓ Intelligence
- ✓ Uniqueness
- ✓ Lover
- ✓ Great mother
- ✓ Intense
- ✓ Proactive
- ✓ Warrior woman
- ✓ Cordiality and politics
- ✓ Celebrated and courted
- ✓ Adored
- ✓ Balanced Yin and Yang polarity

Shadow:

- ✓ Narcissism
- ✓ Authoritarianism
- ✓ Arrogance
- ✓ Loss of vanity due to excess self-esteem
- ✓ Solving other people's problems in excess

✓ Dealing with the Shadows of Envy (can attract / manifest disaffection, criticism, and even betrayal in the professional scope.)

3. Marilyn Monroe

Seduction, sensuality, strong Yin, femininity beauty
"An Archetype descended to Earth. A lamb is not among wolves. She came to teach us the malice of truth. Shine like a star, Illuminated all women... Love overflowing, beautiful as Aphrodite... Immortal."

- Helio Couto

The Marilyn Monroe archetype possesses a powerful energy, especially when the goal is to bring out intense feminine energy. Regarded as one of the greatest legends in Hollywood history, the muse is always remembered for her great talent and beauty.

Throughout her life, Marilyn Monroe participated in several films. However, they all portrayed her in the role of an extremely beautiful and sexy blonde woman endowed with little intelligence. All this made the human being who lived behind this character more depressed and hurt. The blonde had already gone through a series of failed relationships, miscarriages, and panic attacks that added to Marilyn's feeling

A true understanding of the archetypal image of Aphrodite, the one that would allow Marilyn's true face to appear, had denied her: her appreciation for literature, her work as a poet, and her natural curiosity and sensuality were erased. There was only room for the beautiful, promiscuous blonde, with a sensuality manufactured for the taste of the industry.

Marilyn's producers forced her to act out the stereotypical image of the Goddess full-time. There was no room for spontaneity, and there was a displacement between the real woman and the artificially constructed character in this rupture.

Marilyn Monroe, a.k.a Norma Jeane Baker, was required to

act in permanent seduction, to conquer and win back the public without ceasing. The need to please people at any cost robbed Marilyn of her body, her private life, and consequently, her behavior. This led Marilyn down paths of addiction and self-destruction.

Marilyn was attractive because of her ability to arouse a heightened sense of masculinity in the opposite sex. She had the power to make men feel more like men. Another important point of Marilyn Monroe's archetype is that Marilyn had child-like characteristics. Intelligence has to be on your side. Look innocent, unassuming, with no malice, and you'll have guns in your hands.

The muse was considered a sex symbol. Through this, Marilyn could attract even the most powerful men into her life, as was the case with President John F. Kennedy. Thus, it is correct to say that your energy is mainly related to this characteristic.

You enjoy romance and are frequently seduced by beautiful people who are not necessarily emotionally or financially related to you but whose magnetism and charisma are captivating. These people can change your life for the better or worse if they do so with a strong will and an abundance of self-confidence and respect for themselves and others! This trait shines through in your career, relationships, and daily activities, bringing immense delight to everyone who knows you because they see the person you truly are rather than what you appear to be on the surface.

Light:

- ✓ Magnetism
- ✓ Charm and elegance
- ✓ Daring
- ✓ Charism
- ✓ Intelligence and entrepreneurial skills (Marilyn made her own studio.)
- ✓ Increased libido

✓ Uninhibited
✓ Take care of your body
✓ Natural sensuality
✓ Self-esteem
✓ Strong Yin
✓ Easy-going
✓ Spontaneous
✓ Elevated intuition

Shadow:

✓ Depression
✓ Anxiety
✓ Relationships are not permanent
✓ Lust

4. Aphrodite

Love, passion, sensuality, self-love, self-esteem, beauty, divinity, communication, creativity, charisma

Great Goddess Aphrodite, Goddess of Beauty and Love!

As a metaphor for the natural archetypal qualities present in the feminine spirit, Aphrodite interprets the transformative, life-generating presence, open to connections, with an awareness that is both concentrated and disseminated and enlivening. It represents love, beauty, pleasure, communication, and creativity.

Aphrodite is the goddess to worship to develop self-esteem when learning to love yourself!

Aphrodite is an alchemical, resilient goddess, unlike Demeter, Persephone, and Hera, who relied on relationships with children, parents, or spouses to feel like someone, to feel like their lives made any sense. Aphrodite was neither virgin like Artemis, Athena, and Hestia. They realized in themselves, being able or not to be related to someone but without the weight that the relationship determines their reason for living.

Thus, Aphrodite is the one who relates to delivery. Yes, bringing inspiration, art, passion, renewal of life, and procreation, but without letting herself be possessed or determined by feelings and relationships. Aphrodite gives herself with surrender, but she is free simultaneously. Free and demanding, jealous and proud, not admitting that any beautiful mortal is worshipped or has beauty compared to hers.

Aphrodite is an archetypal lover and has enchantment, magnetism, and "chemistry." It is an expression of pleasure in love, beauty, sexuality, and sensuality. Generative, it is closely linked to the human capacity to create.

However, approaching this archetype must be done very carefully. Taking on the traits of such a strong Goddess during ordinary human experience might entail "playing" with hearts and burning yourself in the fire of passions that will be sparked, and the Goddess is aware of this!

Unlike other goddesses, Aphrodite was never victimized or suffered. She was married to Hephaestus and was a notorious lover of Ares. Aphrodite and Hephaestus form a marriage between Love and Work, Manual Arts, and the field of Invention. Aphrodite and Ares include the unlikely pair of Love and War, with whom she has the children Harmony, Terror, and Fear.

Aphrodite also has a son with Hermes, Hermaphroditus. The presence of Aphrodite, however, is not limited to sexual relationships. It can be present in platonic friendships, in the connection of souls, as an energizing spark of creativity and growth.

Aphrodite is the appreciation of emotional experience with others, whether in casual love marked by great delivery, "may it be eternal while it lasts," and involves the immediate pleasure in knowing and making yourself known.

Aphrodite manipulates the two most powerful energies in the universe: love and passion. In this aspect, the archetype Aphrodite will make an immense force of healing and transformation flow in you because from love always flows attraction, union, and fertilization. This also includes the birth of a new life, a new story, or even a new idea.

The archetype of Aphrodite brings to those components of a will, determination, and intellectual interests. She was born from sea foam when Kronos castrated his father, Uranus. The blood fell into the sea, which began to bubble up into foam, and then a floating shell emerged from the bottom, and within it was the goddess of love. The stimulus of this archetype is the pheromone release.

By analogy, you need to make love for you come from deep inside, for it is already an instinct born with us.

The moment Aphrodite was born, love took hold of all beings. After all, we all have self-love somewhere in the depths of our being. However, only the person himself can bring this self-love to the surface.

The relationship of Hephaestus and Aphrodite means that everyone deserves love and brings the symbology that all work needs to be done with strength and dedication. Work (Hephaestus) together with love (Aphrodite).

"What misfortune threatened?
Why had I called thee?"
"What my frenzied heart craved in utter yearning,
Whom would its wild desire persuade to passion?
What disdainful charms, madly worshipped, slight thee?
Who wrongs thee, Sappho?"
"She that fain would fly, she shall quickly follow,
She that now rejects, yet with gifts shall woo thee,
She that heeds thee not, soon shall love to madness,
Love thee, the loth one!"

- Sappho poem

Light:

✓ Inspiration
✓ The conception of a new life, new projects
✓ The strong power of exciting (sensual, sexual, romantic)
✓ Active intensity
✓ Fertility
✓ Irresistible beauty

- ✓ Communication and communion (in the carnal and spiritual sense)
- ✓ Desire to know and make yourself known
- ✓ Provides a connection between souls, platonic love
- ✓ Empathic understanding
- ✓ Receptive, attentive
- ✓ Makes everything it touches fascinating and beautiful
- ✓ Shows up in all creative work
- ✓ As a muse, he awakens in the other his faith in himself, his work
- ✓ Possesses the look that makes the other possible
- ✓ Heightened sensitivity to stimuli (touch, smell, taste)

Shadow:

- ✓ Its alluring, enveloping, can be illusory and fleeting
- ✓ Easily becomes an object of dispute between men
- ✓ Vengeful and jealous, can't stand to be mocked, ignored, compared, or belittled
- ✓ Enables and fosters forbidden passions
- ✓ Curses making the mortal fall in love with someone inadequate or unable to return that love - behold, love becomes a curse!
- ✓ Demanding
- ✓ Within the Judeo-Christian culture, the Aphrodite woman will feel the weight of guilt and judgment for frivolous/promiscuous sexual and loving behavior
- ✓ Propensity to generate erotic energy in the other (and lose control of the situation)
- ✓ By acting according to their instinctive desires, they disregard the consequences, which can be serious (social condemnation, men who only seek her for sexual satisfaction and resulting low self-esteem)
- ✓ Impulsivity, live the present as if there is no tomorrow
- ✓ Loves intensely in the magic of the moment but leaves along the way a series of bitter, depressed, angry, and broken men

5. Mermaid

Fatal seduction, charisma, magnetism, sociability, self-esteem, fertility, libido, sensuality

The mermaid archetype is linked to the element 'Water. 'That is, it is energy linked to emotions.

The mermaid myth is universal. There was some portrayal of women who "bewitched men till they drowned" in every region where men relied on the sea for their food or life. Some psychoanalysts believe that these representations were personifying aspects of the sea or rivers that are incomprehensible to man and therefore dangerous.

According to Greek mythology, there are three possible origins for these beings:

1. Women who offended the goddess Aphrodite (of Love and Beauty) were punished to live eternally on an isolated island.
2. Persephone, daughter of Zeus (god of the gods, Sky and Lightning) and Demeter (goddess of Agriculture), is kidnapped by Hades. All of Persephone's friends are punished by Demeter for not helping Persephone, being turned into fish women.
3. Sirens are the daughters of the god Achelous (a river god) with Melpomene (Muse of Tragedy) and with Terpsichore (the Muse of Dance).

There is a passage in the Odyssey in which Odysseus, the protagonist, is forced to cross an ocean channel full of mermaids. He advises his sailors to pour wax in their ears, so they won't hear them, get enchanted, and tie him to the ship's mast, so he doesn't leap into the sea.

Mermaids can represent the source of life, purification, and rejuvenation. On the other hand, water may be a formidable foe, with thundering waves threatening to carry us off into the abyss. According to legend, ancients were lured irresistibly to the Sirens 'captivating vocals but were afraid of their abilities.

Our uncontrollable emotions frequently prohibit us from achieving our goals. As a result, the mermaid archetype may help us explore the core of our passions and find answers.

When associated with waters, mermaids have mastered the art of swimming in the seas. They will also help you find a new place where you can start over again, which is often very difficult if you are shipwrecked at sea or have been banished into exile because of your wrongdoing. Mermaids will assist you in navigating these seas, whether stormy or calm. If you adapt to this archetype, you will weave a path through your life despite obstacles and find your way to your goals.

Mermaids may not commit to partnerships, but they surely enjoy a good romance. Here's some raw, uncontrolled sexuality that wants to be noticed. Mermaids traverse a person's most fundamental impulses in the sphere of seduction.

Mermaids are the fantasy of the passionate male desire of the incredibly erotic, bold, and gorgeous woman who offers unlimited pleasures and a small amount of danger. Mermaids go through three stages of seduction:

1. Seduction
2. Intimacy
3. Danger

Mermaids possess knowledge obtained via intuition and observation of those they wish to attract. They intrigue because they promise knowledge, pleasure, and excitement. Their vocals are soothing and charming, promising victims that they will progress. They speak in a quiet, low tone as if you had just awoken. When you speak slowly and deliberately, you tranquilize the listener.

If you practice the mermaid archetype, you should replicate your thoughts by speaking what the other wants to hear. This is a really simple trick that works for any relationship, not just romantic ones! You will say things the other wants to hear, thereby developing their interest in the conversation and getting them to become vulnerable. The other person will let their guard down and speak of their passions and desires.

However, there is another crucial part to comprehending the mermaid myth, which has to do with our vulnerability due to our wants. When we discover that mermaids are an illusion, we recognize that perceiving things as we wish them to be rather than as they put us at grave risk.

People, things, and circumstances are widely perceived as per our desires than their actuality. We are like sailors who see pretty ladies when only wind, stones, and freezing water exist. When we see what we want to, it damages our lives.

As I previously stated, it makes no difference if the archetype impacts men or women, for archetypes are consciences but think about it...How many ladies have ever felt chemistry for a man when they heard his siren song? How many guys have fallen in love with a woman's curves? That is the essence of mermaid virtue!

Would you know how you would feel if you opened your consciousness to comprehend how fashion brands design dresses for women's curves or if you looked at the Starbucks logo directly in front of your cup of coffee? That is the archetype's major secret – it gives you a glimpse of what you desire, to feel confident about yourself.

We can also define a mermaid's archetype as inspiration, as in a woman's attire, since anything that produces energy or feelings generates manifestation or action. For example, if you wear pink to feel feminine and attract love, it represents what you want when you wear pink. The actual color itself and the emotional energy will also produce its actions and results!

Light:

✓ Sensuality

- ✓ Adaptability
- ✓ Knowledge
- ✓ Criterion
- ✓ Divination
- ✓ Seduction
- ✓ Magnetism
- ✓ Irresistibility
- ✓ Self-esteem
- ✓ Beauty
- ✓ Easy to flirt
- ✓ Libido increase
- ✓ Increased libido
- ✓ Stunning and remarkable appearance

Shadow:

- ✓ Illusions
- ✓ Manipulation
- ✓ Falsehood
- ✓ Shortage
- ✓ Feeling of loneliness
- ✓ Exaggerated sexuality
- ✓ Lie and deceive
- ✓ Losing sense of reality
- ✓ Uncontrolled emotions
- ✓ Dishonesty
- ✓ Destroys relationships
- ✓ Unable to establish a relationship
- ✓ Competition with other women

6. Lilith

*Freedom, sexuality, self-confidence,
force, seduction, independence*

Lilith is a goddess to pagans and a demon to Judeo-Christian civilizations. She is hidden or withdrawn from sacred scriptures, feared and loathed, and "demonized."

Lilith is our shadow archetype, containing our anxieties, shame, and guilt. It is, however, where our unlimited possibilities to be, comprehend, heal, and acknowledge ourselves and our potential and self-knowledge reside. This is because "The Shadow" is implanted in our unconscious and represents everything we hide, mostly of a sexual nature, according to Sigmund Freud.

Carl Gustav Jung, a psychiatrist and the pioneer of Analytical Psychology, believes that the Shadow contains the entirety of our existence since we can only be full by embracing, illuminating, and comprehending subconscious concerns. Only in the dark does the seed grow. It is in the womb and the darkness of the soil that life is conceived.

> *"And then we return to what was hidden, to what was disowned. All the biological issues, the sexual urges, what frightened within the dark of the psyche, all these were placed on the woman's back—as guilt and shame for being a descendant of that one who betrayed the will of God. For it was not enough that Eve was inferior, she still had to be blamed for all humanity having lost the paradise of Eden."*

These harrowing tales were what sparked millennia of tyranny toward women. Women had already been accused of having inferior perspectives, indecent urges, and being lustful and familiar with the devil and carnal sins, which the Pharisees despised.

Adam and Eve, the first humans on Earth, are crucial to the myth of human creation. Outside of biblical mythology, Lilith, the first woman, refused to submit to Adam and was exiled from Eden. She would have transformed into the serpent who handed Eve the apple, causing her to commit worldly evils.

Some people claim that the verse in Genesis 1:27, which says that "God created male and female," comes before the quotation of Eve in Genesis 2. This gives rise to the interpretation that there was a woman before Eve. Another point for this argument would be Adam's reaction to saying "yes," as if there was another woman, see Genesis 2:23 "This is now bone of my bones and flesh of my flesh; she shall be called 'woman, 'for she was taken out of man."

Lilith, Adam's first partner, is made of the same material as him, is full of blood and saliva, and boasts demonic passion and vigor, which irritate Adam; nevertheless, she is also the one who gives you orgasmic pleasure. The man's dominance of being on top of the woman, which she does not tolerate, causes the relationship to be disrupted, and she pulls away from him. This myth represents the feminine impulse as exhibited in her sexuality and the quest for sexual and social equality in the face of macho.

Therefore, the myth follows a spectrum of domination, subjection, sexual suppression, and the fight for female sexual and social independence. Femininity is a totality, yet this myth focuses on one aspect of a share: the sensual woman, the prostitute, but with the power of individualism seen in today's feminine struggle for balance.

Healers, herbalists, prayers, midwives, and slain "witches" are all honored by Lilith. Lilith is a tribute to the raped Indians and black women in the Americas. Lilith pays tribute to the women confined in asylums for "hysteria" as they wailed the feminine sufferings that a sick and dishonest society won't discuss.

This energy comes to alter us, and Lilith will symbolize everything you have inside you that is eschatological. Still, you might interpret Lilith as much more of what has been elevated or suppressed within us if what you have subconscious is another picture of revolt, independence, and self-confidence. There's more because, like any archetypal energy we name "god and goddess" (regardless of whether you worship it as a religion or not), something unique and specific for each person will arise since it is also a symbol that may represent and indicate according to our own experiences.

What is your stifled potential and your worry of not being good enough, of not being noticed? Are you afraid of discovering you're more intelligent and capable than you've been led to believe? Do you dread being held accountable for everything that affects you?

Lilith, like all the goddesses who inhabit me, tells me to seek the cure for an ancestral female pain, to scream the voices that have been silenced, to say the words, create movements, and dance the dances that have been forbidden, that have tethered our bodies and minds to pre-determined equations of what it means to be a woman or, more importantly, of what it means to "be a good woman, the ideal woman."

The Lilith archetype can generate an inflated sense of self-sufficiency, even solitude if practiced for a long time. If the driver sees any additional undesirable effects, the advice is to merely "turn it off," meaning to cease utilizing the connections, symbols, and instructions.

Light:

- ✓ Independence
- ✓ Sexuality
- ✓ Fertility
- ✓ Liberation
- ✓ Strength
- ✓ Seduction
- ✓ Sensuality
- ✓ Strong Yang

Shadow:

- ✓ Lust
- ✓ Exaggerated self-sufficiency
- ✓ Repudiate
- ✓ Uncontrolled sexual practicing

7. Athena

Independence, intelligence, wisdom, victory

Athena is the female and male archetypes of intelligence, strategy, wisdom, and bravery. The Athena archetype is found in persons with significant willpower, such as professors, brilliant students, executives, and other professionals with a high level of intelligence.

Commitment to the Athena archetype works effectively in every scenario. People who practice this archetype are skilled, organized, have a rational mind, and are logical masters. Your conflicts are accomplished initially in your personal reality, and your strength is in your thoughts.

Athena is the goddess of wisdom and Zeus 'favored daughter via Metis, the goddess of cunning. Metis is as clever as Zeus. Wisdom, which is Athena, emerges from the combination of Creation and Cunning.

Athena was born from Zeus's head as an adult, clad and equipped with a spear and armored, releasing a battle cry as soon as she was born. She bowed before her father and surrendered her weaponry, saying she prayed she wouldn't have to use them because her battle was just intellectual.

As a result, Zeus was thrilled with his daughter, who was born especially for him. She became his favorite daughter and her father's advisor due to her knowledgeable mindset. Nobody else on Olympus had done anything like that. All of the decisions were made by Zeus, although he always sought wisdom from his daughter, the goddess Athena.

The Owl was Athena's favorite bird. The owl denotes intellect and instincts, which must operate together to overcome obscurity. Athena and Poseidon fought for the city of Athens. The deity who provided the people a "useful gift" would acquire control of the city. Poseidon smote the ground with his spear, causing a stream of salt water to come up, allowing only males to conduct physical labor. Athena, who was the wisest at the time, grew the Olive tree, which favored both men and women. The city then picked Athena as the city's patroness that would eventually become known as Athens.

Poseidon, unwilling to acknowledge failure, challenged the goddess to a fight. With no trepidation in her heart, Athena rose to the challenge to confront the sea god. Poseidon was the god of the seas, representing emotions, while Athena was the goddess of knowledge, representing reason... That is, the symbolism of logic vs. passion when they clash.

Ares, the god of war, was similarly despised by the goddess because he enjoyed bloodshed. Athena would always challenge Ares in battles. For example, Ares was impetuous, but Athena was methodical. Additionally, the goddesses Hera and Aphrodite competed to distinguish the most beautiful goddess Athena. She attempted to influence the judge in this case by offering him the virtue of knowledge and war success.

But, having lost the challenge to Aphrodite for vengeance, Athena, together with Hera, demolished the city of Troy using only logic and deception.

Light:

- ✓ Independent, autonomous, focused
- ✓ Decisive
- ✓ Defined objectives
- ✓ Courageous and daring; knows how to face challenges
- ✓ Problem solver
- ✓ Logical, intelligent, and insightful
- ✓ Sense of reality, clarity, and transparency of thought
- ✓ Triumphant
- ✓ Change driver
- ✓ Leader
- ✓ Resilient and dedicated

Shadow:

- ✓ Cold-hearted

- ✓ Manipulative
- ✓ Corrupt
- ✓ Arrogant
- ✓ Elitist

8. Artemis

Individuality, independence, freedom

Artemis is a strong and independent woman who bravely accomplishes her dreams in a difficult environment.

Artemis is a feminine archetype that inspires a woman to act independently, have an identity and a zest for life, and experience wholeness and competence. The goddess was the twin sister of Apollo and the daughter of Zeus and Leto. The Romans called her Diana.

Artemis 'mother was pursued by the terrifying serpent Python and wandered the earth searching for a secure place to give birth after a high-risk pregnancy.

Light in the Darkness

After nine days of excruciating suffering, clutching to a palm branch in the dead of night, the goddess Artemis was born, bringing the uniqueness we all possess. Our freedom and place in society, to have our viewpoint, and to be is given birth.

The goddess had already demonstrated her skills shortly after her birth. She assisted her mother in the birthing of her sibling at the time. In this sense, the goddess's stance demonstrates that action is the only tool that can carry the vision to life. It is undoubtedly the desire to complete tasks. Apollo is born second, giving light and consciousness to the world.

Artemis was so appalled by what unfolded for her mother, Leto, that she petitioned Zeus to grant her father the gift of eternal virginity. She wields a bow and arrow, just like her brother Apollo, implying vision, determination, and dedication in the quest for her ambitions. She conspired with Apollo to murder

Niobe's children, who had offended their mother. Agamemnon made sacrifices to all the gods during the Trojan War, but he omitted her. Artemis was so offended that she blocked the winds from blowing the ships away from Troy.

Artemis not only despised Hera for what she did to Leto, but she also refused to obey Aphrodite's laws. Because they were self-sufficient gods, Athena, Artemis, and Hestia frequently clashed with the goddess Aphrodite on Olympus. She killed Actaeon for seeing her naked during her bath. She was brave and vindictive, stern and brutal.

The Archetype of the Myth

Artemis was far from a helpless victim. Her valor persevered in every situation to protect her from any scenario. She assassinated the Allodia, two brazen giants who had attempted to rape her, and she was courageous enough to set up a trap to murder them.

Artemis accidentally murdered Orion by shooting her arrow through his head. This exemplifies the impulsive behavior associated with the goddess Artemis archetype. The more "wild" Artemis was, the less of a mother figure she became (and vice versa). However, her more nurturing side is evident in stories where she takes on the role of protecting and nurturing others. She may be protective of women and children, especially when they are in danger.

The "unconscious" side of Artemis 'personality is represented by an arrowhead, while the "conscious" side is a diamond. The two aspects of her personality are in constant battle with each other. Artemis can either be one or the other depending on the circumstances and events of her life at any given time and the state of mind of those around her at that time (including her inner circle). Artemis also has dual personalities within herself, which make up the internal struggle between the conscious and unconscious sides of her psyche

Those who resonate with Artemis believe they are alive

cause of constant motion. Those who do not resonate with Artemis equate their life to death or invite the sense of victimhood, which Artemis would never accept.

While many people might consider relaxing, going on a vacation to discover the best answers, sacrificing, or waiting to see what happens at a time of difficulties, global crises, or calamities, the Artemis person is the one who never ceases. She always seeks answers, creates initiatives, and forges her path.

The Artemis archetype is about more than simply momentum. Every silver arrow launched by this precise archer's bow has a reason, a cause, and an intention. Artemis 'archetype then harvests the will, perseverance, and resilience to achieve her purpose or die trying for herself and those she loves.

Artemis archetype inspires us to take action in our lives because we understand that we cannot wait for things to get better; we must be proactive and make changes that help us reach our goals today and tomorrow as well as build upon them for generations to come by making it better for ourselves and those around us, as well as giving back to society through philanthropy and volunteerism when possible!

Artemis is all about moving forward with the times and not standing still as many other archetypes have done throughout history.

Light:

- ✓ Free and independent
- ✓ Self-confident, firm, and decisive
- ✓ Copes alone
- ✓ Sense of justice
- ✓ Naturalist
- ✓ Environmentalist
- ✓ Humanitarian
- ✓ Successful
- ✓ Complicity between women
- ✓ Objective, persevering, and persistent

✓ Focused
✓ Courageous
✓ Pragmatist
✓ Health-conscious

Shadow:

✓ Impulsive
✓ Lonely
✓ Selfish

Most actions are based on the emotions

9. Medusa

Resilience, strength, power, protection

The story of Medusa is one of the best known in Greek mythology. In the legend, the terrible gorgon with serpent hair and petrifying eyes is decapitated by the hero Perseus and used as a war weapon. Anyone who has seen the film Percy Jackson and Clash of the Titans is well familiar with the scene, reproduced at length, about the dangers of confronting the gorgon.

Priestess of Athena

Before turning into a monster, Medusa lived with her sisters in the temple of Athena, the goddess of war and wisdom. According to the Greek poet Hesiod, who wrote between 750 and 650 BC, Medusa was a beautiful woman with elegant features and enviable hair. Daughter of the marine deities Phorcys and Ceto and sister of Steno and Euryale, Medusa was the only mortal in the family. She respected the teachings of Athena, remaining a virgin and chaste to continue to exercise the priesthood.

However, Medusa's beauty attracted men from many cities. These men came to the temple not to make offerings but to observe her, which infuriated the goddess. One of these men was the god Poseidon, Athena's uncle, who never got along with his niece. The land of Attica was disputed by two gods in legends about the birth of Athens, and it was up to the populace to pick which deity would be the patron of the place, that is, the one who bestowed the most valuable gift on the inhabitants.

Poseidon created a water source, and Athena provided an olive seedling, useful for making olive oil. The city then named her the local patroness, which sparked a family feud between the two gods.

Obsessive Poseidon

Poseidon was aware that Athena's priestesses should be pure, but that didn't stop him from courting the beautiful Medusa, who constantly evaded. Tired of denials and dominated by passion, the god of the seas decided to rape the priestess inside the temple and in front of the statue of Athena, who, furious, chose to punish her.

The Curse

By violating her temple, Athena turned Medusa into a terrible monster. Her hair turned into snakes, her body grew scales, and her teeth were transformed into boar tusks. And the worst: the curse determined that all who looked at her would turn to stone, which condemned Medusa to terrible loneliness. Expelled from the temple, the three sisters took refuge in a cave in the far east of Greece, where they could live without major conflicts - until the warriors of Greece came to visit the place to confront her and take her head as a weapon.

One of them was Perseus, a young demigod forced by the king of the island of Cycads to decapitate the monster. If Perseus didn't, his mother would have been raped by the king. Asking the gods for help, the young man received gifts that helped him in the endeavor, such as a helmet that made him invisible and a beautiful sword. With these aids, Medusa, who had already been raped, cursed, and later beheaded.

When the hero Perseus defeated Medusa, a drop of her blood came into contact with the water, and a great thunderclap was heard. Then a white foam appeared on the water, and a beautiful white horse with wings emerged - it was Pegasus, son of the relationship between Poseidon and Medusa. Yes, the goddess's rape in the temple had spawned a pregnancy. In addition to Pegasus, the giant Chryseis also emerged due to the relationship between the two.

Experience the Myth as an Archetype

Athena is the goddess of wisdom. Remember that everything is within you, desecration, wisdom, curse, everything was built from within you. You are Perseus, the hero. Perseus received a mission because the goddess of wisdom punished Medusa. The punishment caused Medusa's hair to turn into snakes, and her eyes stoned everyone that faced her. Consequently, someone had to defeat Medusa.

Perseus received an extremely difficult mission; killing someone you could not look at was no easy task. Perseus received a shield and sword from Athena. She guided the hand of Perseus when he cut Medusa's head off. He won the battle only because the wisdom represented by Athena guided his hand. Perseus did not let himself be guided by anything else than Athena.

Perseus could have been stopped from moving past Medusa's ability to stone anyone who looked at her, limiting Perseus's progression of beheading Medusa. However, wisdom (Athena's guidance) allowed Perseus to progress from the stoning thoughts Medusa would have brought had he looked at her.

Now, what does it mean to be stoned or to have stoning thoughts? Well, because of the common parlance and comprehension of the words "stoned" and "straight," the non-materialist, non-intellectual mechanism of perspective is referred to as "stoned thinking." Stoned thinking depends on hunches, probabilistic logic determined by direct encounters, and intellectuality. In simpler terms, stoned thoughts are mostly the beliefs that limit us, our irrational fears of the unknown and uncertain, or any notion that hinders our pursuit of progress.

Stoned thoughts prevent us from moving, walking, and growing. These thoughts are concrete, limiting us from moving past them. Do you have any thoughts on that stone? Or do you have thoughts that prevent you from moving forward?

For example, some people think, "If I don't commit to anything, I will be free." This thought comes from someone completely enslaved like Medusa through their stone thoughts. If we make an analogy, the only thing that saves us from collective is our ideals, choices, and dreams.

When a person devotes himself to his dreams, he liberates himself since dreams point us on one path rather than allowing us to be thrown in other directions. Those who do not commit to themselves, humanity, family, or dreams, on the other hand, are those who do not live but merely exist. They go through life mechanically, performing a narrow set of tasks predetermined by their genes and environment but have no inherent meaning for them whatsoever.

Another example of stoned thinking is, "If I'm not with people physically around me most of the time, it means I don't love them." Clinging to people makes us more dependent and a slave to passing desires. The human mind is a very sensitive instrument, which the emotions of others can easily influence. Since it's an essential part of who we are, other people's emotions significantly impact how we feel about ourselves.

Many people have become victims of their success or have been held back by a lack of success because they aren't aware of what they want in life and what they need to do to achieve it. Such people are unaware that they may take charge of their life by removing themselves from the influences and ideas of others about who they should be and what they should be doing, thinking, saying, and believing. To do so, one must learn about themselves, their goals, and ambitions to use these things to better themselves.

There is nothing better than learning to become a better person, gaining wisdom, and using this to bless others. Wasting time having fun is good, but remember that fun alone won't do anything for people around you. Whereas lessons that made you a better version of yourself can work as a guiding light for others.

Plato once said, "People are like dirt. They can either nourish you and help you grow as a person, or they can stunt your growth and make you wilt and die." The same goes for our relationships with other people, and that's why we have to learn how to take care of ourselves before we expect anyone else to do so for us. It's up to you whether you want to be in their presence and allow them to affect you.

Do not meet people with the idea of pleasing them. Like Perseus, we are all given a choice to reach our goals or let the people we stumble into on our path stone us. It is up to us if we choose wisdom and guidance in the form of self-awareness and ambitions so we do not falter in our path. The only way to defeat Medusa's stony hair is the hand of wisdom.

You are rewarded with guidance and self-nourishment when you cut through any limiting beliefs, thoughts, self-doubts, and fears. Look back at Medusa's example. As soon as the head was cut off, a Pegasus was born from the foam of the waters. It was a white horse with wings to fly. Similarly, you can create flight, wings to soar high to guide you through life when you cut through any stoning thoughts.

Light:

- ✓ Resilience
- ✓ Protection
- ✓ Knowledge
- ✓ Conscience elevation

Shadow:

- ✓ Fury
- ✓ Fear
- ✓ Stagnant

10. Hestia

*Inner strength, female power, transmutation, faith,
confidence, self-knowledge*

Hestia is the goddess of fire in the home. The first step toward healing your body is recognizing it as a temple of the Spirit. Our body requires care and protection just like any other living creature—and, like you, it has its spirit or consciousness that exists outside of this physical world but is inextricably linked to it through the power of love and light.

Our bodies are a part of nature in its entirety, and we must live in harmony with all aspects of nature if we are to maintain a sense of balance within ourselves, society, and the world at large; this is the foundation for our health and happiness, allowing us to reach beyond the limitations of our daily lives into the realm of true freedom and fulfillment—the realm of spiritual life itself! We must be free of the tyranny of fear and anxiety to achieve our potential as human beings completely. We must become aware of and actively connect with the power of love and pleasure inside each of us.

It is precisely this inner fire that gives you security and self-confidence. This same fire brings peace, order, and energy to you and whoever is by your side. As a result, Hestia learned that she could know why things were happening around her by looking within herself.

Hestia was the daughter of Cronos and Rhea; of the six brothers, she was the eldest. After being swallowed and Zeus saving them, she was the last to emerge from within Kronos. However, it seems she didn't like leaving Kronos. Hestia asked Zeus for the privilege of being a virgin forever.

In short, Hestia became a housewife who took care of Olympus. All gods need Hestia. She is a fundamental presence in the lives of all gods, bringing inwardness and insights into their lives. Hestia appeared very little, with a veil on her head and discreet. Therefore, she did not participate in the quarrels and intrigues of the gods. Hestia is that peaceful goddess who wants peace.

Hestia was always described as quiet, gentle, peaceful, serene, reserved, dignified, and balanced. Athena and Artemis could hardly have had these qualities. Hestia's power was silent, as all honors and prayers were offered to her first. Beautiful, like all the other goddesses, Hestia didn't get emotionally involved with anyone. However, once Priapus tried to rape her. A donkey started screaming, waking everyone up, and letting Hestia escape in time. As a result of being away from sex, she lived outside the norm.

Hestia became the family's strength and a never-ending source of warmth and the focus of life, its core. Hestia represents the inner experience. It's your inner fire that keeps you going.

Light:

- ✓ Observant
- ✓ Reserved
- ✓ Introvert
- ✓ Warm
- ✓ Wise
- ✓ Reflective
- ✓ Rational
- ✓ Steadfast
- ✓ Quiet
- ✓ Intuitive
- ✓ Imaginative
- ✓ Harmonious
- ✓ Cultivate solitude
- ✓ Peace and harmony

Shadow:

- ✓ Reclusive
- ✓ Unambitious
- ✓ Inhibited
- ✓ Lack of communication skills
- ✓ Low emotional and physical vitality
- ✓ Reluctant
- ✓ Apathetic
- ✓ Prefer anonymity
- ✓ Anxious
- ✓ Sedentary lifestyle and lack of interest in the health of the body.

11. Hera - The Queen

Loyalty, partnership, queen, regality, kindship

The goddess Hera symbolizes the feminine archetype of the wife and companion. This is the archetype of the woman who wants to get married, who has no goals of her own, precisely because her focus is on her partner, so she wants to help her spouse achieve success in life.

The goddess Hera's feminine archetype sees marriage as a life success first and foremost. Hera, unlike Athena, Artemis, and Hestia - who are independent deities to do whatever they want, whenever they want, without the need for a companion - felt lonely without a spouse by her side. In other words, Hera's focus was mainly on her partner and not on herself.

Hera is the type of woman who follows her husband's every move, treating his career growth as her own. The goddess Hera, daughter of Cronos and Rhea, sister and wife of Zeus, became the queen of all the gods and mistress of Earth and Sky despite all her infidelity. When the other gods come together, she is respected equally with Zeus.

Despite all the lovers of Zeus, only the goddess Hera can sit beside him on the golden throne of Olympus, bearing a royal scepter. However, Hera will never be able to have full power over her husband completely. Zeus was always a womanizer, and he managed to deceive the goddess several times to have his extra-marital affairs with other goddesses, nymphs, and even mortals.

Zeus 'infidelity was the great pain of the goddess Hera, a wound that brought a lot of emotional suffering and impotence in the face of betrayals. As a result, her psyche was seriously un-balanced. Hera was extremely beautiful and intelligent but jeal-ous, vengeful, and violent. In such a way that to punish the lovers and harm the bastard children of Zeus, she created all kinds of intrigues and punishments possible.

Additionally, Hera's hatred was not just for the betrayal of her husband Zeus; her anger was for the fact that she didn't want to lose her power or position as queen. Hera hated Athena because Zeus gave birth to a daughter without her help. In the same way, he hated Aphrodite for being a seductress and for having lost the beauty contest to the goddess of love.

Hera was always vigilant about her husband. She had great power for observation and seeing between the lines. Zeus would always represent creation, which was why Zeus couldn't be faithful to Hera. He needed to have that bunch of kids, as the power of creation was in his hands. Alternatively, by analogy, Hera means fruitfulness and dedication to strengthen the whole work of creation.

Everything that is created needs protection and dedication. That's why Hera is the one who takes care of and protects so that everything prospers and the conquests are consolidated.

The planet we live on needs to be protected from any nega-tive energies or influences leading to problems such as health issues. The same applies to a relationship. If your partner feels neglected, they will not feel fulfilled in their lives, which leads to unhealthy situations.

When you do not take good care of yourself and the people around you, nothing is left for anyone else. It is a vicious circle that cannot be broken until one person starts changing.

Light:

- ✓ Confidence
- ✓ Rational
- ✓ Morals and ethics
- ✓ Loving
- ✓ Dedicated
- ✓ Values relationships
- ✓ Upholds family values
- ✓ Team-spirited - knows how to make partnerships
- ✓ Distinguished, respectable, and sober
- ✓ Communicative
- ✓ Sociable
- ✓ Authoritative and commanding
- ✓ Polite, disciplined, and rigorous
- ✓ Faithful and loyal
- ✓ Harmonize relationships
- ✓ Persuasive

Shadow:

- ✓ Selfish
- ✓ Lack of aspirations
- ✓ People pleaser
- ✓ Low sexuality and sensuality
- ✓ Jealous, vindictive, and possessive
- ✓ Obsessive and controlling
- ✓ Tyrant
- ✓ Fragmental sense of self
- ✓ Needy to being honored in relationship
- ✓ Perfectionist
- ✓ Competitive

12. Demeter

The mother, fertility, unconditional love,
affection, creation, realization

This archetype inspires and stimulates a woman, whether physically, psychologically, spiritually, or via pregnancy. This mother archetype nourishes and relishes in providing for and feeding her offspring, whether biological or not.

Demeter was a sister of Zeus who, after defeating the Titans and establishing himself as king of the gods on Olympus, named Demeter as the goddess of agriculture, giving her the power to take care of the Earth so that it would bear fruit and that there would be food for both humans and the animals.

This decision of Zeus was wise and right. No one on Olympus loved and cared for the plains, animals, and humans as passionately as Demeter. She was willing to do this difficult task. Demeter, the goddess of seeds, fertilized the Earth and soon made the fields green and abundant with fruit.

In those times, humans did not know how to cultivate land. They lived like wild animals fighting each other in hopes of survival. And it was the goddess Demeter who helped them and taught them how to cultivate the land and create their luck.

The goddess was grieved and went into severe despair shortly after her daughter Persephone was abducted by the god Hades. She deserted her duties and ceased performing and producing. As a result of Demeter's great sorrow over her daughter's kidnapping, the countryside became barren and lifeless.

Demeter used to be a goddess who had a cool and collected demeanor amid daily tumult and understood how to solve all difficulties properly. Her heart was filled with anguish, and then everything on Earth began to resemble a desert. Sadness is typically the feeling created to inform us that something is wrong in our lives and to point us on the proper route.

The Demeter archetype is the earth element linked to creation, achievement, and action. In this way, Demeter and Persephone were responsible for the seeds, and they depended on the flowering, the fruits, and the well-being of the collectivity.

Every desire, in the beginning, is still a seed. This seed is inside you, under the ground for a while, then you water it, giving it form inside, preparing the Earth, and fertilizing it with the available materials.

The actions of both made the seeds grow and prosper. In conclusion, when you have the right attitude and tools, what you want to bring to life manifests itself.

Light:

- ✓ Sensible
- ✓ Motherly affection
- ✓ Nurturer
- ✓ Loves selflessly
- ✓ Calm, sensible, and patient
- ✓ Doer
- ✓ Experienced
- ✓ Achiever
- ✓ Resourceful
- ✓ Inspirational
- ✓ Confident
- ✓ Amiable
- ✓ Caring

Shadow:

- ✓ People pleaser
- ✓ Acquiescent
- ✓ Lack of insight
- ✓ Uncontrollable desire to be a mother
- ✓ Lack of purpose
- ✓ Overprotective
- ✓ Stubborn
- ✓ Alexithymia

- ✓ Obstinate
- ✓ Reckless

Chapter 11

Spiritual Archetype

"Complete surrender to God unveils the truth. Nothing is hidden; only the ego is blind. Reality lies just beyond the mind. Out of the fear of becoming nothing, consciousness."

- David R. Hawkins

Spiritual enlightenment may seem like the hardest thing to reach, but that's not the case. Reaching the tree of life means moving forward from one stage to the next stage of consciousness.

David R Hawkins was a psychiatrist and pioneer in the evolution of consciousness. He dedicated his life to healing people physically, mentally, and spiritually. David Hawkins performed selfless work internationally, providing clinical care, lecturing, and writing books that inspire people on the path of self-healing and spiritual enlightenment.

The knowledge required to overcome this level of self-enlightenment, according to David Hawkin, is Divine Love, which is non-linear and devoid of a subject, object, form, or conditionality, and the Void's mistake is to deny even Divine Love by conflating it with the love of the human egoist state of possession. It is the constant exchange of effort for delivery.

Enlightenment is a continuous surrender to the Divine, something greater, Buddhahood or Christ consciousness; it doesn't matter, for they are all the same. Spiritual Enlightenment is Presence. Presence is not the absence of thought but detachment from mental phenomena like thoughts, ideas, opinions, judgment, emotions, and any other distractions from the ego.

Enlightenment is the state of not believing in the mind, which deconstructs the belief that we are our minds or bodies. Enlightenment offers us the ability to accept what is in front of us at any given time and the ability to observe rather than judge.

The power of observation is perception, commitment to presence, focus on the essence, flow, seeking the truth, self-honesty, reality, acceptance, and surrender, focus on the journey, unification, and understanding.

Otherwise, the shadow of judgment is the notion of what it is or will be, consistent with the past, content-focused, violent, elusive, self-deceptive, frustrated, resistance, and effort, concentration on destiny, separation, and condemnation.

Discernment is the experiment of knowing that we don't know anything. If we think we know, we are closed to learning the new, and without learning, there is no evolution.

There are several stages of enlightenment, as consciousness is constantly evolving.

According to the Buddha's descriptions, the earliest steps still occur in the realms of consciousness of Love and Unconditional Love:

1. **The Sotapanna Stage** is deemed to enter the flow when the measured level of gratitude reaches 510. The ego and the mind (Maya) belief in oneself as separate from the Whole, attachment to rituals, and doubt about the Way to God have all been broken by this entity (enlightenment).

This Being will be reborn a maximum of seven times to learn enough about Spiritual Enlightenment and leave Samsara, the continuous and uninterrupted cycle of physical births and deaths. Salvation through Jesus Christ is equivalent to a consciousness level of 540, or unconditional love within the Christian concept.

2. **The Sakadagami stage** is the second stage of Buddhist enlightenment. It corresponds to 570 levels of consciousness and is said to come back just once. Because it has already broken

three bonds, it weakens the bonds with two more: sensory cravings and evil intents. You'll only be reincarnated once more to clear your karmic debts.

3. **The Anagami stage** is the third stage of enlightenment. It is equivalent to the calibratable level of 600 or called the state of peace. This Being is considered not to return unless it is of Divine Will to guide humanity. This being permanently severed the first five mentioned ties and is no longer reborn in the realm of the senses; it is reborn in a formless paradise and becomes enlightened there.

At this stage, the Being becomes the observer and witness who intervenes in the world when summoned. There is no longer the need to do something to feed your pleasures, no matter how much the characteristic preferences of that human life remain because there is no need to be altered or set aside if they are of pure intention since the state is of full acceptance.

This level of consciousness is of great spiritual masters and saints like Laozi, Saint Francis of Assisi, S.N. Goenka, Alan Kardec, and Chico Xavier at the end of their lives when they were no longer teaching, among others.

In this third stage, Dr. David R. Hawkins explains that there is an evolution with differentiated characteristics to the level of consciousness of Self-Realization at 700. From this level and beyond, we meet the great spiritual prophets who dedicated their lives to saving humanity and taught us the basis of all the classical religions we know like Christianity, Islam, Judaism, Buddhism, Hinduism, etc.

The Grace of Being is described as ineffable (indescribable, nameless, and indivisible). At this level of consciousness, we find sages like Muhammad, Mahatma Gandhi, Mother Mary Teresa of Calcutta, Teresa of Ávila, Nisargadatta Maharaj, Ramana Maharshi, Master Dōgen Zenji, Adi Shankara, Adi Shankaracharya, Meister Eckehart, and others.

4. **The Arhat stage** is the fourth stage of enlightenment. After this stage of gratefulness, we find the much talked about and requested by Buddhist monks, the Arhat stage, which means

'the deserving one 'or 'the one who deserves Divine praises.'

This entity has broken the five lower bindings of the first three stages and the five subtle higher bonds: yearning for existence with subtle form (heavenly skies), craving for existence in the formless realms, conceptions, restlessness, and ignorance (colorable to level 800). You will never be reborn. It has gained Nirvana or Full Enlightenment and is still in the early stages of this state. This is the level of Nirvikalpa Samadhi in yoga when there are no remnants of the ego.

At these levels, the number of sages is uncommon (In the last 1,000 years, 50% of the time has passed without one of these beings.) Vedas, Upanishads, Shrimad Bhagavad Gita, Pali Canon, New Testament, and Zohar are among the same teachings, although originating in diverse countries, eras, and civilizations.

The great masters of this level and above and their teachings emanate extremely powerful fields of high-frequency energy into the collective consciousness of humanity.

At this level of consciousness, we find prophets and sages like Abraham, Moises, John Baptist, Huangbo Xiyun, and the 12 apostles of Jesus.

5. **Last Stage of Consciousness.** As the last possible state of consciousness to be awakened in the physical world, there is the level of Totality, which calibrates at 1,000. The last vestige of the collective ego disappears in the silence of the presence. This is the level of Divine envoys, or children of God, or Avatars, where we find Jesus Christ, Buddha, Krishna, and Zoroaster.

The totality of creation as Divinity emits immense perfection and beauty; the State's motto is "Gloria in Excelsis Deo." All these levels of consciousness are available to all human beings at all times and in all cultures.

1. Jesus Christ

*Perfection, enlightenment, peace, unconditional love,
transformation, transmutation, resurrection, unification,
spiritualism, and transcendence*

If we deeply analyze the life of Jesus, it is possible to perceive the influence of all archetypes in one.

Several witnesses attest to Jesus 'unification with God. For example, in John 10:30, it says, *"I and my Father are one."* and in John 10:36, *"What about the one whom the Father set apart as his very own and sent into the world? Why then do you accuse me of blasphemy because I said, 'I am God's Son'?"* When a person achieves a high level of consciousness, such as Jesus Christ, he realizes that everything is one, that all of the consciousness or archetypes that he desires are already inside him.

We can find any archetype in the life of Jesus. He ruled by the archetype of the rebel by going against all the teachings of that time by preaching love. He broke taboos by showing love, affection, and respect to the women of that time and confronting Pharisees and authorities by telling the truth. The master archetype ruled Jesus with the teachings and training given to the disciples.

Jesus was luminous; his presence was enough to captivate the attention of others. He was a wizard. Miracles and alteration of matter were works performed by Jesus that transformed water into wine, healed the sick, walked on water, calmed the storm, etc. He's also known as the Hero, the Mediator, and the Revolutionary, among other archetypes.

One of the most interesting archetypes that influenced Jesus was Detachment. I believe it was the hardest thing for people to let be influenced by him (detachment). I also believe it was the main basis of Jesus 'teaching to manifest miracles, which we also call "let it go," as the main key to wisdom and proof of faith.

One of the most expressive texts is found in the book of Matthew 6:31-34 *"So do not worry, saying, 'What shall we eat? 'or 'What shall we drink? 'or 'What shall we wear? 'For the pagans run after all these things, and your heavenly Father knows that you need them. But seek first his kingdom and his righteousness, and all these things will be given to you as well. Therefore, do not worry about tomorrow, for tomorrow will worry about itself. Each day has enough trouble of its own."*

In part, we can see what Jesus meant in the question, *"What shall we eat?"* He knows the essential needs of human survival, *"What shall we wear?"* He knows every human material needs, *"Heavenly Father knows that you need them."* Before human existence, God created everything so that humans would never miss anything.

"But seek first his kingdom and his righteousness, and all things will be given to you as well." Everything will be given to you by His grace. The Father wishes for everyone to be joyful. What exactly are you looking for? Do you want a house, boats, property, etc.? Fine, you may have it; the Father almighty has given you everything; He is the owner of galaxies, planets, and multiverses; He would never be concerned with material necessities, and neither should we. Because Father has everything, you may have everything because He is in you. Detachment is also referred to as trust because it is something that we cannot see but know is present.

For example, Thomas was one of Jesus 'disciples. After all, he witnessed what Jesus performed, but his refusal to believe in his resurrection demonstrates that he was enslaved to the material and intellectual world, which believes only in what can be seen. The book of John 20:29 says, *'Jesus saith unto him, Thomas, because thou hast seen me, thou hast believed: blessed are they that have not seen, and yet have believed."*

What makes you suppose someone is carrying a valuable stone in his clenched hands? Faith! If this individual opens his hands, your trust is instantly shattered since you can see, but you know and feel that something or someone is in there.

Why did Jesus use metaphors, tales, and symbols to teach? Because words that come from inside and inspire others to think about them are the best method to communicate with the soul. That is why most people could not grasp Jesus 'teachings and did not even try to stay still and think about it.

Poets, literature, and fiction are all examples of the unconscious mind connecting one soul to the souls of others.

For Jung, the Christ symbol is the most important symbol in psychology, and it is likely the most developed and distinct emblem of the Self, second only to the Buddha image. The breadth and richness of the predicates assigned to Christ, which correlate to the psychological phenomenology of the Self, can be used to judge this.

Jesus is the personification of the wholeness and interconnectedness of all things. It is vital to transform to achieve an evolved state of consciousness. When Jesus chose the disciples, for example, their names were altered, like Jesus becoming Christ, Siddhartha Gautama becoming Buddha, and Saul of Tarsus became Paul of Tarsus. When the ego is laid aside to become a servant of the Self or the spirit, the

No one can change a behavior or a habit if he doesn't change who he is. Jesus taught as an example in the book of Luke 9:23, *"Then he said to them all:* "Whoever wants to be my disciple must deny themselves and take up their cross daily and follow me." Why is it hard to deny ourselves?

Because the ego is attached to us as the cause of our individuality, it is part of our flesh. For the transformation to happen, a sacrifice must be made for the love of the Self, or perhaps through the path of pain.

Unconditional love is one of the main archetypes of Jesus. The book of Matthew 22:36-40 says, *"Teacher, which is the greatest commandment in the Law?" Jesus replied: "Love the Lord your God with all your heart and with all your soul and with all your mind. This is the first and greatest commandment. And the second is like it: 'Love your neighbor as yourself.' 'All the Law and the Prophets hang on these two commandments."*

We can imagine how difficult it was for Jesus to teach about love in those times. He lived in a time of terrible political strife, his works in Capernaum were doing well until he came back to the land of Nazareth, where persecution started. For those times, the term "love your neighbor as yourself" was the maximum level that could be said. But if we analyze the love of Jesus and everything he did, we can easily notice that he loved others more than himself. Later the book of John 13:34 says, *"A new command I give you: Love one another. As I have loved you, so you must love one another."*

In my experience, I felt a deep inner peace when I activated Jesus's archetype. Even if the whole world blows up, I would be still, and nothing in this world would take away my peace. Sometimes I imagine the great leaders that impacted the world with their jobs, some of them died doing their job. Jesus died to see everyone happy, prosper, and fulfilled.

John 14:12 says, *'Verily, verily, I say unto you, He that believeth on me, the works that I do shall he do also; and greater works than these shall he do; because I go unto my Father."*

Those leaders understood all of Jesus 'teachings, perhaps in different ways, but to the same point: when one reaches a higher level of consciousness, the fear of death fades away. I'm sure every leader knew what they were doing would result in death, but nothing could remove their inner peace. They understood that death is not the end but a new beginning in another world's plan where they await the next mission.

One of the most controversial and contentious sentences from Jesus, when he was dying, was written in Matthew 27:46 *"About three in the afternoon Jesus cried out in a loud voice, 'Eli, Eli,[a] lema sabachthani?"* (which means "My God, my God, why have you forsaken me?")

We infer that there is a problem with this phrase based on

reasoning. If you look at Jesus 'demeanor throughout his life, you'll see that he never said anything like that, even though he had a wonderful relationship with the Universe and nature. He would never complain about anything in a psychological or psychiatric examination. What exactly did he say? *"Father! How much do you glorify me?"* (Couto, Akhenaton, 2020)

Jesus knew after what he had done, dying the way he died, the message would reach generations, and everyone would know or hear about him. It worked! It finished! I won! Do you understand the difference? Do you separate weeds from wheat? Do you know what was written? Is it distorted? Or changed? Just read, and your intuition will respond to you. How do you feel when you read something like that? Jesus knew that God was doing the world's best thing for him and humanity.

After all, the love was rejected. John 3:19 says, *"And this is the condemnation, that the light has come into the world, and men loved darkness rather than light, because their deeds were evil."*

Jesus cried when he saw what was about to happen in Israel - destruction! In the year 70 b.c, the Romans invaded and destroyed, fulfilling Jesus's vision in Luke 21:5-6, *"Then, as some spoke of the temple, how it was adorned with beautiful stones and donations, He said, 6 "These things which you see—the days will come in which not one stone shall be left upon another that shall not be thrown down."*

Who decides to turn on the light? You are a person who lives in the light. Who wants to be in the dark? You dwell in the dark. This isn't a punishment; it's an electromagnet camp for everyone. Similar people attract other similar people. Throughout his sermons, Jesus attempted to explain many times, but rejecting love explains the evil due to the lack of love, good, light, and peace.

2. Buddha

Prosperity, transcendence, enlightenment, spiritual awakening, detachment, positivity, self-knowledge, inner peace, and abundance

The term Buddha does not exactly refer to a God but to a state of consciousness, and whoever attains this superior condition understands the true essence of life and can teach it to men. According to certain schools of thought, the Buddhas appear to teach dharma, which is Sanskrit for "universal law" or "ethics."

Siddhartha Gautama, born in 556 BC in Kapilavastu, the capital of a small kingdom near the Himalayas on the present-day Nepalese border, was an example of a Buddha. Siddhartha, the son of King Suddhodana, was trained as a guerrilla to be the heir to his father's realm.

Siddhartha studied with the best tutors, practiced sports and martial arts, and was gifted with unique intelligence. His life was filled with riches and comforts, but when he left the palace and was confronted with poverty, illness, and death, he became restless and wanted to comprehend human suffering.

Against his father's wishes, at the age of 29, Siddhartha decided to leave the palace. He set out to find the wisdom to release man from pain and provide him peace. For six years, Siddhartha traveled around his country looking for spiritual masters and meditation practices.

Siddhartha became a disciple of ascetics, who believed that abstaining from psychological and physical pleasures was the way to find emotional development and balance. Siddhartha practiced asceticism with great discipline for six years.

Asceticism preached severe fasts, and during one of these periods without food, Siddhartha went to a river to purify himself and fainted. A woman offered him food and his fellow ascetics, seeing Siddhartha eating, believed that he had betrayed their principles and abandoned him.

On a walk along the banks of a river in northeast India, the pilgrim prince spotted a fig tree and leaned back to meditate. Sitting under the treetop, he promised not to move until he found the Supreme Wisdom Pragya - in Sanskrit. The concept of Pragya does not relate to a logical or intellectual pursuit, nor does it refer to information obtained from the literature.

This is a knowledge that goes beyond the capabilities of the ordinary mind and is linked to the Universal Mind, something like the creative principle of everything, the Cosmic Soul, the primordial source, or God. Whoever understands Pragya becomes unique with this generating force of things and knows the fundamental truth of life. Buddhist tradition calls this nirvana. A condition of maximum freedom, in which sufferings (dukkha) are extinguished, and the adept attains enlightenment.

At 35 years old, Siddharta still hadn't reached that level of consciousness, but he carried within him the uncontainable urge to achieve it. So, he crossed his legs in a lotus position, closed his eyes, and began a silent journey towards the depths of himself.

There is a staunch enemy of every candidate for enlightenment: Mara, the demon who rules the realm of illusions. To reach full wisdom, it is necessary to leave Mara's territories. However, this demon does not let us climb its walls with ease. Mara is made up of fears, temptations, doubts, greed, and ignorance, among other imperfections. Strictly speaking, Mara is similar to the concept of the Ego, described by the psychoanalyst Sigmund Freud as the conscious part of the mind.

Some sources say that Siddhartha reached a state of omniscience by transcending his mind, and understanding all the plots that sustain human existence. From then on, Siddhartha began to introduce himself as Buddha - The Awakened One - and began his teaching path. Siddhartha had the talent to carve his name out of history.

Buddha is a great archetype for self-knowledge. In my experience, the only way to manifest our goals and dreams, release pain and suffering, and attract good results is to look inside and heal the shadows. Rather than believing in love manifestation through thoughts, I must first accept it without resistance, live the love, enter the unconscious world, and get close to the Father, God, Universe, or whatever name we choose to call it.

3. Akhenaten

"My God is Aton."

- Akhenaten

A psychic Helio Couto presented his narrative through canalization. "The city where Akhenaten reigned was not an ordinary place 3300 years ago. The city was like a temple; there was no suffering, and it appeared to be a paradise on Earth. The greatest scientists, sages, sculptors, and writers went to Amarna to minister seminars and scientific lectures.

Amarna was a suburban city with water features, plants, geese, birds, and gardens all over the place. The city contained benches where people might sit, relax, and gaze at Aton and other necessities of existence. Akhenaten worked on pedagogy, books, and all the supplies needed for Egyptian children to learn to read and write.

In Pharaoh's times, people liked big things, but the goal was always to serve Aton. Thus, it was necessary to show the grandeur of the concept. There were three 2624.67-foot-long hanging gardens in the palace. It was also the principal temple of Aton, measuring 656.168 x 164.042 feet. The temple was an open place with no statues or physical objects, just an open space for meditation and connecting with the universe.

Why did people not use statues or anything physical to worship Aten during the Pharaonic period? That's because the name 'Sun 'has archetypal meanings of light, brightness, lighting, vitality, and so on, and Akhenaten recognized that he was within everyone.

Akhenaten attempted to explain the presence of only one God and single energy; the notion was philosophical. Thus it was not a star in the Solar System. It was the only way he could shift the paradigm and introduce polytheism, but other skeptics wanted to keep believing in Amun and claimed that Akhenaten was trying to replace one deity with another, and it was also difficult to give gifts to the sun.

For those who live in darkness, killing men who strive for the light has always been the preferred method of blocking progression. It was enough to smear a woman's image and ruin her reputation, as happened with Marilyn Monroe. Deluca, Akhenaten's father's second wife, taught Aton, the Universe. The priests were aware of the threat this posed. What influence did the negatives have? Deluca and her son were slain and thrown into the river. The story's beginning ended in tragedy.

The negatives continued to ruin society by bribing individuals to turn against Aton until it was impossible to live with them any longer. The struggle against Akhenaten and everything he intended to accomplish was well-known. Akhenaten attempted to alter people's perceptions by demonstrating that they were all brothers and sisters." (Couto, Akhenaton, 2020)

What people from darkness don't understand is that there is no possibility of stopping God. The light side has strength, just like the dark side has its strength. Only God has the power as He is the owner of all the galaxies that exist. Akhenaten was like Jesus; he cared about people of any social class and treated them like brothers and sisters. Akhenaten radiated pure love all the time.

Many people wanted Akhenaten to start a War against the worshipers of Amun, but he was reluctant because he understood all about the electromagnetic field. What you emit comes back to you sooner or later. That's why Jesus said in Luke 6:29, "If someone slaps you on one cheek, turn to them the other also. If someone takes your coat, do not withhold your shirt from them." You don't have to pay back or become one of them, but you can stop someone else's hand without being angry or resentful, right?

Because it was Jesus laboring in Akhenaten's heart as an archetype, Akhenaten didn't have much of an option except to make peace. Akhenaten made it obvious that he was the forerunner in creating a setting for the arrival of the Lord Jesus; the day of Jesus 'birth had to be postponed if this development was halted.

Who ran Egypt with Akhenaten? The glorious Nefertari. She took care of everything and managed to run an empire's bureaucratic part.

Akhenaten didn't think about anything other than Aton. He thought about how to spread it, how to make people understand. This caused Akhenaten to become distant from the social world. He was fused with God and no longer had to worry about the concerns of this world, such as what clothing to wear or what to eat. None of this mattered. Why should it anyway? Don't we dress up because we have to, eat because we have to? Importantly, since Aton is well-versed in both, why should Akhenaten have bothered with worldly possessions when striving for the Divine?

Being spiritualized and ruling an empire like Akhenaten is not the same as being unified with God as a citizen. The activities of a leader who emits a low degree of consciousness or emits a negative frequency contract with one's interests and makes economic decisions that make people's life miserable and promote poverty. That is why a Christ figure must descend to teach love, a feeling that addresses all environmental, economic, social, health, and political issues.

After Akhenaten was poisoned, civil strife erupted in Egypt until the negatives retook control, slaughtered all of Aten's followers, gathered the remains, and tossed them into the desert for the vultures to feast on.

Imagine people who worship Aton with peace, love, and joy, and then an army invades the city and kills everyone who lives there in less than an hour. The emotional trauma that has been passed down through generations, causing their lives to crash and become imprisoned, is the leading cause of life stagnation; the only treatment is forgiveness and a fresh start to trauma.

Consequently, Akhenaten became the dictator, trying to impose a new god on Egypt. The negatives persecuted and tried to sabotage Akhenaten's teachings in many ways. The allies communicated, informing Amarna that there was a problem with the Hittites and that the negatives were being armed were destroyed before they reached Amarna. The situation was intolerable when the message eventually arrived.

Akhenaten was building another city in Syria and another in Nubia. Alas! Traitors were everywhere, and everything was made for money and business.

Akhenaten and Nefertari were a solar couple or two people who became one. If one person died, the entire process would have been disrupted. Nefertari was also poisoned; she was handed a package containing a poisoned rose, which she was to inhale. She died instantly as soon as she smelled it.

Nefertari oversaw the entire administrative procedure and brought Akhenaten's life to a close with passion and emotional harmony. Without her, it was nearly difficult to complete any endeavor; this is unconditional love, and comprehending this sensation allows one to comprehend what occurred when she died.

The hymns and praises to Aton were only of thanksgiving. Have you ever imagined any religion without supplication and request? Just giving thanks...a religion of gratitude? That is exactly what Akhenaten did, worshiping Aten and teaching love and peace to prepare the way for the Lord Jesus 'arrival. A psychic Helio Couto presented his narrative through canalization.

Akhenaten was a living example of a spiritualized politician who was united with God, and if all leaders from all nations were like him, the earth would undoubtedly be a Paradise on Earth.

4. Sacred Geometry

*Expanding awareness, spiritual evolution,
manifestation, and harmony*

Many teachings have described sacred geometry as the blueprint of creation and genesis, the origin of all forms. Sacred geometry is considered an ancient science that explores and explains the energy patterns that create and unify all things and reveals how the energy of creation organizes itself. It is said that every natural pattern of growth or movement returns to one or more geometric shapes.

It is believed that the ancients considered the experience of Sacred Geometry to be essential for the education of the soul. They knew that these patterns and codes symbolized our inner realm and were significant for higher consciousness and self-awareness. Sacred geometry amplifies our connection to spirit and creates harmony within us, between us and the outside world.

Ancient cultures that studied these patterns believed the patterns were repeated throughout the universe. Today scientific studies show that sacred geometry reproduces the molecular structure that forms the basis of all life in the universe.

The sacred geometry can improve your life! Sacred geometry brings certain healing, harmonizing, and rebalancing effects on all levels. It connects the internal and the external, uniting everything.

Understanding energies that intervene in any therapy such as chromatherapy, crystal therapy, Feng shui, or any other vibrational technique inevitably leads us to mathematical proportions, geometry, and quantum physics.

What is the biggest reference in the world of shapes? Nature. The natural world that surrounds us and to which we belong is closely related to the values of geometry and all the energy implications.

Every existing form contains in its formal field a hidden language. To learn this mysterious language of shapes, we need to understand the "mother of shapes," the basic patterns that give rise to all others, such as triangles, squares, pentagons, hexagons, heptagons, octagons, circles, etc.

Mystically, we can say that unlimited space is manifested through the symbolic language of geometry. God, the source of all things, the unified field, through the symbolism of forms and archetypes, manifests the true deep being, its creative power, and its modulating action of harmonious forms. This is one of the reasons why the adjective "sacred" is added to geometry, to incorporate psychic and metaphysical values into that technical geometry that we were taught in school, to give each pattern of geometry the value of an archetype related to our spirit and our psychic behavior.

Triangle - Platonic solids are considered the "building blocks" of the sacred geometry of the Universe that were taught in the Greek Mystery Schools 2,500 years ago. They are tetrahedron, hexahedron, octahedron, dodecahedron, and icosahedron. The triangle is an underlying symbol for all of them. The triangle symbolizes balance, harmony, and completion. Rising upwards, the triangle raises us to Higher Consciousness.

Circle - Wholeness, unity, endless circle/cycles of life, the eternal constant, cycles of change, unity, perfection, inclusive, limits. It is said that God's first thought is represented by a circle, which exists by itself and then creates a replica of itself.

Square - Foundations, solidity, grounding, practical, "ground," stability, reliability, security. The base of a pyramid creates balance/stability.

Cross (2 lines) - The intersection of two lines is where "heaven and earth" meet, and the result of their union is humanity (symbolized by the cross).

The Flower of Life - Is a physical representation of the connection to all living things in the universe. It is considered a sacred symbol universally and is said to contain within itself the "blueprint of creation," the "building blocks" of the universe - which we call the "Platonic Solids."

These are models through which the basis of life can be expressed. The Greek Mystery Schools 2,500 years ago taught that there were five perfect 3D shapes - the tetrahedron, hexahedron, octahedron, dodecahedron, and icosahedron.

These Platonic solids are considered the foundation of everything in the physical world, revealing the unity in all things. However, breaking these Platonic solids into their simplest forms will form the triangle, square, circle, spiral, and straight line.

A natural pattern is not merely an aesthetic arrangement of shapes; it has its mathematical properties, allowing us to observe the "perfect" laws governing our universe.

5. Eye

*Spirit, vision, activity, future, inner vision, divinity,
perception, vigilance, omnipresence, wisdom, penetration,
magic, and protection.*

The Eye of Horus is an ancient Egyptian symbol. It is very controversial. Different people have different interpretations of it, which is acceptable, because, as Carl Gustav Jung mentions in his sixth volume, "A symbol loses, so to speak, its magical force, or, if you like, its redemptive force, as soon as a solution is known."

The Eye of Horus is an Egyptian symbol that reproduces the open and righteous gaze of one of the Egyptian gods of mythology: the god Horus. This symbol, also known as "Udjat" and "Wedjat," means "whole eye."

The Eye of Horus represents the Sun (right eye) and the Moon (left eye), while the two eyes together (Udjat and Wedjat) symbolize the entire Universe and the forces of light. This concept resembles the symbol of Tao, Yin, and Yang, in which one is the Sun, the other the Moon, and together they form the forces of everything that exists in the universe.

Horus was considered the god of the heavens, son of Osiris and Isis, and had the head of a hawk. His eye has become a lucky charm that has been used since ancient times.

The right eye of Horus represents concrete information controlled by the left side of the brain. This side is responsible for understanding letters, words, and numbers and is more universe-oriented in a masculine way.

The left eye represents abstract information, is represented by the moon, and symbolizes a feminine side, with thoughts and feelings, intuition, and the ability to see a spiritual side.

The Eye of Horus is the exact graphic representation of the region of our brain that houses our pineal gland. In the symbol of the Eye, it is possible to find exactly the drawing of the Thalamus, the Corpus Callosum, the Hypothalamus, and the Medulla Oblongata.

The philosopher René Descartes associated the pineal gland with our spiritual side, and he even described it as the shelter of the soul. In other words, the pineal gland is a gateway to our Divine Spark. She is a third eye that helps us see beyond matter, beyond the physical, and connects us with the Divine that dwells within us. Our "divine self" sees through this "eye."

Do not confuse Horus's eye and the providence eye.

The providence eye in the dollar money represents God's eye upon human beings. The triangle symbolizes the Holy Trinity and the rays of divine power. It is a powerful reminder that the great architect of the Universe is always watching over human beings.

While the Eye of Horus is a liberating sign that connects us to the Divine inside us, the Eye of Providence is a castrating symbol that places the Divine on the outside, looking over us with a punishing stare. It shows that God or the Divine is within each one and puts responsibility in our hands.

"When the mind explores a symbol, it is led by ideas that are beyond the reach of our reason."

-Carl G Jung, Man and His Symbols

Turn off the keys of reason and immerse yourself in this dreamlike experience that is the Eye of Horus. Immerse yourself in understanding that the Divine is within you. There is no punishment!

6. Sun

Light, intelligence, life, fertility, resurrection, heat, justice, power, prosperity, success, and happiness.

The sun symbolizes the principle of vital energy, the creative force of life, and the will to live and express who you are. The sun gives you energy and the opportunity to shine and radiate who you are for the benefit of the other members of this wonderful community. The sun signifies the heart of our mission: to participate in the production of life and the expansion of consciousness so that we can make the contributions that are acceptable to the world.

The sun is a source of light and life in our solar system, providing heat and energy to planets. Our planet's life is dependent on the sun, which lies in the galaxy's center. The sun is a glowing rock that produces its own light. It is necessary for the survival of plants, animals, and humans. It keeps the planet's temperature stable so that it can be inhabited.

The sun is related to the Thalamus in mind, which, according to Indian yogi Paramahansa Yogananda, is a type of HD in humans. We associate the sun with the heart, the center of intrinsic wisdom that guides and reveals the truth, suggesting what is relevant to the soul, spirit, and mind.

The people of ancient Egypt worshiped Ra, the sun god. The ancient Greeks had in the sun the representation of the God Helios. In India, the God Indra was symbolized by the sun. In Babylonia, the God Shamash was associated with the sun. All these gods were related to balance, strength, and achievement.

The sun is connected with energy, life, strength, spiritual force, and rebirth in Christianity. Also connected to healing and happiness, the book of Psalm 30:5 says, *"For his anger lasts only a moment, but his favor lasts a lifetime; weeping may stay for the night, but rejoicing comes in the morning."*

The sun signifies the creative force that emanates and inspires from what is most true, authentic, and genuine in you. And having the bravery to follow the impulse of this spontaneous energy is the greatest act of love for yourself, others, and the world! How can I make something like this? Developing the understanding that the sun and its interactions in the birth chart show the path of what we need to assimilate into ourselves to progress.

7. Water

Purification, spiritual awakening, self-knowledge, deep memories, emotions, and prosperity.

Water is considered an archetype in literature, dreams, memories, etc., for birth, creation, resurrection, fertility, and growth.

The sea, for example, is associated with a mother figure - the protective amniotic fluid that surrounds the fetus. The island represents the mother figure, the sheltering uterus. Numerous myths and legends point to the importance of the water and islands in creating the world and culture. These images and depictions can be found across literature and art.

The sea, according to Jung, represents maternal, fruitful, and creative waters, as well as the unconscious. The sea or any wide expanse of water represents the unconscious in dreams or fancies. The water's maternal aspect corresponds with the nature of the unconscious in that the latter, particularly in man, can be understood as the mother, the matrix of the unconscious.

The water is also preexistence. This can be seen in the book of Genesis 1:2, which says, *"Now the earth was formless and empty, darkness was over the surface of the deep, and the Spirit of God was hovering over the waters."*

We can notice that water existed before the formation of the planet. What God did was divide the water into two parts as Genesis 1:6-8 says, *"And God said, "Let there be a vault between the waters to separate water from water." So, God made the vault and separated the water under the vault from the water above it. And it was so. God called the vault "sky." And there was evening, and there was morning—the second day."*

Science proved that our body is 70% water, and the whole planet has more water than Earth.

Baptism represents the rebirth of the spirit and purification, the water set slaves free with Moses as their leader, the flood during Noah's times(Genesis 7:11), God healed the Land when Elijah threw salt on the dirty water(2 Kings 2:19-21), Naaman healing (2 Kings 5:10), and the healing of the blind man John 9:7 are some examples.

The water is also where our deep memories live in the book of Micah 7:18-19 says, *"Who is a God like you, pardoning iniquity and passing over transgression for the remnant of his inheritance? He does not retain his anger forever because He delights in steadfast love. 19He will again have compassion on us; he will tread our iniquities underfoot. You will cast all our sins into the depths of the sea."*

If you watch any documentary about people who explore the oceans for a living, you will notice that there are many places in the ocean that the sun cannot reach because it is so deep. These areas are where our memories are, especially the shadows.

This experience is accessible to everybody! Place a cup of water near some derogatory music with lyrics, or try saying bad words with negative energy in the water. When viewed microscopically, the composition of water will change. If you freeze the water into ice blocks, you can see how the molecules change. Now think of it this way - if our bodies are 70% water, how does it react when we hear negative affirmation? Naturally, our brain will be affected physically too. Notice how your mood changes when you listen to awful music or fuel your mind with negative thoughts; you feel physically heavy as if a weight has been placed on your shoulders.

A good example of positive affirmations and water is when Jesus had a lot of energy and changed water into wine without becoming weary. The water is also the spirit of God. For example, we can find the story of the good Samaritan woman in John 4:14 *"Jesus said to her, "Everyone who drinks of this water will be thirsty again, but whoever drinks of the water that I will give him will never be thirsty again."*

Nicodemus in John 3:5, *"Jesus answered, "Very truly I tell you, no one can enter the kingdom of God unless they are born of water and the Spirit."* While the Good Samaritan asked, *"Give me this water so I will never get thirsty again."* Nicodemus said, *"How can this be?"*

Nicodemus was a wise man, while the Good Samaritan was just a simple woman, yet she felt the message.

That's why the bible says in 1 Corinthians 1:27, *"But God chose the foolish things of the world to shame the wise; God chose the weak things of the world to shame the strong."*

The water brings fulfillment to the spirit in Revelation 21:6 says, *"He said to me: "It is done. I am the Alpha and the Omega, the Beginning, and the End. To the thirsty, I will give water without cost from the spring of the water of life."*

The words of Jesus were very deep, not fiction or poetry, but something real. He was talking to their unconscious mind, soul, or spirit. I don't see differences because everything is linked and unified. But for anyone who believes in separation, Jesus 'words must be remembered as words of wisdom that may be unbelievable but are never refutable.

8. Flames

Twin flames, purification, transformation, transmutation, rebirth, sexuality, divinity, and regeneration. Fire is one of the four fundamental elements of defense and light.

Flames are not destructive fires. The unconscious recognizes this Sacred Fire as a sacred symbol associated with the Divine Holy Spirit and the Divine Rays. There are recordings in your mind and memory that point to the dharma's freedom, to the purification and redemption that this Flame signifies.

The mind is an "empty" space that mirrors the universe. The Violet Flame erases and dissolves the mistakes made by the children of God and transmutes depressive states into a happy and peaceful state of mind. It is magical and relieves physical, emotional, and mental pain.

The Violet Ray, like the God Rays, is a part of God's mind. As a result, it contains the Father's intellect and volition. The Violet Ray can tell what may and cannot be cleansed and transmuted into Light in the individual who invokes her.

The Violet Flame dispels delusion and ignorance, exposing divine Truth. Only by knowing the Truth can a man be set free.

Saint Germain brought the energy of love from the ruby pink ray, symbolizing the Holy Spirit. This is the age of justice, of liberation from the oppressed, of liberation through the truth, which comes with the transmutation of Karma through the correct use of the Violet Flame. The Violet Flame is the blending and union of love in service, the pink ray, and the power of blue ray justice, beginning an era of freedom, peace, and enlightenment.

The Violet Flame is high vibrating frequency energy that penetrates the atom's nucleus, flows through our cells, transmutes mental states, and regenerates aging or damaged cells. It is an action of the seventh ray of God's consciousness, an aspect of the Holy Spirit.

Flames are associated with twin souls when two people become one through love. In Christianity and Judaism, a couple becomes one in marriage when consumed via sex, known as the unification ritual. However, for certain spiritual beliefs, the unification begins when they meet again, which we know as love at first sight; once the soul was unified in previous lives, they will be unified forever.

Others conclude, "Not all energies, entities, or creatures desire to be twin flames." As a result, they have distinct travels than those engaging in this form of union. The energies you pick are drawn from the greatest levels of your consciousness to experience pure love or comprehend the universal laws that govern such a union.

Probably anyone who allows this archetype to influence their lives without resistance, a new paradigm and a new mind start to flow within them.

9. Tree

Expanding awareness, wisdom, unification of spirit and material worlds, mother, virility, love, relationships, protection, and the elevation of consciousness

Since ancient times, humankind's destiny has been associated with trees. Much evidence regarding severing the connection between humans and trees cannot be ignored. In the context of a tragic relationship between humans and nature through domination and perversity, we no longer can ignore the consequences of those world deforestation.

We can find ways to save our trees by starting to awaken our connection with them. The tree represents the connection with the world of matter. This is since its roots are connected with the earth element. On the other hand, the tree also signifies the connection with the spirit world, thus symbolizing the expansion of consciousness.

From the seed, the tree holds the full potential of becoming within itself. Some seeds even only "wake up" if they go through conditions such as drought, fire, and even the digestive tract of some animals. In this context, the tree only begins to become a tree if it goes through the waking process. The one who does not discover the conditions to awaken may never become a tree, despite its potential already existing.

During this process, the plant will need to develop environmental resilience to play a role in a broader system. Few trees can survive on their own; many require the presence of other trees, including other species, to live and, in certain situations, to assist the environment around them to grow more suitable for themselves and others. By removing leaves and decaying sections, the tree provides food to the soil and its micro fauna, converting the waste into food for the tree and its surroundings.

From birth to death, the tree performs photosynthesis as a fundamental process of its existence. The tree feeds on photosynthesis, which converts sunlight and mineral salts from the soil into food for its upkeep and growth. As a result, it forms a link between heaven and earth, causing natural elements to combine and produce life.

Another phenomenon that occurs as trees ascend to the sky is the depth of their roots. Large trees with shallow roots are bound to die young. The quest for roots in deep soils has two purposes: first, to anchor the tree to the earth so that its crown, which is taller and leafier, can endure the elements; and second, to find water and nourishment in deeper places. During this process, the roots frequently "mimic" the crown, taking on the same size and shape or, in some circumstances, becoming larger than the aerial section of the plant, allowing some species to survive even fire.

The tree takes in nutrients from the soil. Simultaneously, it absorbs sunlight and converts it into wood, leaves, flowers, and fruits, thus merging material and immaterial and changing them into substance. It eliminates carbon dioxide from the atmosphere and replaces it with oxygen. The tree is a living vehicle that allows itself and others to exist.

The tree represents life, cycles, work, our interaction with the environment, and the various stages. We must, like the tree, always seek our sacred self in the skies while also deepening our roots and seeking ourselves in the unconscious, remembering our history and the marks it leaves on us and building new meanings from it.

We must live life in its phases as trees live through the four seasons. There are times when we grow, blossom, bear fruit, and rest, but we must always seek to grow, learn from the environment and be this vehicle of constant exchange between heaven and earth, which provides a true expansion of consciousness.

"If you want to reach the skies,
your roots must reach the hell."

-Helio Couto

Tree of life

The tree of life has a lot of meanings. Some people believe it is a magical tree that must be found and touched to reach immortality. Since the bible was written, practically everyone has been trapped on the tree of knowledge due to this misconception.

In general, the Tree of Life climbs towards the sky with roots in the soil. Fulfilling the cycles of your life is a sign of the human being's ascent and growth via spiritual expansion, exploration, and learning, as well as his existence on Earth.

From the tree used as a symbol by the Assyrians, a people who dominated Mesopotamia derived the symbolic tree of each of the cultural vehicles such as Egyptian Mythology, Kabbalah, Bible, people of Babylon, and Islamic Religion.

The palm or branch represents the Tree of Life in Kabbalah and is a Jewish symbol. It is formed from Ain Soph's ten emanations, known as Sephiroth. These emanations appear in more dense layers on four separate planes that connect the ten sephiroth. The four layers are:

1. Atziluth, the World of Emanations – Kether Chokmah Binah
2. Beriah, the World of Creations – Chesed Geburah Tiphereth
3. Yetzirah, the World of Formations – Netzach Hod Yesod

4. Asiyah, the World of Actions – Malkuth

Trees, groves, and wildlife are emblems of life and protection adopted by Great Britain, Ireland monks (druids), and Gaul in Celtic Tradition.

The Persians thought that the Tree of Life carried immortality-granting resin.

In ancient traditions, the Scandinavians believe that the tree's roots store all knowledge and wisdom.

Irrespective of different cultural beliefs, one thing remains common - the tree is related to our psyche and the Holy Spirit in most cultures. For the psychoanalyst Carl Jung, the tree was an archetype, a symbol of our Self, Psych, and Unconsciousness.

If we analyze Genesis 2:9, we see that the tree of life and knowledge were in the same place. One offers immortality, and another offers death. The tree of life provided numerous advantages to Adam and Eve's consciousness. That was an archetype they were enlivened by, full of brightness, riches, immortality, control of the animals, and ownership of the grounds till the frequency dropped.

Eve was the first woman to fall. What was Adam doing when this happened? Walking, distracted, or busy? How many couples let something like this happen? The man was distracted as the woman talked to the snake in her head and looked at the shadows rather than the light. That's a metaphor; when Buddha extended awareness, he sat on a tree.

The tree is linked to two worlds, spiritual and material. It shows us that both sides are one, which is how to change everything for the worst or better. As soon as Adam and Eve were seduced by their own ego, the planet's energy changed. The effect was wild animals, physical changes, death, fatigue, natural disasters, etc.

If you believe in the tree of knowledge of good and evil, your life will be good and evil. Solomon showed an example in the book of Proverbs 11:30 *"The fruit of the righteous is a tree of life, and the one who is wise saves lives."*

In Revelation, we find a lot of passages about the tree of life. The change in many people's consciousness is happening, slower, but it is happening. Every bride must be prepared for the wedding, as every human being must be prepared to unify to the Whole, God, Universe, or any other name that can be called.

The Tree of Life has multiple branches, but they all seek and need light. The Tree of Life symbol is a metaphor for the expansion and growth of beings.

The following are teachings of the Tree of Life for each of us:

- Rise and renew yourself
- Live your mission
- Fructify through your gift
- Spread your seeds with your actions
- Feed from the earth with respect
- Be generous and grateful for what you receive from life
- Practice bestowal with the expression of love and magnification of wisdom through your existence.

The Tree of Life symbolizes our psyche and our spirituality in various mystical knowledge and science, such as Psychology, Philosophy, Astrology, Yoga, Kabbalah, Taoist Tai Chi, and Esotericism in general.

Nothing beats the earth's natural beauty. It is up to us only to admire, register, value, and preserve.

Chapter 12

Children Archetypes

As we learn different archetypes, the Children archetype is an important aspect we need to understand to help us develop a better version of ourselves. Archetypes are the most fundamental building blocks that make up our personalities and character traits as they represent our deepest inner selves with the help of our parents 'guidance during childhood development. It would be good if you could identify your personality, character traits, values, strengths and weaknesses, goals, etc., as it all comes from your archetype of childhood experiences you had with your parents and caregivers in your early developmental stages.

Children's archetypes are everywhere, from toys, cartoon movies, clothes, and playgrounds to theaters, theme parks, etc. All these archetypes are part of children's lives, forming personalities until adulthood.

Recently, raising and educating children has become a complicated mission to fulfill. The amount of information that adults and children receive in the brain because of technology results in a "mess" in emotions, and physical and mental health can have consequences if not learned how to control. We all live in an era when so much information is available at every moment of the day. It is no wonder many parents are overwhelmed with navigating through all this content and finding time to interact with their kids about important issues such as family values, morals, religion, etc... This makes it hard for them to keep up with the constant barrage of media messages that bombard us every day without even knowing what these messages really mean or how they affect us emotionally, physically, mentally, and spiritually.

Parents ask themselves, "What do I do?" Resorting to parenting books seems to be the only option to find the best ways to solve a problem, which in reality does not mean exhausting the energies to raise a child, just doing it correctly.

I wrote earlier in chapter 6 that we have to follow a protocol for a relationship to work. Rules make the universe; if you go against the whole protocol, the result will be negative. For example, if we observe traffic rules, we will get to our destination safely; otherwise, we may arrive late or with problems. The same protocol can be carried out for parents of toddlers or adolescents. There is no difference - self-knowledge is for all ages. This is where the Children archetype steps in. When we pay attention to the Children's archetypes around us, we can make better and more conscious decisions for the betterment. So, let us delve into the various archetypes surrounding our children to better understand them and support them in developing to their greatest potential.

The Process of Self-Knowledge and Identification

In order to begin the journey toward self-awareness, it is critical to first recognize your own identity. Spiritual labels and classifications like "rainbow," "diamond," "Starseed," "crystal," and "indigo" may be used to describe certain types of personalities in children. However, I shall only stick to the demonstration of Indigo and Crystal traits in this book.

Indigo Children

Indigos are advanced beings born between the decades of the 1950s and the 1990s. They are youngsters who dislike Earth yet are aware that they have a purpose here. Indigos have the spiritual ability to connect with other dimensions, as well as to see, feel, and speak with spirits without bodies. Additionally, because of the richness and complexity of their minds, they are naturally inquisitive and want to know why they must follow certain rules set down by their parents. Indigo children often rebel against authority figures, question the validity of accepted social norms, and even look their parents in the eye to declare that they will not do as they are told. It is owing to the fact that there aren't enough external mechanisms for them to manifest the high potential they harbor within. Living in the shadows may cause the vibration pattern of such children to drop, which can lead to issues like anxiety, despair, attention dyslexia, and different phobias. They have such a high level of conscience that they are able to utilize telepathic communication to acquire what they want from their parents. Indigos may have a difficult time in school because they see it as a waste of time to repeat the same lessons and assignments over and over again.

On the other hand, Indigo adults have a strong desire for autonomy. It often leads them to pursue positions of authority within an organization. However, their wide range of skills makes them excellent candidates for self-employment, while they may succeed in fields such as management, coordination, direction, governorship, and more. Most judges, promoters, and attorneys who identify as Indigo are whistleblowers who expose corruption in their organizations. It is primarily because their life experiences and sense of morality do not let them be a part of the corrupt status quo. Indigos are warriors who despise injustice and would always put up a good fight. Furthermore, they are usually passionate about environmental protection and despise anthropogenic devastation. Indigos are the minds and souls of the future generation.

Crystal Children

The children of the twenty-first century are the embodiment of pure love and heavenly light. They are the first reincarnation of humanity and the hope for a better future. They love everyone and ask their parents why they are well-fed when other children are starving, yet they are not tied to material things. They are calm little beings with high consciousness, capable of reading a book even when it is closed. Additionally, they are sensitive to their surroundings and can distinguish between good and negative energy. Parents that are not prepared to deal with crystal children believe that children won't have a future because they don't have ambitions for the business. However, crystal children are healers, and their future jobs will be in acupuncture, nursing, medicine, psychology, holistic treatment, or anything linked to wellness. Mahatma Gandhi was an excellent example of a crystal kid. He responded to intolerance with patience and a smile. Similarly, Jesus was also among one of the most enlightened children of all time. Crystal children are the revolutionaries of truth and missionaries of the world. The contemporary world is undergoing constant evolution, and crystal children are active in the process.

1. Toys

Children gravitate toward toys. One of the stimuli caused by toys is dopamine; children can be very happy when playing or throw a tantrum if their toys are confiscated. Since they were created, one of the goals of toys was to cause distraction or entertainment. Alternatively, the parent's goal should be to control the number of toys. Why? The more toys, the more distractions. Furthermore, the selection of toys is important since they are archetypal models that will create more stimulus in the child, eventually building personality in the unconscious.

Math toys, logical thinking, science, and art activities are the finest options for parents who want smart kids. For parents who desire their children to be inspired by the Hero archetype, options such as police car, firefighter, nurse, and so on are wonderful options. Toys with a dark side are those inspired by villains or figures that inflict havoc. Many adults identify with the bad guys as they do with the good guys in movies and TV shows. The archetype will undoubtedly influence any child who idolizes a fictional character or an archetypal toy for the rest of their life.

2. Movies, Series, and Music

Many archetypal projects for all ages have been developed through writing, characters, special effects, and all the enchantment of cinema. Different stimuli are employed in movies to elicit the desired emotion in children. Because of their screenplays and use of archetypal imagery, films that gross tens or hundreds of millions of dollars at the box office have become the norm.

Writers and directors found that researching psychiatric material yielded fabulous profits in cinema. Even movie actors express the archetype so well that our emotions are almost imperceptible, and we forget it's just a movie. This is even more profound in children since they are purest.

Magic, enchanted kingdom, castle, prince and princesses, animals, children and monsters, beauty, freedom, obstacles, courage, and so on are the best ways to apply an archetype in a movie in the children's world.

3. Words

Words also develop stimuli in the brain. Hence, daily affirmative words are valuable in keeping a child happy and motivated, unlike negative words that inevitably result in negative reactions. In children, the result is faster and more uncontrollable because of sensitivity and not knowing how to have self-control.

The child's unconscious is like a blank paper that archetypal models are implanted on all the time, and this information can manifest as shadow or light. The child's feeling is like a light bulb that requires energy to stay on, which means that each word he hears is automatically transferred to the feeling, such as if a foreign nanny says "Yo te amo" to a kid. The unconscious of an English child will grasp that the nanny said I love you, and the child will be happy even if they do not understand what was said.

Words don't need to be spoken directly to children; words can be indirect. If someone wants to implant an archetype in a child's unconscious, just create a story/music without showing the symbology. For example, if someone wants to influence a child to be governed by the caregiver archetype, give the child a baby doll to care for, adopt a pet, or tell stories about animals that care for puppies, activities that must be done daily until the child develops her own will to care. This will be a sign that the archetype has been activated.

4. Baby

When a baby is born, he has his mother as his first love and affection. He smiles even when she is not smiling. He loves unconditionally. His purity is like that of lilies. Babies are pure perception because what they see and touch is with feeling. A baby also sees his parents as gods because they understand that everything he has comes from them. Babies are pure universe energy, clean, and without any negative energy. They don't care about what's missing or not enough; they just love and are happy.

5. Toddler

Years 1 to 3 are the age range during which the ego and personality develop gradually. One example is an emotional lack of negativity or non-acceptance of an event, irritation, difficulties communicating, and not getting what a toddler desires.

Because of ego development, toddlerhood is also the beginning of paradigm creation. Due to the sheer addiction to electronics and toys, it becomes much more difficult to overcome the materialistic paradigm after technology. The child's brain receives unlimited information, but this merely paralyzes the process of completely experiencing an archetype because he still does not know how to manage his thoughts or emotions.

The child can also be taught to live moments of stillness, normally in the Toddler stage, if their interaction with technology is limited. If the child is encouraged to participate in physical games and activities instead of watching cartoons or playing online games, the child's mind will learn how to process everything in real-time. This will let their brain develop analytical skills. In addition, children should get a chance to interact with parents and other adults by asking them questions about anything they may want to know about life, sports, art, science, and more on an ongoing basis throughout childhood and into adulthood so that it doesn't feel like the information they receive is based on one particular topic or event in their lives only, but rather as part of a continuous experience for their entire lifetime, as well as for those around them who are interested in what their kids are thinking.

Even the timeouts given to toddlers allow them to understand what reflection is, how to self-reflect, and build the ability to distinguish between good and bad for themselves based on the reflection they will perform on the bad behavior they committed. Toddlers start to live in the tree of knowledge of right and wrong and learn from the first experiences of life. Thinking is the best option if it seems complicated to teach a child to meditate. Greek philosophers expanded consciousness by contemplating the art of thinking. To encourage your child to think, take them out near a lake as the water is an excellent archetype for the unconscious or an open place. Sitting near a tree and a lawn without any toys or electronics to distract your toddler are good options for a process of detachment from the material world.

6. Child

The phase of questions, curiosities, talent and skill development, the paradigm guided but not signed, and everything taught begins to be experienced throughout the childhood phase. There is no opposition, but because the ego does not yet have power over itself, any new paradigm and instruction supplied to the kid will be received because the mind is still receptive to new experiences.

Curiosity means a new perception of reality. Children admire everything they see as babies. When they grow up, they want to know the why of things, reasons, motive, cause, and how things happen. When the child is in the process of self-knowledge, he will probably ask himself, "Who am I?" "Do I do it here?" and "Where am I going?"

Questions are the essence of every human being in discovering what is beyond this life; the archetype of love is the main influencer in answering these questions. The love archetype makes all things make sense, and the answers manifest themselves naturally, including improving skills and talents, as children will develop the perception of seeing people happy as being worth more than anything else with the thought of "making the world a better place."

Parents provide the main experiences with the archetype of love in children's lives. The more love there is, the more endorphins in their brains. Children learn that all this love given to them during life needs to be shared with others as a form of gratitude. Not just parents, but we also know that not everyone will get love the same way that others do; this is part of the universe's plan to increase compassion, complicity, and solidarity with others. What would happen if a person the family never loved starts to be loved by someone he has never seen? A light will walk over darkness, lighting paths, breaking paradigms, and becoming a guide to what is new.

7. Teenager

Teenage is the phase where children put everything they have learned into practice. They learn to take responsibility so that they have more freedom and less parental control. The teenager will face a life of trial and error, learning to deal with life's experiences since they acquired information but did not learn to regulate or separate the wheat from the chaff. Many believe you have to suffer to achieve enlightenment, but this is incorrect. Learning to love or suffer is a choice where teenage is the stage where you start to make things work and conquer dreams.

For example, the work of Jesus when he was a boy and the three years of ministry in adulthood before he died, from boy Jesus to twelve years old, he preached to the wise men in the temple of Jerusalem. From an early age, Jesus already performed miracles, and such works quickly became notorious. For reference, see Luke 2:39-40, Luke 2:51-52, and Matthew 13:54-56. Similarly, an enlightened child is always aware of what he was created to do and does not start in the future. Because the enlightened child knows that life is too short to waste time, the child feels that it is necessary to prepare for growth as soon as he reaches his level of consciousness.

One of the main shadows that teenager carries is nonconformity and confrontation. The thought that "everything is wrong," "dad and mom can't prove what they say," or "this isn't fair" feels like an emotional mess out of control. It becomes much more perplexing when parents instruct their teenagers to do something they've been taught their entire lives as improper. For instance, when parents instruct their children to lie after teaching them as a child that lying is unacceptable. When a teenager recognizes the parents 'shadows and recognizes that any rule can be broken because the ego thinks, "I can; I do," the self thinks, "I can; I shouldn't," but the ego does not like to be addressed.

The ego wants to confront and do what it wants without bowing to rules. Everything that is forbidden encourages you to do it because, for the ego, nothing is forbidden. Shadows and ego inflation can be healed through the process of self-knowledge. Any teenager can understand what myth they are living in so they can live in the light to achieve whatever goals they desire.

Sometimes parents think, "I wish my child would choose books over electronics," but are you like that? Since children revere their parents as if they were gods, not only capable of teaching but also someone with whom they can mirror and think, "I want to be like them." Children tend to be like their parents when they grow up. So how will addicted parents raise spiritual children? You will have to walk the path your children choose until they are as mature as you to do so. It seems impossible! There are rare and honorable exceptions as more sensitive children, who are already born spiritual and tend to be influenced by the spirit world. These children need a mentor to show them the way, but it's not for everyone.

Children admire their parents more than any other individual. Admiration for parents ends when perception changes from one phase to another. The feeling of being used and not loved takes over the previous admiration for parents. Teens ask themselves, "So many demands for what?" Even the parents don't know how to answer this, leaving the children to find out for themselves when new perceptions and new experiences arise.

Ultimately, for any problem to be solved, it is necessary to look within. There is no way to escape a problem. Before someone solves any problem in life, they always look for the origin of the problem to understand how it all started. Likewise, looking at the unconscious works similarly because that's where the thought of God is. The challenge of facing the shadows causes resistance in hopes of curing a problem, and that's why problems are perpetuated. When you learn to look inside yourself from childhood, children grow up enlightened as they put light where there is shadow.

8. Adult

Only the lessons given during the adult phase can be evaluated during the result phase. It takes work to be prosperous in all facets of life. In the adult stage, parents switch from being educators to counselors to give their kids the freedom to make decisions and assume responsibilities. The choice for adults to live on the light or dark side will depend on whether they want to live by the reins of life itself and all the archetypes they applied as children.

9. Process of Self-knowledge

Parents can identify their children's archetypes, but they also need to go through the process of self-knowledge because perception is the primary attribute of an expanded or advanced state of consciousness. In order for children to have a minimum of self-knowledge, they will need to learn about myths, understand philosophy, and discover what myth they are living in.

Every one of us is an imitator, making it simple to exert influence over others via tricks or by being unconscious of them. Since parents are the primary influencing archetypes on children as father and mother gods, children worship their parents. Children model their parent's behavior and are influenced by what they see in their parents. It makes sense that if we love someone dearly, we naturally want to emulate them.

When parents introduce anything to their children that incorporates a symbol, story, name, nickname, toy, room decoration, etc., archetypal impulses are triggered in the child. Archetypes start to affect attitudes in childhood and throughout life as everything becomes a part of a child's life.

10. Princess

The Princess archetype has always been the most used in children's world, especially among girls. The only problem is that parents do not have the king and queen archetype.

The archetype of a royal family has a very deep meaning.

Since ancient empires, the king and queen have always been in a position of authority. The princess also has authority, but she is not above the orders of the king and queen; princesses must be instructed and prepared to reign when the father and mother (king and queen) die.

Typically, children influenced by the princess archetype tend to be feminine, dream of a prince, dreamy, creative, and loving on the light side. The shadow would be authoritarianism. It rules the parents without them realizing it. This is the archetype's great trick! The child's authoritarianism can persist into adulthood since the knowledge in the unconscious is not deleted; nevertheless, as you become a woman, you may find it challenging to establish close friendships, in addition, because your unconscious is programmed to believe in castles and prince, romantic relationships will also become challenging because her illusion is part of the shadow.

11. The Hero

The hero is a very popular archetype in the children's world. It is linked to both genres. Marvel and DC movies have been the great influencers of the Hero archetype.

It is not necessary to exercise a profession influenced by the hero to be a hero; anyone can save the other using skills, sharing information, and helping the other within the possibilities. A child, for instance, can save a day of chaos while parents are resolving an important challenge by providing all the pertinent details about what occurred. A child can also be a hero by assisting a classmate who is falling behind in their school work.

Despite the strong influence of the hero, the experience becomes more evident in adulthood. It's no surprise that many young people are unsure of what they want to do in life and choose a career. As I previously stated, a person can be influenced by more than one archetype experiencing shadow or light, and children live surrounded by symbolism everywhere.

This is because they keep changing their minds until they find what they were truly born to do.

One of the most popular activities for kids who can swim is playing with a baby doll in the pool that has to be saved, taking on quests to discover a kidnapped doll in the woods, freeing a cat from a tree, etc.

12. The Butterfly

The butterfly is one of the best archetypes for a child to experience as it is always in constant change and transformation. A caterpillar changes into a chrysalis, then transforms into a beautiful winged insect, just like our human lives do!

The caterpillar will shed its skin, transform into a chrysalis and then emerge as a new being with a completely different appearance and personality that looks back on what came before, not knowing how others will view it; it has no choice but to fly away from the cocoon and leave everything behind and never look back – a very painful and difficult process for the butterfly to go through and yet a necessity to become stronger and more confident than ever before and to begin life afresh.

It is common to see butterflies in kindergarten all over the place, especially in the Toddler stage. Butterflies influence children from the inside out; when perception changes, reality also changes along with the worldview.

13. The Heart

The heart activates the heart chakra. The archetype of love is the main influencer of the child from the beginning of life even before existence. The heart is a deep archetype that awakens universal and unconditional love, perfect to be kept in the child's life until adulthood. What makes this so important is that we are given it at birth, which means we do not have to "acquire" it (in the same way you can acquire language). What I am getting at here is that your baby's heart will always feel like it is still fresh, unscarred, pure, and uncorrupted by outside influences (because it has been so well cared for and loved from birth). It is, therefore, easier to connect with people if you just remember how pure they are.

14. The Tree

The tree is a common archetype in schools and libraries. It is a perfect archetype for self-knowledge. The connection between the child's earthly mother and father and the cosmic energy will influence a new perspective on reality. Attitudes will be based on emotions and rationally balanced, as long as the parents do not resist and allow it to flow naturally in the child. When the child has access to this frequency, he will have more control over himself, regardless of feelings or decisions.

A new set of attitudes will develop and become stronger as we move through this process from infancy to adulthood: We begin with a strong need for safety, security, love, warmth, attention, acceptance, nurturance, protection, and support from both our inner world and outer world – or 'inner child '("child within") and "outer child" (the environment). The tree represents the "tree of life" or growth path.

15. The Horse

The horse is an archetype that influences the child to have self-control, especially on the emotional side, which is the dream of many parents. The horse is a powerful archetype of independence, as a foal starts to take its first steps a few hours after birth. No, there is nothing to worry about because they respect hierarchies and authorities as a matter of honor. The only possession the horse wants to have is itself.

The world of archetypes is infinite. Knowing about them will help children succeed in the future in every area of their lives.

Chapter 13

Health Archetypes

Health archetypes are influential in all areas of life - the physical, mental, spiritual, social, and emotional. They majorly impact your beliefs, perceptions, behavior, attitudes, relationships, career choices, and how you make sense of your world and experience it in its totality. We can imagine that you are a star with five arms. Each arm represents an aspect of your life, and they are all integrated, united, by a center or star body. However, as the health archetype affects all realms of our life, it does so at the expense of our energy. Since our body is made up of energy, it needs to be recharged. The energy, while used as a central aspect ourselves, needs to be recharged in all five aspects like a star. To understand how we can recharge ourselves, we must look at the health archetype.

As every archetype has its meaning, the areas of health are also divided by different representations:

1. Physical Health: Concerns your physical body and taking care of it through food, physical activity, breathing, rest, etc.
2. Mental Health: Concerns your thoughts, beliefs, and worldview.
3. Spiritual Health: Concerns the eternal aspects of your being, which gives life and animates your body.
4. Emotional Health: Refers to your basic feelings and how you feel and react to things that happen to you.

5. Social Health: Refers to the way you relate to other people, to other beings, to the environment, to your profession, and to money.

In physical health, one of the things that people most seek is the ideal weight or body shape. However, achieving the goals without dealing with anxiety first is impossible. It is like fighting against yourself instead of reeducating and adapting the body to a new routine. There are also those who seek a cure for an illness or treatment.

The physical body keeps the internal environment balanced through the process called homeostasis, which detects imbalances at an early stage and, through a delicate means of self-regulation, corrects them without realizing it. So long as we don't interfere, the body will heal itself, and if it has the necessary physiological reserve, it will react forcefully.

We are also equipped with a complex defense system that fights internal and external aggressors. When the strength of the aggressive agents is greater than the competence of the defense system, disharmony, initially energetic, occurs. If it is not corrected, the disharmony becomes functional; that is, it changes the functioning of the organs, and, finally, the disorder can settle in them, also changing their shape. If this continues or is too intense, it leads to the death of the biological body.

- Potentially aggressive agents for the physical body are:
- Inadequate diet
- Lack or excess of physical activity
- Postural errors
- Lack of rest
- Climatic factors (wind, heat, cold, humidity)
- Physical trauma
- Intoxication by food or chemical substances
- Electromagnetic radiation
- Microorganisms (viruses, bacteria, fungi, etc.)
- Genetic predisposition

- Unbalanced and prolonged emotions such as fear, anger, anxiety, worry, and sadness
- Contraction of consciousness
- Expanded consciousness as the foundation of life and health

The contraction of consciousness happens when the person resists the present moment and reality as it presents itself; when a person holds on and doesn't let go. The signs of this contraction in a person who feels annoyed, frustrated, or depressed for not having his desire fulfilled see situations as a struggle. There is always a lot of effort involved in what a person does. Anxiety and fear of failure are present to a greater or lesser degree, along with mental confusion, inner conflict, and physical and mental exhaustion.

The more you try eliminating the problem, the more you are trapped by it. It is important to differentiate that the body is not an object; it is a process.

One of the best female archetypes for those who want to achieve body shape is the goddess Aphrodite! Self-love and high self-esteem teach us to love new things that bring us energy. The answer to what we do with our body is how we feel when we eat and what kind of food brings us energy and makes us happier. On the contrary, what do we eat to feel low in energy and with less self-esteem? Why do we never feel satisfied when we eat? And why are there people who gain weight despite having a good appetite and no lack of exercise? The answer is simple: they have not understood how to manage their emotions and, therefore, cannot achieve a state of well-being through their eating habits (this is also true of bulimia). Some people seem to eat without ever feeling happy or contented, whereas others always feel happy and satisfied when they eat but often binge on food when they don't want to.

Few people live only on light, without the need to eat. Of course, this only works for those with an advanced stage of consciousness, but we cannot forget the benefits that fasting brings to human life in the physical, mental and spiritual. Leaders like Moses, Jesus, and Buddha were incessant practitioners of fasting. When deeply immersed in the unconscious, we forget about material demands and pleasures without making any sacrifices. Even after going without food for hours, we don't feel hungry when we sleep.

In mental health, the hummingbird is the archetype that stands out the most for inner healing, trauma, attachments, and dark pasts because it vibrates in the frequency of unconditional love. Therefore, it has the power to heal the shadows.

For spiritual health, any archetype linked to love is wonderful - heart, hummingbird, lotus, lily, tree, cross, etc. Because of the number of minerals they contain and their link to cosmic energy, stones have tremendous archetypal power in addition to serving as a means of energy cleansing and a way to maintain a connection with the Whole.

In emotional health, the horse is one of the most admirable archetypes for having self-control and being a strong symbol of independence. The Yin and Yang poles are also part of emotional control because it teaches us to think emotionally and rationally in a balanced way.

Social health is present in many archetypes mainly because the human being is a social being. Even if he is not friends, he is among people in different places, hospitals, markets, banks, libraries, etc. Even if they are on social networks, the interaction can be different. However, there is interaction because emotions and information are constantly influenced. Examples of communication and personal magnetism are the magicians, masters, leaders, and fortunate archetypes. If we are teaching, leading, helping, and doing business, we are interacting, and all these things will attract results.

Prosperity in all areas requires a deep knowledge of yourself. There is no problem facing the shadows as they only serve to present us with the light; health is part of this light. Because of the materialistic paradigm, many people do not believe health is part of the spiritual path. Consequently, success needs to be in all areas because everything is connected. If one side has a defect that is not corrected, all the others will have a defect, and health is as important as the other areas because the attitudes we take result in our inner being before manifesting on the outside.

Chapter 14

Magical Archetypes

Magical archetypes are linked to mythological creatures. As a child, fairy tales and any character who can manifest and transform any matter into something else by manipulating the forms of reality are firmly believed in.

The purpose of these archetypes is not to create illusions but to influence. We know that every person has an electromagnetic field surrounding them that constantly transmits information to the universe. Eventually, this information will be reflected in everyone as a wave or a particle (information or matter). It doesn't matter if the creatures are myths or characters created in comics. They are pre-existing information in other dimensions, and the human being's mission is to manifest them in the material world with an impulse of symbols. All archetypes are as real as we are. It is not an allegory like the story of the prince of the white horse; myths are like a reality told through metaphors to be transmitted in the human unconscious.

1. Phoenix

The Phoenix is a mythical bird known for its power to rise from its ashes. In addition to immortality, the Phoenix possesses supernatural and extraordinary strength. In some tales, it is said to be able to lift an elephant. It is the universal symbol of death, fire, the sun, life, renewal, resurrection, immortality, longevity, divinity, and invincibility.

The Phoenix myth dates back to ancient Egypt. The Egyptians associated the Phoenix with the solar cycle, and they believed that the Phoenix could live for 500 years. However, it is possible to make a parallel between the Phoenix's phases with the sunrise and understand its association with the king.

The rebirth of the Phoenix took place at dawn, and she became powerful at the morning's peak. In the afternoon, the Phoenix lost her strength. At night, moments before she died, she started a magical self-combustion process until she completely incinerated herself. The Phoenix, before dying, laid an egg that was protected and heated in its ashes. This phase is represented by the total absence of the Sun at dawn.

At dawn, the egg cracked open, and the Phoenix was reborn.

The Greeks also gained access to the Phoenix myth through Egyptian influence. As the Egyptian Phoenix was associated with the Sun, the Greeks associated it with Heliopolis (the city of the sun.) It was believed that the moment the new Phoenix re-emerged, it would take the ashes of the old Phoenix to an altar in Heliopolis to honor it.

The Phoenix was described by Roman authors Tatius, Ovid, and Pliny (the Elder) as a majestic bird of great strength that could control fire and emerge from its ashes. The most widely recognized version today, it swept throughout the western world.

The Persians believed that a Phoenix existed. In 1177, the poet Attar from the city of Nixapur wrote the work "The Conference of Birds," where he narrated the saga of thirty birds that flew together in search of King Simorgh. In this work, the Phoenix is an example to be followed, as she knows exactly the day of her death and can prepare for it.

In the Middle Ages, the Phoenix was a sacred symbol for Christians, and it represented the resurrection of Christ and the triumph of life over death.

1) (Re) Birth - Dawn

This phase is when the Phoenix hatches from the egg. Extremely positive period, action energy is at its peak. Hope, motivation, will, strength, claw, personal power, and courage are present. It's a dopamine bath for the body, mind, and spirit.

2) Life - Dusk

This phase is the time when the Phoenix is maturing. It is the period of life with the greatest energy mastery. It is self-knowledge being improved. Action energy is still in great amounts. It is a phase of fullness. A process of intimate reform makes possible a great leap in consciousness.

3) Self-combustion - Dusk

This phase is ambivalent. Minutes before it dies, the Phoenix unleashes its maximum power, starting a process of self-combustion. This phase represents the moment when the being reaches its potential. It is the moment of the greatest achievement of personal evolution. This can be reflected in any area of life or all simultaneously, as everything is interconnected.

4) Ashes - Dawn

After burning in flames, the Phoenix extinguishes itself in ashes. This phase can represent a period of lack of courage, and it is the period that follows the best moments of our lives. Life goes on, and now there is an unconscious weight: making the next few days as pleasant as the ones you experienced. This phase is very emotionally complicated. But it must be remembered that the Phoenix always leaves an egg in its ashes: there is life, there is hope.

As a cyclical archetype, the Phoenix is an archetype of ups and downs, which activates the Law of Polarity to the fullest extent possible. The ups and downs are the shadows of this archetype. There is no moderation or restraint; everything or nothing. For instance, as shown in his brand design for Queen and other symbols, Freddy Mercury, infamous for his life's ups and downs, was heavily affected by Phoenix.

Another example is the January 9, 1988 issue of the Economist magazine, which featured the strong expression "Get ready for a world currency" and a Phoenix to represent the demise of paper money and the birth of digital currency. At the time, the economy and cryptocurrency were both known for their ups and downs.

Light:

✓ Rebirth
✓ Hope
✓ Positivity
✓ Stateliness
✓ Self-sufficiency
✓ Fearlessness and courage
✓ High self-esteem
✓ Elevated self-confidence
✓ Energy transmutation
✓ Personal power
✓ Natural magnetism
✓ Transcendence
✓ Connection with your ancestry
✓ Elevated intuition
✓ High performance
✓ Proactivity
✓ Detachment
✓ Solitude
✓ Self-knowledge
✓ Determination
✓ Self-criticism and absolute presence
✓ Boosted Yang Energy

2. Fairy

The archetype Fairy is for those who want to feel an impulse on their projects or set goals.

As supernatural beings, fairies have a variety of powers. Fairies are born with a kind essence, being able to spread feelings of joy and love wherever they go, consequently getting younger for millenniums.

Depending on the fairy's kind, every species has a distinctive ability, some even magical. They are renowned for showing compassion to all living things and for protecting and appreciating nature. Fairies are typically exceedingly friendly and use their abilities to help individuals. The Fairy is an air element strongly connected to the priestess archetype and the great mother.

Fairy has a luminous essence and radiates light. It assists and guides, comforts, and imparts the impulse of transformation. It shares with the sorceress, whose celestial form is the absolute power of metamorphosis.

The imaginary brings to the scene the sorceresses, an old woman who represents the dreamer's shadow or fairies who symbolize the strength of the soul. The fairy in the dream immediately proclaims its heavenly belonging. She is the inextinguishable light, the source of life, the mother of the child of hope and love.

The fairy infuses all that has to do with the feminine essence of the manifest world. She is a mother representation, a force for destiny, and a reflection of the global Mother. Her favorite areas are the grotto and the fairy rocks. Although the fairy is from the sky, she enjoys gliding over the water. One of the most beautiful forms it takes is the character of the dragonfly fairy. The dragonfly's multicolored wings are radiant, light, swift, and translucent, captivating the eye. The fairy displays a tremendous desire to align ourselves with fate's energies through the star that forms her wand.

Light:

✓ Beauty
✓ Creativity

- ✓ Imagination
- ✓ Freedom
- ✓ Luck
- ✓ Elevated self-esteem
- ✓ Intelligence
- ✓ Sweet
- ✓ Zealous
- ✓ Intuition
- ✓ Healing
- ✓ Glamour
- ✓ Mediumship
- ✓ Femininity
- ✓ Kindness
- ✓ Clairvoyance
- ✓ Animal affinity
- ✓ Mother nature affinity
- ✓ Youth
- ✓ Strong Yin

Shadow:

- ✓ Hate disorganization
- ✓ Excessively dedicated
- ✓ Kindness can be explored
- ✓ Obsession with action and achieving goals

3. Dragon

Dragons previously coexisted peacefully and close to humans on Earth. As the planet ascends, they are returning in large numbers from the upper dimensions to help us in the effort to uplift it.

In Fantasy Literature, Dragons appear from the beginning as guardians of treasures, transmitters of knowledge, and sovereigns in the mysteries of magic. The idea that dragons could communicate directly with the gods and serve as intermediaries between them and humans may have originated orally. An enormous magical pearl that resembles an egg and can multiply anything it touches is frequently shown in its claws. The egg also represents the Great Wisdom.

Guardian of "The Effulgent Pearl," the Dragon is a strong good luck charm and a sign of spiritual excellence. It is described in some literature as a massive magical pearl with the capacity to multiply anything it comes into contact with. The pearl stood for wisdom, the most priceless of all goods.

The Oriental Dragon is good because eastern traditions have long understood that since the beginning of life on Earth, Earth has had access to much of the cosmic/ancestral information that reaches the west. The Dragon is also the master of the primordial force and ruler of the four elements that make up matter (Fire, Water, Earth, and Air), the protector of unbounded space, and the mentor of the moral consciousness that directs behavior.

The symbology of the Dragon that emerges in opposite directions represents the paradox of the human condition itself in this evidence of duality:

- Light × Shadows
- Female × Male
- Good × Bad
- Creation × Destruction

This archetype encourages our contact with the psychic nature and the look capable of discovering and seeing the "wonderful" that lives in us.

Dragon symbology is associated with evil and terror, but at the same time, it also symbolizes the protection of treasures. Fighting and defeating the dragon translates initiation and evolution through the ordeal. This mythological animal is also a symbol of immortality, the union of opposites, and divine power.

Each dragon specie and color have its meaning. In Christianity, the Bible expresses the dragon trying to devour the woman's child at the moment of its birth in Revelation 12:4, which refers to Herod the Great's attempt to kill the baby Jesus in Matthew 2:16. We can see the great shadow of the dragon is the wrath.

The dragon species included are Big Shadow Wing, Small Shadow Wing, Fire Tail, Flame Whipper, Silver Ghost, Fire Caterpillar, and Red Death.

The Oriental Dragon is a traditional symbol of countries like China and Japan and means wisdom, strength, power, protection, and wealth. It looks like a giant snake with four claws.

The Red Dragon is associated with luck, fire, passion, and the heart, and it is the dragon of summer and the south. Other Chinese associations with this color include vitality, enthusiasm, and creativity.

These dragons inhabit all kingdoms. Many are also in the waters and interact directly with Nature on Earth. They control the rain, rivers, lakes, and seas. Earthquakes and tidal waves are associated with dragons for the force their movements exert in the depths of the Earth.

According to Chinese mythology, it was one of the four sacred animals summoned by Pan Ku (the creator god) to participate in the world's creation. It is a mystical being, a mix of several mystical animals: tiger eyes, snake body, eagle's paws, deer horns, ox ears, carp whiskers, and so on. It represents the energy of fire, which destroys but allows the birth of the new, cleaning, and transformation.

1. Bixi: similar to a giant and strong turtle. It is often used as a base for ornamental carvings. Symbolizes longevity.

2. Chiwen: similar to a beast endowed with good eyesight, he is believed to be able to extinguish the fire. Because of this, he is often decorated on roofs. It symbolizes the capacity for broad vision, the power of vision beyond the eyes, the one that allows us to see the different possibilities in the face of situations that present themselves.

3. Pulao: is a small dragon. According to legend, it likes to howl. It is used as decoration on the bells. It symbolizes the annunciation. That is, it activates our senses for the new events to

come.

4. Bi'an: similar to a tiger and quite powerful, he would be able to tell right from wrong. It is carved into prison doors to frighten prisoners, symbolizes protection, and guards against invaders from the astral and physical planes.

5. Taotie: symbolizes gluttony and is used as a decoration in food. It calls us to reflect that we should pay attention to what we eat because everything we ingest is transformed into energy that works in us.

6. Kung fu: The sixth son loves water, and his image is used to decorate bridges and fountains. It symbolizes the search for balance in the field of emotions and drives us to pay attention to the feelings we produce when we go through certain situations.

7. Yazi: Found on swords and knives. It symbolizes the strength of the warrior that we often put into action in the pursuit of dominance from our invaders (internal saboteurs)

8. Suanni: similar to a lion. It is usually represented on festive days. It acts by exploding fiery energy like fireworks, helping us to expand joy and gratitude for achievements.

9. Jiaotu: Shell-like and hates to be disturbed. It is carved into the front door or doorstep. It represents the inner withdrawal that is often necessary for us to meet our Master of Inner Wisdom. It drives us to find in our well of knowing the answers that we often expect to come from outside, while in fact, all the answers are within ourselves.

Lord of all elements, the Dragon enlivens the invincible Fire of Transmutation in us. He teaches us to understand that fear is the only place where we can awaken true courage. Dragons are powerful guardians that guide us through multidimensional portals towards completely unknown horizons and the mysteries of our inner hiding places. By blowing the golden flame of the Wisdom of the East, the Dragon invites us to balance to the middle path. Awakening the Dragon is awakening our healing power, our infinite divine faculties.

The Dragon inhabits what Jung would call the collective

unconscious, an intangible "something" that actively operates within all of humanity, beyond the limits of the ego. In this non-individual territory, we find eternal myths and archetypes.

Light:

- ✓ Wisdom
- ✓ Prosperity
- ✓ Transformation
- ✓ Power
- ✓ Leadership
- ✓ Organization
- ✓ Self-acknowledgment
- ✓ Conscience elevation
- ✓ Protection
- ✓ Intuition
- ✓ Spiritual connection
- ✓ Clairvoyance
- ✓ Libido
- ✓ Freedom
- ✓ Transmutation
- ✓ Unification of Yin and Yang

Shadow:

- ✓ Wrath
- ✓ Destruction
- ✓ Duality
- ✓ Separation
- ✓ Egocentrism

4. Unicorn

The Unicorn is a mythological being that, in addition to being well known in fables, myths, legends, and stories and being used as an esoteric, alchemical, and spiritual symbol, is increasingly present in pop culture.

The Unicorn reveals itself to those who can see the beauty of the Sacred Path beyond the gray clouds of illusion. A magical creature of rare power heralds Mystery's return to the ordinary dimension of existence. He teaches us to re-establish contact with the spiritual world and our Divine Self from contemplating the entirety of our Being and polarities. He is one of the guardians of Mystery and Magic, the bridge to the world of dreams.

Jung used the horned horse archetype to illustrate duality, the complementation of seemingly irreconcilable opposites. For this reason, the Unicorn represents purity and lust, the good and the bad, and the unification or integration of both polarities like dragons.

In Ancient Greece, around the year 2 B.C, the Unicorn was considered a myth associated with purity and strength. In the Middle Ages, Christians began associating it with the Virgin Mary and the power of the Holy Spirit.

In the Old Testament, it is possible to find Biblical passages that symbolically allude to a one-horned animal. There may be reports about the Siberian Unicorn, as there are indications that it lived in other regions and would have had contact with humans.

These verses can be found in Psalms 22:21, 29:6, 92:10, Job 39:9–10, and Numbers 23:22. Although the Bible has undergone numerous translations, it is difficult to pinpoint precisely what animal is described in Isaiah 34:7 and Deuteronomy 33:17. This is due to the Greek word Monokeros, which means "one horn" or "unicorn," being used in place of the original Hebrew term Re'ém in the translation.

The Unicorn teaches us to break the illusion of duality and travel through the Universe's immensity. It is time to move, to abandon the old pretexts and attachments to seek heights never reached. To see the colors and lights that reveal infinite possibilities. Allow yourself to see life with another vision. On the frontiers of the unknown, the mysteries that our Spirit longs to rediscover are hidden.

Light:

- ✓ Calm
- ✓ Goodness
- ✓ Luck
- ✓ Protection
- ✓ Sweetness
- ✓ Affectionate
- ✓ Healing
- ✓ Power
- ✓ Purity
- ✓ Inner sacredness
- ✓ Sensuality
- ✓ Beauty
- ✓ Unification of Yin and Yang polarities
- ✓ Freedom
- ✓ Spirituality
- ✓ Peace

Shadow:

- ✓ Lust
- ✓ Duality
- ✓ Separation

Chapter 15

Popular Archetypes

We are constantly immersed in advertising campaigns that use many iconic symbols. The end goal of such campaigns is always to create a neuro-association between the product and human emotions. This linkage may be made with the company's logo and any product. Any business that employs the appropriate archetype in its marketing will see a rise in revenue. On the flip side, it may backfire if clients are repelled by the archetype and stop buying from you.

Destructive emotions and behaviors, including self-sabotaging thoughts and actions, anxiety, and depression, may be sparked by negative archetypes. For instance, images of skulls, demons, and pain are typical of how the media portrays death. This method employs skulls disguised among other pictures to elicit a negative emotional response without the target being aware of the manipulation.

Let's look at some well-known and often used archetypes and their function to better understand how marketing gimmicks employ archetypes to create purchase behaviors in humans by utilizing symbols to identify particular ideas and products.

1. Star
The star is a positive ideal with widespread appeal, particularly affiliated with Hollywood actors and actresses. It signifies the spiritual realm, heavenly direction, and divine protection

with the microcosm of the human experience. In Sumerian mythology, the goddess of fertility, Ishtar, was represented by this star. In occult philosophy, the significance of the number five is associated with the bridge between the physical and the spiritual realms. The increased delivery of the actors and actresses ingrained in their personas is, in fact, no accident. This occurs because the roles are archetypal, and their usage transforms the performers into another person. This trance is usually conveyed to the audience. Professor Oliver Schultheiss was an early pioneer in demonstrating the impact of movies on hormones.

2. Films

All cinematic works are archetypes, as I discussed at length in Chapter 12 on Films and Series. Archetypes include scripts, situations, and mythology-based storylines that generate excitement and ensure box office success.

Cinematic archetypes may be used to explore themes such as philosophy, life, and death, wizardry, sorcery, sex, sexual symbolism, heroism, villainy, messianism, vampires, ego, monsters, beauty, honesty, dishonesty, business, slavery, freedom, youth, love, romance, etc.

'The Matrix' cleverly depicts the dilemma of knowing what is real and what is not. The movie reveals how an entire generation may be duped into believing in a false world. Any film whose goal is to emotionally connect with its viewers will inevitably achieve this goal and find financial success.

Even horror films about monsters, vampires, or any other iconic figure who drains human energy tend to do well commercially. The trick is to come up with a strong storyline, which may be similar to other horror films since the tropes they utilize are embedded in our collective psyche.

3. Politics

Similar persuasive strategies are used in both politics and the film industry. Marketing, metaphors, oratory, and dress are all components of an archetypal model. The purpose of such models is to evoke emotions in the unconscious of voters. The "savior" Leader who can fix everything would be the ideal paradigm. A candidate's words must elicit a response from the listener via their sentiments, emotions, paradigms, and social context until they fully embrace the candidate's position. With this technique, the energy or frequency may be sent to the subconscious of every person on the planet, making it simple to trigger an emotional impulse in any person. Therefore, the proportion of sensible voters to emotional voters always remains low.

Voters may explain their choices without seeming irrational because they are human and use language to mask their true feelings. They constantly claim they are voting for the greatest option, but their true feelings may be buried deep within. This is one of the main causes of the heated political competition we often see. It has been shown that if you carefully survey 3,000 individuals during elections, you can predict their voting behavior practically and precisely. One can only win an election by appealing to archetypes.

4. Sports

Athletes may be pushed to their mental and emotional limits with the help of certain strong tools. However, it should be noted that even if such tools are used, some veteran athletes lack the motivation to keep competing as they age. The Greeks were the pioneers in sports, and thus the Olympics were first held in Greece. However, modern mankind has not yet retrieved ancient Greek knowledge from the realms of history.

Neurotransmitters impact more competitive sports as they are the brain's inherent chemicals that provide the will and motivation to compete. Other activities may include listening to music with metaphorical lyrics connected with the hero archetype or seeing yourself as a hawk, tiger, horse, or panther. The Nike archetype was essential in influencing one of the world's greatest corporations, founded on the ideal of sporting competitiveness.

5. Artists

Art is part of a mood and exerts a swift impact as any professional area. The speed at which an artist may become successful from one day to the next is legendary.

This door to the archetype is always open in the artist's subconscious, regardless of whether they are a musician, actor, dancer, painter, or designer. A living archetype would be someone like Mozart. Leonardo da Vinci, a sensitive creator and designer, painted about his most personal emotions and thoughts.

The archetypes we encounter in life are significant symbols that demand our attention and respect. For instance, in his role as Achilles in the movie Troy, actor Brad Pitt injured his Achilles tendon. This exemplifies how re-enacting a story may lead to the same myth outcomes. However, if one is properly oriented and has a thorough understanding of the archetypes, such shadows can be adequately addressed.

6. Hospital

The hospital is a universally recognized emblem of health care and healing. However, the outside signage of both the outside doors and the vehicle conveys the prospect of a treatment or a potential means to feel better. We may think hospitals hold the key to our health issues, yet there are reminders of sickness and death around us.

Employees of hospitals often speak openly about the psychological challenges they face when confronted with patient deaths and illnesses. In order to maintain a healthy neurotransmitter level, these workers would have access to different archetypal tools. A number of employees usually take care of the patient since they don't believe they have long to live, and they're probably right. And sure enough, after a few hours, the patient dies. It is mostly owing to the fact that the unconscious may interact with another unconscious—especially if the patient is deficient in dopamine, serotonin, endorphin, etc.

7. Employees, Managers, and Entrepreneurs

Today's businesses are marked by increasing competition

and will increase further in the next few years. Entrepreneurs need to keep their emotions under check, so they do not make any rash choices. Without equilibrium, strategy, and skill, it would be impossible to do things right while being objective and rational.

The firm will stagnate if it hires lackluster archetypes. It would be harder to compete in the market with workers without the potential for advancement. Many businesses use this strategy, and it has proven effective. The more neurotransmitters an employee has, the better they will perform in every interaction with consumers. The executive staff is sometimes referred to as Alpha males due to their stereotypically masculine traits of ambition, dominance, and competition that can be reiterated through different archetypes.

8. Lawyers

Archetypes are well suited to work in the legal profession due to their willingness to defer to more powerful authorities, such as the law, the judge, the jury, and the client. To win cases, you need to hone your oratory skills and understand the archetypes of both your client and your opponent's lawyer. A lack of emotional control on the part of a client might result in a case loss. For instance, experts prepare ministers from several nations before they appear before a panel; if the Orestes myth has any impact on any jury, they will reach a verdict before the trial even starts.

9. Restaurants, aesthetics, and decorations

A restaurant's ability to draw in guests depends on its ability to provide an ambiance that appeals to its diners. It can be via the provision of a nice ambiance, a decent selection of music, a live performance or orchestra, photographs, clips, or popular television shows. If the restaurant has a show-house vibe, choosing music or putting on a performance that makes customers happy is a great option with optimal benefits.

The same technique is used for facial aesthetics, drainage, etc., at beauty salons, massage parlors, spas, etc. Plants, soft music, pale walls, and a stack of glossy magazines on a glass coffee table are all standard elements of environments designed to make people feel good. Consequently, a boost in serotonin and endorphin levels is experienced by customers, particularly in the realm of feminine beauty care.

10. Media

Strong stereotypes are used in studio or show marketing for captivating television programs, vlogs, and podcasts to attract a certain audience, depending on the show. By introducing some excitement to the topic, presentation, and circumstance, we should expect a massive increase in the number of viewers. People are more likely to become devoted fans of a show and bring in new viewers when they are left feeling uplifted, satisfied, motivated, and curious. As I demonstrated with the movie analogy, there is an audience for stories that use negative archetypes. On the other hand, I am committed to universal well-being via positive archetypes.

Chapter 16

How to activate an Archetype?

Through our lengthy archetype mapping in this book, I hope you understand how archetypes are requisite to prosperity, health, joy, better relationships, and, most importantly, more flexibility to create a better life. We believe they are powerful, though the first step is to learn how to create them in your life step by step. This book aims to give you practical tools for creating more powerful archetypes and transforming their presence in your life into something greater than before. Now, all you need to work on is the focus on archetypes as an essential part of a toolbox that can help you to build your own "archetypal self" — your true self within who you want to become — so that you have a solid foundation upon which to grow more powerful archetypes and create the reality you desire.

The archetype definition depends on the worldview of each individual. Archetypes contain a vast ocean of information that requires the application of logic, thought, human behavior observation, inspiration, sentiments, intuition, or scientific verification. It's not uncommon for archetypes to be interpreted in different ways by various people as they are influenced by their own cultural and emotional background, which is reflected in their understanding of what an archetype means, how it manifests, and why this archetype is meaningful for them and/or professionally. Regardless of how you interpret an archetype, the outcome will remain the same – it will create your reality.

Archetypes are sources of energy and information that are expressed through symbols. Therefore, we can use strong and positive symbols in the decoration of environments and in objects of personal use to activate, for example, energies of prosperity, success, and joy. Knowing the influence of archetypes on the people around you, whether for love, friendship, or family relationships, allows you to grasp their worldview, skills, issues, and behaviors, which can improve the understanding and dynamics of your relationships.

As entrepreneurs, we can positively influence people, sell more, and prosper in business using archetypical design. It is the creation of a visual identity for the company (logos), or archetypical branding, which is the construction of a brand based on the study of the company, the partners, your manufactured products, and the target market while leveraging the emotional power archetypes have on us. After all, archetypes are critical components of effective communication.

We can learn to communicate with the richness of the contents of our unconscious through understanding the archetypes that appear in our dreams. This helps us have more mental and emotional balance, and dreams are related to our psychic and physical health.

Carl Gustav Jung said, "Since psyche and matter are contained in one and the same world, and moreover are in continuous contact with one another and ultimately rest on irrepresentable, transcendental factors, it is not only possible but fairly probable, even, that psyche and matter are two different aspects of one and the same thing."

Knowing which archetypes influence us is a precious source of self-knowledge. Archetypes work in our minds from birth, helping to shape our worldview and revealing our abilities, tendencies, thoughts, feelings, and behaviors. According to the stage of life, new archetypes are activated in us; with that, we are also changing, always gaining more information, brain complexity, and expanding consciousness.

Because the archetype may modify personality, energy frequency, and thinking, activation is simple but needs responsibility. If we use the Leader Archetype as an example, we may explain the activation through logical and rational means. Search books or relevant content about leadership on the internet to activate the Leader Archetype: how a leader behaves, what he does, what he doesn't do, and what his virtues and abilities are. After researching the archetype, the next stage is to try incorporating its characteristics into your daily life. You must embody the archetype and act as he would.

Another way to activate an archetype is through affirmations. Affirmations are phrases that evoke the power of each archetype. Just as mantras have power, affirmations do, too, if done with intent, concentration, and feeling.

Another way to activate an archetype is to use symbols of power in decoration or personal items. For example, you want to work the joy in you. One way to do this is to use dolphin images in your home. Dolphins encourage joy and happiness. They can be paintings, statues, images on your computer or cell phone screen, or even jewelry as pendants.

Mythology is another approach to awakening an archetype through intellectual life. Myths are universal stories that represent many archetypes. Any civilization's mythology contains a character who represents wisdom. This narrative is associated with the goddess Athena in Greek mythology, Minerva in Roman mythology, and so on.

Choose an archetype that represents a quality you love and want to possess or to help you in your moment, study everything about it, search the different pantheons and see which gods and goddesses appeal to you. There are countless pantheons of gods: Greeks, Egyptians, Indians, Celts, Norse, American Indians, Chinese, Africans, etc. After those, it's time to connect to your archetype. You must enter a meditative state, listen to ethereal music or any other music that puts you in a dreamy sense, and meditate for five, ten, or more minutes, feeling as if you are in a human body with the spirit of a wolf or any other symbol, an animal of power, god, or goddess. An active imagination is similar to using images; the difference is that it is done exclusively within your mind.

Carl Jung was the first to come up with the idea of 'active imagination 'for psychological self-discovery and used it in his work. That is the way fiction books and movies influence all of us with imaginations full of symbols. This method of activating an archetype is so effective that it will provide you with numerous insights. Then, when you're finished, ask the archetypal questions and thank them.

Physically embody your archetype. Temporarily assuming the behaviors and attributes of the chosen archetype is a great way to activate the structure of the archetype and its personality. For example, if you want to connect with the seductive or sensual side of the goddess Aphrodite and her nature, why not choose a sensual perfume, a beautiful piece of jewelry, or an elegant outfit to wear? Profoundly simple changes in our physical appearance affect our mood and emotions.

The connection with archetypes is deeper than knowing about them; loving them is the key to unification. That is the way you live the archetype fully.

Chapter 17

Reasons Why Archetype Effects Don't Work

One main reason that archetypes manifestations might not work is that negative feelings like anxiety, fear, ego, comfort zone, envy, tabus and prejudice, paradigm, self-sabotage, resistance, and ignorance can make your journey full of obstacles.

It is important to understand that archetypes are not miraculous, magical, or enchantment. Archetypes are 'Primordial Energies 'capable of expressing themselves in the physical world. Therefore, studying and "activating" them is an ongoing practice that requires a process of intimate reform.

Knowing or understanding your intentions behind the archetype you choose is important. For example, if you choose the Eagle as an animal of power or someone important like Akhenaten or King Solomon, you may ask yourself... What am I going to do with it? Do you want to become a leader or build an empire? Akhenaten was a divine and unified being with the universe and worked hard day and night. His main dream was to make people happy on a large scale. Do you want to do the same? Are you sure about Akhenaten? The Eagle results in great levels of dopamine. Are you ready to become an Eagle? Can you control your emotions or anxiety to avoid living in the Eagle's shadow? Do you have trauma to heal? What about in relationships? What archetype are you and your partner living? Flamingos, Goddess Aphrodite? What if you want to activate Cleopatra or Lilith's archetype?

Archetypes have different frequencies. While Aphrodite is romantic and lovely, Cleopatra is empowered. This change could be good or bad for your partner. As I mentioned in Chapter 6 about relationships, we all live under the Heisenberg principle of uncertain momentum, and position is linked with changes. Consider this before deciding to make that sign a part of your life.

Living the archetype is followed by four steps: Presentation, communication, transformation or unification, and action with the affirmation, "Me and the Archetype Are One; One Are We."

Archetypes must be activated with responsibility. Make sure of what you really want. Once you are ready to activate your archetype, focus on the following aspects that will be affected by the archetypes.

1. Ego

Sigmund Freud divided mental life into two parts: Conscious and Unconscious. Like the visible part of an iceberg, the conscious portion would be small and insignificant, representing just a superficial view of the whole personality. The immense and powerful unconscious portion, the submerged part of the iceberg, would contain the instincts, the driving forces of all human behavior.

Freud proposed the conscience and unconscious concepts in 3 parts: Id as a psych energy source, superego as a moral of personality, and ego as a rational aspect of personality.

In Carl G. Jung's conception, the ego would be the center of consciousness like thoughts, ideas, feelings, memories, and sensory perceptions. Although the ego has to do with matters such as personal identity, maintenance of personality, continuity over time, mediation between the fields of conscious and unconscious, etc., it must also be considered as an instance that responds to the needs of another, which is superior to it. It would be the Self, the ordering principle of the entire personality. Initially, the ego is merged with the Self, but it must differentiate. Jung describes an interdependence of the two: the Self, which has a more holistic view, is supreme. The ego's function, however, is to confront or satisfy, as the case may be, the demands of that supremacy.

The ego is like a reptilian brain, or R-complex, a deeper ancestor of our brain, responsible for self-preservation. Through his action, the individual does not think; he reacts by instinct. It can be seen how much he is responsible for the life situation of a person, whether their finances, health, or relationships, as well as power struggles within society. The reptilian brain is linked to negative feelings influencing negative behaviors.

2. Comfort zone

If the observer creates his reality, as quantum mechanics proves, why aren't people deliberately creating a better reality for them? That is because of the system beliefs that govern their lives, mainly at an unconscious level. All these statements form a model of reality, and they create a program that runs in that person's mind, obstructing any possibility of growth. We noticed that limitation does not exist, but one creates and sustains limitation himself.

Knowing about this, why don't individuals free themselves from these imposed programs? We call the behavior a comfort zone! It is a nice name for laziness or accommodation. Can you understand how someone can be chronically lazy? How can someone be against achievement, progress, well-being, happiness, and evolution? We are inherently atomic beings, therefore, in constant vibration and perpetual motion, with the need to grow and evolve. We can find an example in the Bible, John 5:17

says, "In his defense, Jesus said to them, "My Father is always at his work to this very day, and I too am working." When we impede our growth, we suffer somatizations and inevitably get sick.

Think about it, why do health problems always come from someone who does nothing? We could think about retired people, though not only do older people feel pain after retirement, an expressively high number of youth get sick by living in their comfort zone. The problem could be mental, physical, or emotional; One of the most common doctors 'advice is to undertake exercises; your body needs movement!

In relationships, the comfort zone is the same thing. It is assumed that finding a partner is the final step. The number of official and unofficial separations is enormous because it permits a vibrant relationship to devolve into monotony, stagnation, and death.

3. Fear

Fear causes an individual to seek absolute security all the time. The space/time continuum does not exist for the reptilian brain. Therefore, any trauma brought to memory causes the same first-time reaction. Think of the reptilian brain's power to shape your emotions, feelings, and behaviors. For example, some people like to become Mahatma Gandhi but think, "If I activate, I will be like him, and I might die like him." These people get afraid of the shadow of the archetype. They might want to become someone great, but they are afraid of dying like Gandhi, consequently attracting the situation and his reality created through thoughts and feelings.

We have two kinds of suffering: Good and bad. In front of an event, we are the ones who determine whether there will be one or the other; the fact itself is neutral. The main fear of the human being is death, which, as an analysis, is the fear of the ego losing its grip. Ego is an illusion; the person thinks his individuality is real, but this does not exist. There is only one consciousness.

All mystics teach, "When they transcend the ego, everything happens. Health, relationship, prosperity, money, all. Everything flows magically as soon as one leaves the ego aside." But the person's fear of losing their individuality is so great that they don't allow it. They want to find the solution to their problems and the world's problems within the material paradigm. Therefore, everything they do is to improve the material world, more money, features, looks, and everything within material rules.

The same happens with fear of other things like scarcity, loneliness, punishment, condemnation, growth, and evolution.

4. Anxiety

Patience is required by anyone who wants to take a quantum leap and perceive the archetypes that govern their lives. Without patience, we observe the occurrence of the delay effect, which stops atomic decay. That's why you won't see results or anything else you wish. You need to let go, not be anxious about the results! Have fun, watch something comedy, and take your mind off the problems! Pressure the archetypes; you pressure yourself.

5. Envy

Envy is a feeling of frustration at another person's good, which causes a desire to destroy it, consciously or unconsciously. It represents the emotional pain for the good of others. It is a cause of great suffering for many people, both the envious and their victims. The person who is the target of envy receives a negative emanation that can suck your energy if you don't keep vibrating at high and good frequencies.

The envious are perpetually unhappy and harbor deep hatred toward others who have something they desire but cannot obtain or refuse to work for to achieve success, money, happiness, power, freedom, and love. Envy can be expressed through destructive criticism, insults, domination, rejection, rivalry, revenge, and defamation. Let us remember that everything that emanates returns to the one who emanated it through the principle of electromagnetism.

6. Taboos and Prejudice

All taboos and prejudices are nothing more than implanted content in people's minds during childhood or misconceptions embraced during adulthood. Prejudice, whether based on gender, color, nationality, religion, and sexual preference, or socioeconomic class, results from those unable to understand the wider picture of life.

Have you ever thought that the feeling of love that emanates from God does not condone any discrimination, taboo, prejudice, torture, and war made in His name? How difficult is it to question this?

Some men would think, "Women are no good." "There are two types of woman, saints, and harlots. He marries the saint, who will be the mother of his children, but marriage doesn't work. Why? Because he treats that woman like a saint, and "saint" he does not touch. He goes to the street and picks up a harlot for that." When did the concept come out? It was five thousand years ago when they "invented" male dominance.

Women's thoughts are also the same thing dominated by emotions. We live in a universe ruled by physical rules, such as strong nuclear force and weak electromagnetism and gravity, and all other laws flow from them. What reality will you have in your little universe if no one is good? It will draw someone who verifies your prophecies.

7. Paradigm

The information transmitted by parents or educators over the years is part of personality formation, particularly in early childhood. The transmitted contents are more than interpretations of truth accepted by the same people who educated us. It is their beliefs, good or not, that are instilled in us at a stage of life when we are vulnerable to the influence of the authorities. Our beliefs are just interpretations of their reality.

Part of our beliefs is formed due to our life experiences and the everyday influence of the media, educational institutions, and scientific and religious institutions. Beliefs function as real filters, determining how we capture sensory stimuli and, as a result, how we experience the world. We can perceive a person's paradigm in several ways. How do they dress? How do they eat? How do they walk? How do they express themselves bodily? What do they read? What do they buy? What are their deepest thoughts? What are the underlying feelings? How do they behave? How do they work? What do they study? How do they talk to friends, colleagues, boss, and partners? How do they treat a woman/man? How do they treat their husband/wife? How do they treat their children? How do they plan for the future? How do they drive a car? Where do they travel? How do they treat relatives?

If you ask someone these questions instead of observing, that person may answer one thing and do another. But the facts of your and their lives don't lie from what happens to all of us.

It's in our belief system; all these feelings, thoughts, and behaviors emit certain waves with specific frequencies that attract similar frequencies to us by electromagnetism. So we attract what we emit; different life circles are exceptions.

8. Self-sabotage

Among so many limiting factors that emerge from our unconscious, self-sabotage is one of the most nefarious. It's an inferior force that impels us to look for justifications to stay where we are, to prevent growth.

The self-saboteur "pulls the rug out" unconsciously when opportunities for personal growth arise. That happens when, after a variable period of growth, a boundary where the limiting programming (belief) is. In these cases, there is usually fear of growth and success. That's why we see people who start over many times, always presenting a behavioral pattern of failure and self-destruction. People create a limit to growth, a well-defined boundary that can be a salary range, a quota of personal happiness, or a level of commercial success.

9. Resistance

Anyone who wants to grow needs to live the Hero archetype; there is no escape. The Hero walks alone - not in a pack. Only a few army troops win an honor medal, and whoever survives the war counts, but the others do not believe it because they have not experienced it. This dilemma is because you say, "Friend, I went there, the journey, and it is true; everyone is welcome." You resist instead of accepting because the material judges everything.

The picture characterized by the individual who does not want to leave childhood and refuses to mature is the Peter Pan complex. This syndrome is characterized by certain immature behavioral, psychological, sexual, or social behaviors. The individual tends to show outbursts of irresponsibility, rebellion, anger, narcissism, dependence, and denial of aging.

In the so-called civilized world, where materialism has advanced and created a minimum of material bounty on Earth, so much effort is no longer needed to survive. One can stretch this time of psychological childhood. Children up to nine years of age don't want to know anything except to play. They are in an alpha state all the time, at the brain frequency of 7-12 MHz —

that's why it's hard to make a child study or do something because they are playing all the time; they don't go off that frequency.

There is soccer, horse racing, surfing, etc. Everything that is
entertainment has a money guarantee. This is the entertainment planet: Bars, restaurants, nightclubs, games, and anything
in the distraction business is extremely profitable. All this is a
collective escape. However, don't let it fool you. Let the archetypes guide you. Connect to your inner being you will have a relationship with the Whole.

Conclusion

After a long journey of archetypes, we realized there is no difference between symbols, metaphorical stories, myths, and legends; they are all real beings that influence everything that exists on the planet, from divine creation to human creativity.

People are completely committed to positive planetary change through love, fraternity, evolution, and action. Remember and feel your most joyous, strong, productive, loving, and fulfilling experience! The emotions are the most diversified, such as a huge triumph, a goal scored, love rediscovered, and so on. The archetype is another mechanism for the cosmos to work in you.

We all have more than one talent and ability. However, there is only one talent that we excel at the most: the archetype that we experience from birth, a specific archetype that the universe gave us when we were created. Have you ever envisioned doing a job that no one else can do better than you because you have such a talent that can make a difference in the entire world? This does not imply abandoning other talents but rather enhancing them; passion for what we do makes us better at what we do; if you are a driver, be the best. If you are a waiter, be the best. If you are a salesman, be the best. If you are a nurse, be the best. Be the best in everything you do.

One of the most important things about seeing an archetype play out explicitly is perception. People who are inspired by an archetype do not detect changes in life cycles, ups and downs, some negative results, some positive results, and so on. Perception is completely effective with the expansion of consciousness. Archetypes are a part of a transformation process; everything changes, energy, thoughts, tastes, loss of interest in

watching programs, changing habits, and all the other processes of change occur naturally, almost imperceptibly, as a result of the awakening of the Self, abandoning ego desires and
living in full consciousness.

Archetypes are like physics; whether you understand them
or not, it is being applied to you. One indigenous living in tribes
may have never heard about Isaac Newton, but the Law of Gravity works for him. He may not have heard of Carl G. Jung, but the
archetypes still work in him. It is not required to explain physics
to indigenous people; all he needs to know is that he must not
jump from a higher tree. That is why archetypes manifest themselves in various ways; that is how God teaches. However, if
some of the sharpest indigenous people comprehend Jung and
Isaac, they will most likely control someone else's reality.

For many people who belong to great powers, it is in the interest of humanity to remain where they are. Otherwise, expanding consciousness will be bad for business, the weapons
factory, the music industry, the world currency, and ego interests. Many negative and frozen heart beings are also thinking
about their successful moments: a perfect heist, a successful
rape, a murder, raising their power. The Divine Light shines on
them and makes them see the consequences of these acts on
their future and all suffering they brought for themselves. Some
kneel and regret what happened, while others remain unyield-
ing because they believe they were a channel for a negative god.

Only a radical change in the worldview can save humanity!
At the time, Earth is in a sluggish state, like death's sleep before
her final breath, and accommodating people is virtually the
usual. The numbing of human consciousness towards the esca-
lating economic catastrophe, weapons of destruction in which
man no longer engages in warfare but clicks buttons, and so on.
The list is extensive. The Second World War was predicted by
Wotan, the Norse God of War.

All this and much more result from a materialist, Cartesian,
and reductionist paradigm. This worldview, in which the Whole

does not exist, and only matter exists, has resulted in these outcomes. The only thing that can reverse this situation is a change in consciousness. Expand it to integrate the Whole into one's daily life, experiencing the power of the "I AM."

Children, adolescents, and adults must understand myths since it is our story. Analyzing any old story reveals the same problems, drama, and truths. The Greeks and Romans recognized this and knew they were discussing the same God under different names. The question is always mental in that we choose the symbols we wish to deal with in our emotions via neurotransmitters. Choosing appropriate symbols for the individual, company, institution, or country must grow.

God pours out love to all humanity all the time; otherwise, humanity would cease to exist in a second. God collapses humanity's wave function all the time, and all of this can be talked about theologically or scientifically to see if it changes the current situation. God cannot be understood; how can part understand the Whole? The Whole is greater than the sum of the parts. What we can do is feel God's love as much as we can, the love of the Whole. As our capacity to love grows, our perception of the love of the Whole will get stronger; this depends on the state of our conscience. The more It expands, the more you will be able to love unconditionally. Loving any archetype you choose will immediately become part of your life and potentializes your vibration.

As we come to the end of our journey of discovering archetypes, I hope you, my dear reader, can now relate to archetypes as the vehicles that carry the energy of God's love into your being and manifest it as a new reality in your life (and in the world). Therefore, to experience more love in our lives, let's raise our consciousness to a higher level by becoming conscious of our soul development. Through prayer, meditation, group, and individual work, let's receive and transform these new energies from our Higher Self into real-life experiences.

Bibliography:

50 Meanings Of Diamond (Scientific, Religious, Psychologic, Political, Marriage). (n.d.). Retrieved from SomethingBorrowed: https://somethingborrowedpdx.com/what-does-diamond-mean/

Altschuler, R. T. (2017, January 24). *Plant Archetypes: insight and references on living virtues, blueprints for sanity and wholeness*. Retrieved from Essence Mentoring: https://essencementoring.com/plant-archetypes-references-sanity/

Andrews, T. (2002). *Animal Speak*. Llewellyn Publications.

Anra, A. (2019). *The Dragon Within*. Invoke Healing International, LLC.

Ashley, J. (2016, November 3). *Advertising Persuades Human Behavior*. Retrieved from Medium: https://medium.com/@James.Ashley/advertising-persuades-human-behavior-772c5cbe65fd

Atkinson, W. W. (1908). *The Kybalion*. Simon & Schuster.

Berens, E. M. (2020). *Mythology*. New York: Crestline.

Blavatsky, H. P. (1889). *The Voice of the Silence*. Kshetra Books.

Briggs, J. (2000). *Seven Life Lessons of Chaos*. Harper Perennial.

Bryn Farnsworth, P. (2019, August 27). *EEG (Electroencephalography): The Complete Pocket Guide*. Retrieved from Imotions: https://imotions.com/blog/eeg/

bulfinch, T. (1867). *Bulfinch's Mythology*. Lee & Shepard.

Burrows, J. B. (2004, September). *Musical Archetypes and Collective Consciousness: Cognitive Distribution and Free Improvisation*. Retrieved from ResearchGate: https://www.researchgate.net/publication/298329739_Musical_Archetypes_and_Collective_Consciousness_Cognitive_Distribution_and_Free_Improvisation

Byrne, R. (2006). *The Secret*. Simon & Schuster.

Cameron, J. (1992). *The Artist's Way*. Tarcher.

Campbell, J. (1962). *Oriental Mythology The Masks of God, Volume II*. Penguin Books.

Campbell, J. (1964). *Occidental Mythology The Masks of God, Volume III*. Penguin Books.

Campbell, J. (1991). *Primitive Mythology : The Masks of God, Volume I*. Penguin Publish Group.

Campbell, J. (1991). *The Masks of God, Vol. 4: Creative Mythology*. Penguin Books.

Campbell, J. (1991). *The Power of Myth*. Anchor.

Cherry, K. (2022, May 2). *What Are the Jungian Archetypes?* Retrieved from VeryWell Mind: https://www.verywellmind.com/what-are-jungs-4-major-archetypes-2795439#:~:text=Archetypes%20are%20universal%2C%20inborn%20models,passed%20down%20from%20our%20ancestors.

Chopra, D. (1994). *The Seven Spiritual Laws of Success*. New World Library / Amber-Allen Publishing.

Cialdini, R. B. (2006). *Influence, The Psychology of Persuasion*. HarperCollins.

Clifford, G. C. (2021, September 24). *Dragon Symbolism & Meaning (+Totem, Spirit & Omens)*. Retrieved from World Birds: https://worldbirds.com/dragon-symbolism/

Couto, H. (2015). *Mentes Informadas*. Sao Paulo.

Couto, H. (2016). *Marketing e Arquétipos Símbolos, Poder, Persuasão*. (I. L. F. Silva, Trans.) São Paulo: Linear B.

Couto, H. (2018). *16-Paixão*. Retrieved from YouTube: https://www.youtube.com/watch?v=tEW_RFWNNqU

Couto, H. (2019). *Amar, a Bioquímica do Amor*. (I. L. F. Silva, Trans.) Linear B Editora Ltda.

Couto, H. (2020). Akhenaton. In H. Couto, *Akhenaton* (I. L. Silva, Trans., p. 64). Sao Paulo: Linear B Editora.

Daniels, E. (2022, February 8). *Plant Symbolism Guide: 31 Plants for Every Personality*. Retrieved from ProFlowers: https://www.proflowers.com/blog/plant-symbolism-guide/

de Saint Exupéry, A. (1943). *The Little Prince*. (R. Howard, Trans.) French: Reynal & Hitchcock.

Dias, M. C. (n.d.). *O luminoso*. Retrieved from Artetipos:
https://www.artetipos.com/arquetipo-luminoso

Ecavade, S. (2020, April 16). *An Ultimate Guide to Plants Meaning & Symbolism*. Retrieved from GiftaLove:
https://www.giftalove.com/blog/an-ultimate-guide-to-plants-meaning-symbolism/

Edinger, E. F. (1992). *Ego and Archetype*. Shambhala.

Estés, C. P. (1989). *Women Who Run With the Wolves*. Ballantine Books.

FRESH, F. (2016, June 1). *Orchid Meaning and Symbolism*. Retrieved from FTD by Design:
https://www.ftd.com/blog/share/orchid-meaning-and-symbolism

Gandhi, A. M. (2015). *The Gift of Anger*. Simon & Schuster.

Gimbutas, M. (2001). *The Living Goddesses*. University of California Press.

Goldsmith, J. S. (1947). *SPIRITUAL INTERPRETATION OF SCRIPTURE*. DeVorss Publications.

Helmenstine, A. M., & Ph.D. (2019, May 6). *How Is Gold Formed? Origins and Process*. Retrieved from ThoughtCo.:
https://www.thoughtco.com/how-is-gold-formed-4683984

Jinpa, T. (2015). *A Fearless Heart*. Avery Publishing Group.

Jordan, L. (2020, September 10). *THE SYMBOLIC MEANING OF A DIAMOND IN THE MOST POPULAR COLORS*. Retrieved from LexieJordan:
https://lexiejordanjewelry.com/blogs/posts/symbolic-meaning-of-a-diamond

Jung, C. G. (1968). *Man and His Symbols*. Dell Publishing Co., Inc.

Kenneth Maiese, M. (2022, April). *Neurotransmission*. Retrieved from Merck Manual:
https://www.merckmanuals.com/professional/neurologic-disorders/neurotransmission/neurotransmission

Kubler-Ross, E. (1993). *On Death and Dying*. Scribner Book Company.

Lama, D. (1988). *Ocean of Wisdom*. Clear Light Publishing.

Lesses, R. (1999, December 31). *Lilith*. Retrieved from Jewish Women Archieve:
https://jwa.org/encyclopedia/article/lilith

Lowin, R. (2021, October 22). *Thanksgiving Cornucopia Meaning: Why Is the Horn of Plenty a Symbol of Thanksgiving?* Retrieved from CountryLiving: https://www.countryliving.com/entertaining/a286219 09/thanksgiving-cornucopia/

McLeod, D. S. (2018). *Carl Jung's Theories: Archetypes, & The Collective Unconscious.* Retrieved from Simply Psychology: https://www.simplypsychology.org/carl-jung.html#:~:text=Jungian%20archetypes%20are%20d efined%20as,%2C%20literature%2C%20art%20or%20 religion.

Moore, E. (n.d.). *Plotinus.* Retrieved from Internet Encyclopedia of Philosophy: https://iep.utm.edu/plotinus/

Morsella, J. A. (2008, June 26). *The Unconscious Mind.* Retrieved from PMC PubMed Central: https://www.ncbi.nlm.nih.gov/pmc/articles/PMC2440 575/

Nestler, D. E. (2001). *Molecular Neuropharmacology.* McGraw Hill.

Neurotransmitters. (n.d.). Retrieved from Cleveland Clinic: https://my.clevelandclinic.org/health/articles/22513-neurotransmitters

Orwell, G. (1949). *1984.* Secker & Warburg and Harcourt Brace in New York.

Pataki, A. (2017). *Sisi: Empress On Her Own.* Random House Publishing Group.

Pearl, E. (2002). *The Reconnection: Heal Others, Heal Yourself.* Hay House.

Pollack, R. (2019). *Seventy-Eight Degrees of Wisdom.* Weiser Books.

Porter, E. H. (1913). *Pollyanna.* Simon & Schuster.

ReFaey, K., Quinones, G. C., Clifton, W., Tripathi, S., & Quiñones-Hinojosa, A. (2019, May 23). *The Eye of Horus: The Connection Between Art, Medicine, and Mythology in Ancient Egypt.* Retrieved from PMC PubMed Central: https://www.ncbi.nlm.nih.gov/pmc/articles/PMC6649 877/#:~:text=The%20Eye%20of%20Horus%20was,bet ween%20neuroanatomical%20structure%20and%20fu nction.

Reich, W. (1973). *The Function of the Orgasm*. Farrar, Strauss & Giroux-3pl.

Rhys, D. (2022). *Fairy Symbolism and Importance Through the Ages*. Retrieved from Symbolsage: https://symbolsage.com/fairy-symbolism-meaning/

Rhys, D. (2022). *Lotus Flower – Symbolism and Meaning*. Retrieved from Symbolsage: https://symbolsage.com/lotus-flower-symbolism-and-meaning/

Rhys, D. (2022). *What Is the Meaning of the Phoenix Symbol?* Retrieved from Symbolsage: https://symbolsage.com/phoenix-symbol-meaning/

Rodsky, E. (2021). *Find Your Unicorn Space*. G.P. Putnam's Sons.

Rowling, J. K. (1997). *Harry Potter*. Bloomsbury in the United Kingdom and Scholastic Press in the United States.

Schmitt, H. (2022, September 17). *Introduction to Sacred Geometry*. Retrieved from Rare Earth Gallery: https://www.geometriasacra.com/en/sacred-geometry.php

Sedgwick, I. (2020, March 7). *Meet Fortuna, Goddess of Luck, Abundance, and Fate*. Retrieved from Icy Sedgwick: https://www.icysedgwick.com/fortuna/

Shakespeare, W. (1559). *Julius Caesar*. Simon & Schuster in 2004.

Shakespeare, W. (1597). *Romeo and Juliet*. Simon & Schuster in 2004.

Shayne, T. (2016, September 29). *Indigo, Crystal, & Starseed Children: Characteristics Revealed*. Retrieved from Gaia: https://www.gaia.com/article/indigo-crystal-starseed-children-characteristics?gclid=Cj0KCQjwy5maBhDdARIsAMxrkw1le4sC4xmSDA-OoigwiC6GPAE-3pJO3zZrJ34hBVMHYy-Juxhn_YEaAqOFEALw_wcB

Singer, J. (1989). *Androgyny*. Sigo Press.

Smith, E. M. (2022, August 15). *How are Natural Diamonds Formed?* Retrieved from Only Natural Diamonds: https://www.naturaldiamonds.com/diamond-guide/how-are-natural-diamonds-formed/?gclid=CjwKCAjw7p6aBhBiEiwA83fGulVZfcj0

u3enG1OsENJ2Bryg2yTYtPYBCSoYI2j7bkG7fvzvdeS8wB
oCXWwQAvD_BwE&gclsrc=aw.ds

Sones, B. a. (2018, October 9). *Strange but true: 95 percent of brain activity is unconscious.* Retrieved from The Oklahoman: https://www.oklahoman.com/story/lifestyle/2018/10/09/strange-but-true-95-percent-of-brain-activity-is-unconscious/60496296007/

Tello, M. (2020, March 25). *Healthy lifestyle: 5 keys to a longer life.* Retrieved from Havard Health Publishing: https://www.health.harvard.edu/blog/healthy-lifestyle-5-keys-to-a-longer-life-2018070514186

The Holy Bible, New International Version (NIV). (2011). Michigan: Zondervan. Retrieved from Dream & Zodiac.

The Meaning of the Dragon Symbol in Chinese Culture. (2020, December 30). Retrieved from Chineasy: https://www.chineasy.com/the-meaning-of-the-dragon-symbol-in-chinese-culture/

Tolle, E. (1997). *The Power of Now.* 1997 (Namaste Publishing) 1999 (New World Library).

Tuzzio, E. (2021, September 21). *The Curious Symbolism of Apples.* Retrieved from The Muse in the Mirror: https://themuseinthemirror.com/2021/09/21/the-curious-symbolism-of-apples/

Ury, W., Fisher, R., & Patton, B. (1991). *Getting to Yes.* Penguin Books.

Watson, J. (n.d.). *Ancient Egyptian Symbolism.* Retrieved from Tour Egypt: http://www.touregypt.net/featurestories/symbolism1.htm

Wen, B. (2015). *Holistic Tarot: An Integrative Approach to Using Tarot for Personal Growth.* North Atlantic Books; Illustrated edition.

Wilber, K. (2007). *The Integral Vision.* Shambhala.

Wilde, O. (1890). *The Picture of Dorian Gray.* Lippincott's Monthly Magazine.

Yablonski, B. (2022, January 13). Retrieved from Petal Republic: https://www.petalrepublic.com/snake-plant-meaning/